T0320738

MatConvNet Deep Learning and iOS Mobile App Design for Pattern Recognition:

Emerging Research and Opportunities

Jiann-Ming Wu
National Dong Hwa University, Taiwan

Chao-Yuan Tien
National Dong Hwa University, Taiwan

A volume in the Advances
in Computer and Electrical
Engineering (ACEE) Book Series

Published in the United States of America by
    IGI Global
    Engineering Science Reference (an imprint of IGI Global)
    701 E. Chocolate Avenue
    Hershey PA, USA 17033
    Tel: 717-533-8845
    Fax: 717-533-8661
    E-mail: cust@igi-global.com
    Web site: http://www.igi-global.com

Library of Congress Cataloging-in-Publication Data

Names: Wu, Jiann-Ming, 1966- author. | Tien, Chao-Yuan, 1995- author.
Title: MatConvNet deep learning and iOS mobile app design for pattern
  recognition : emerging research and opportunities / Jiann-Ming Wu,
  Chao-Yuan Tien.
Description: Hershey : Engineering Science Reference, 2019. | Includes
  bibliographical references and index. | Summary: "This book presents a
  total solution to developing intelligent pattern recognition apps on iOS
  devices based on MatConvNet deep learning"-- Provided by publisher.
Identifiers: LCCN 2019030373 (print) | LCCN 2019030374 (ebook) | ISBN
  9781799815549 (hardcover) | ISBN 9781799815556 (paperback) | ISBN
  9781799815563 (ebook)
Subjects: LCSH: Pattern recognition systems. | Mobile computing. | Apple
  computer--Programming. | MATLAB.
Classification: LCC TK7882.P3 W83 2019 (print) | LCC TK7882.P3 (ebook) |
  DDC 006.4--dc23
LC record available at https://lccn.loc.gov/2019030373
LC ebook record available at https://lccn.loc.gov/2019030374

This book is published in the IGI Global book series Advances in Computer and Electrical Engineering (ACEE) (ISSN: 2327-039X; eISSN: 2327-0403)

British Cataloguing in Publication Data
A Cataloguing in Publication record for this book is available from the British Library.

All work contributed to this book is new, previously-unpublished material.
The views expressed in this book are those of the authors, but not necessarily of the publisher.

For electronic access to this publication, please contact: eresources@igi-global.com.

Advances in Computer and Electrical Engineering (ACEE) Book Series

ISSN:2327-039X
EISSN:2327-0403

Editor-in-Chief: Srikanta Patnaik, SOA University, India

MISSION

The fields of computer engineering and electrical engineering encompass a broad range of interdisciplinary topics allowing for expansive research developments across multiple fields. Research in these areas continues to develop and become increasingly important as computer and electrical systems have become an integral part of everyday life.

The **Advances in Computer and Electrical Engineering (ACEE) Book Series** aims to publish research on diverse topics pertaining to computer engineering and electrical engineering. **ACEE** encourages scholarly discourse on the latest applications, tools, and methodologies being implemented in the field for the design and development of computer and electrical systems.

COVERAGE

- Applied Electromagnetics
- Sensor Technologies
- Power Electronics
- Optical Electronics
- VLSI Design
- VLSI Fabrication
- Electrical Power Conversion
- Digital Electronics
- Algorithms
- Circuit Analysis

IGI Global is currently accepting manuscripts for publication within this series. To submit a proposal for a volume in this series, please contact our Acquisition Editors at Acquisitions@igi-global.com or visit: http://www.igi-global.com/publish/.

Titles in this Series

For a list of additional titles in this series, please visit:
https://www.igi-global.com/book-series/advances-computer-electrical-engineering/73675

Open Source Software for Statistical Analysis of Big Data Emerging Research and Opportunities
Richard S. Segall (Arkansas State University, USA) and Gao Niu (Bryant University, USA)
Engineering Science Reference • © 2020 • 237pp • H/C (ISBN: 9781799827689) • US $225.00

Software Engineering for Agile Application Development
Chung-Yeung Pang (Seveco AG, Switzerland)
Engineering Science Reference • © 2020 • 330pp • H/C (ISBN: 9781799825319) • US $235.00

Applied Social Network Analysis With R Emerging Research and Opportunities
Mehmet Gençer (Izmir University of Economics, Turkey)
Engineering Science Reference • © 2020 • 284pp • H/C (ISBN: 9781799819127) • US $165.00

Novel Approaches to Information Systems Design
Naveen Prakash (Indraprastha Institute of Information Technology, Delhi, India) and Deepika Prakash (NIIT University, India)
Engineering Science Reference • © 2020 • 299pp • H/C (ISBN: 9781799829751) • US $215.00

IoT Architectures, Models, and Platforms for Smart City Applications
Bhawani Shankar Chowdhry (Mehran University of Engineering and Technology, Pakistan) Faisal Karim Shaikh (Mehran University of Engineering and Technology, Pakistan) and Naeem Ahmed Mahoto (Mehran University of Engineering and Technology, Pakistan)
Engineering Science Reference • © 2020 • 291pp • H/C (ISBN: 9781799812531) • US $245.00

IGI Global
DISSEMINATOR OF KNOWLEDGE

701 East Chocolate Avenue, Hershey, PA 17033, USA
Tel: 717-533-8845 x100 • Fax: 717-533-8661
E-Mail: cust@igi-global.com • www.igi-global.com

Table of Contents

Preface

This book presents a total solution to developing intelligent pattern recognition Apps on iOS devices based on MatConvNet deep learning. The presented solution is a data-driven approach, insisting on training and validating classifiers in Matlab and recognizing patterns on iOS devices. It realizes a classifier by convolutional neural networks derived subject to constraints proposed by a large-scale data set.

Classification is expected to infer a label that properly represents the class of an input pattern according to given labelled patterns. The basic of classification for pattern recognition is therefore translation of an input pattern to its correspondent label. For large-scaled labelled training patterns, it is preferred to realize the classifier by a mapping based on adaptive built-in parameters instead of reserving all original training patterns due to storage and computation limitation. For data-driven classification, human experts play a sole role of labelling input patterns for training, validation and testing artificially. The labelling process means performing classification by human experts and incorporating knowledges and skills of classification to supervised training patterns. Labelled input patterns form paired data, each consisting of an input pattern and a correspondent label determined by human experts in advance. The quality of paired data is a subsequence of the labelling process. Data audition, including relabelling, deleting or expanding, should rise when evidence obviously shows requirement of further improving data quality.

The presented total solution mainly applies deep learning for training convolutional neural networks for classification and pattern recognition. A convolutional neural network (CNN) typically transforms an input pattern to an output label through hidden layers for classification. The CNN architecture employs convolutional filters as adaptable built-in parameters and is extensible to consist of deep hidden layers, each performing a transformation, carrying out either convolution, linear translation, nonlinear translation, pooling, normalization, or softmax operation. Deep hidden layers in neural organization realize sequential transformations. Different type of transformation in a hidden layer refers to special purpose neural processing. Convolution extracts features by filtering. A convolution layer equipped with multiple filters translates a spatial pattern to stacked features. Nonlinear translation of ReLu insists on non-negative signal propagation in the network, pooling rescales sizes of extracted features by down sampling, and soft-max operates to emulate competitive responses or probabilities of being different classes. In the past two decades, researchers have organized CNN architecture by sequential transformations through deep hidden layers. The protocol of sequential transformations combined with built-in adaptable filters as well as interconnections form neural organization portable across different computation platforms.

The portability of CNN neural organization motivates our investigation of deep learning in Matlab and App execution on iOS devices. The presented solution depicts integration of large scaled data sets through deep learning to portable convolutional neural networks, translation of CNN neural organization across different computation platforms and realization of App design on iOS devices. The pattern recognition App is oriented from a large scaled data set. Of course, its performance and acceptability highly depend on correctness and quality of the labeling process. Deep learning on Matlab and pattern recognition on iOS devices are based on the premise that training patterns have been well labelled and there exists consistency among training patterns, testing patterns and executing patterns actually acquired on iOS devices. Skills of human experts for classification are incorporated within the mapping derived subject to labelled training patterns. The only source of learning built-in filters and interconnections of a deep CNN rises from labelled training and validating patterns.

This book mainly employs MatConvNet deep learning toolbox of Oxford University for deriving built-in filters and interconnections of a CNN at early stage subject to labelled training pattern. The MatConvNet toolbox is a third-party product working under Matlab programming environment. Vedaldi and Fulkerson published VLFeat, an open and portable library of computer vision algorithm in ACM international conference of multimedia 2010. Five years later, Vedaldi and Carel published MatConvNet, convolutional neural networks for Matlab, in ACM international conference of multimedia 2015. MatConvNet is an easy-to-use toolbox for constructing CNN in Matlab and can be easily combined with VLFeat and Matlab toolboxes of statistics and machine learning, control system, signal processing, mapping, system identification, DSP system, financial analysis, image processing, text analytics and predictive maintenance. Students and researchers who are familiar with Matlab, in the field of applied mathematics and statistics or the other fields, can directly use this toolbox to construct CNNs for classification, speeding up MatConvNet deep learning by parallel and distributed processes of Matlab and GPU, and realizing preprocesses and numerical experiment with reliable Matlab toolboxes. As described previously, whenever the assumption that training and testing patterns have been well labelled does not stand according to evidence shown by numerical experiments, the developer requires data audition, relabeling, deleting and expanding. Audited training and testing patterns feedback to deep learning of convolutional neural networks for classification. Developers can explore iterative deep learning and data audition more easily and friendly in Matlab. Expert skills and knowledges for pattern classification are essentially incorporated to labelled training and testing patterns of an audited data set. Deep learning in Matlab makes use of labelled training patterns for deriving built-in filters and interconnections and labelled testing patterns for verifying the convolutional neural network. The only source of learning built-in filters and interconnections of a CNN is oriented from labelled training patterns that have been extensively incorporated with expert skills and knowledges for classification of unlabelled pattern through the audition process. This book will share experiences of data audition for developing pattern recognition Apps on iOS devices. The presented solution constructs classifiers in a way other than the rule-based approaches. Human experts play a role of pattern labelling as well as data audition instead of direct rule construction. This will clarify the role of human experts for developing an intelligent pattern recognition App.

The eventual goal of the presented total solution is to develop an App that online executes on iOS devices with reliable and acceptable performance. Therefore, the actual performance is measured over online test on iOS devices and is expected reliable and acceptable for general users. Online execution on iOS devices captures input patterns directly from the equipment of mobile phones. The actual performance of an App on iOS device highly depends on intermediate performances measured over labelled testing patterns in the given dataset. However, due to possible interferences caused by online data acquisition, intermediate performances evaluated during different stages cross variant platforms of translating classifiers do not guarantee acceptability of the actual performance. The performance of a classifier developed in Matlab does not automatically imply acceptability of classification under Xcode environment or on iPhone devices.

iOS mobile devices possess amazing computing power and fruitful hardware equipments for data acquisition. Apple iphone 4 with computing power in CPU speed of 800 MHz and 1.9 GFLOPS has been recognized compatible with Cray-2 supercomputer. Now according to performance evaluation by Primate Labs of Canada, Apple iPhone X has improved iPhone 4 more than twenty folds in computing power. Especially Apple iPhone X has been extensively equipped with modern components of audio, camera, video, three-core GPU, Bluetooth, Wi-Fi, GPS and 3D Touch, and sensors of accelerometer, gyro, proximity, compass and barometer, which provide variant ways of online pattern acquisition for classification. Pattern recognition CNN Apps on iOS devices can thus operate stand-alone for pattern recognition without any linkage to computing servers on clouds. Mounting convolutional neural networks on iOS devices helps designers to build up a stand-alone App that executes for online pattern recognition. A stand-alone App can directly work for online pattern recognition using computing power more than twenty folds of Cray-2 supercomputer and can be published on Apple's App Store for facilitating App access by users. Currently, iOS devices can be locally extended to access portable medical sensors of measuring ultrasounds, EKG and EEG signals. This also extends potential applications of iOS apps to online medical signal analysis and diagnosis.

The iOS Apps presented here include the published handwriting 99 multiplication, handwritten English character classification, and medical image recognition of breast cancer derived from BreakHis datasets. The handwritten digit dataset of LeCun, consisting of sixty thousand training patterns and ten thousand testing patterns, has been considered as a benchmark of performance evaluation of variant approaches for handwritten digit recognition. Recently researchers have extensively applied variant statistical methods, machine learning approaches, supervised learning of multilayer neural networks and deep learning of convolutional neural networks for analyzing this dataset. The rule or classifier derived subject to training patterns is expected to well classify testing patterns. Some methods attain discriminating rules or classifiers that require all training patterns for classification. In general, reserving training patterns at testing or executing stages results in mass storage consumption and is not feasible for deriving classifiers mounted on iOS devices. Supervised learning of multiplayer neural networks derives optimal built-in interconnections subject training patterns for classification. The size of built-in interconnections in a multilayer neural network depends on neural organization. A multilayer neural network translates an input pattern through interleaved linear transformations and nonlinear translations to an output patterns. Its execution is totally defined by neural organization as well as instances of interconnections and requires no reserving of training patterns for classification. A multilayer neural network performs a hybrid of linear and nonlinear transformation and is more suitable for classification by iOS Apps in comparison with training pattern reservation methods and traditional linear methods.

Incorporating convolutional filters to a neural network that is equipped with more than two hidden layers was pioneered by Fukushima for handwritten digit recognition. Neocognitrons of Fukushima are famous convolutional neural networks, in which filters convolve input patterns or responses of previous layer to generate stacked results. Filters play a role of capturing spacial or temporal invariant features of labelled patterns for classification. Filter design is critical for boosting convolutional neural networks for pattern recognition. Relating filters to interconnections of multilayer perceptrons, LeCun pioneered application of back-propagation to calculating gradients of the network output as well as mean square approximating errors with respect to coefficients of filters in hidden layers, opening deep learning for classification. According to the definition of Hinton, deep learning means learning built-in parameters of a neural network with more than two hidden layers in additional to the input and output layers. The goal is to reduce the loss by adapting interconnections subject to labelled training patterns. With several or dozens of hidden layers, the feedforward neural architecture extends to consist of receptive fields as well as convolutional filters. The hidden layer in a deep convolutional neural network executes operations of multi-filter convolution, nonlinear translation, pooling and post-nonlinear projection. The success of applying back-propagation for gradient calculation makes the gradient descent approach feasible for deep learning of convolutional neural networks.

This book presents an integrated approach to deep learning of convolution neural networks by MatConvNet in Matlab, mounting the derived classifiers on Xcode environment and eventually devising pattern recognition App on iOS devices. Thanks for academic contribution to the deep learning framework, Caffe, which appears in the lists of CNN protocol supported by Core ML. Caffe is a bridge, connecting MatConvNet to Xcode through Core ML. In Caffe, a convolutional neural network and its optimization are described by configuration, and the neural architecture is expressive. MatCaffe is an interface from MatConvNet to Caffe, allowing CNN transformation. This book provides details of CNN transformation from Matlab to Xcode, facilitating development of pattern recognition Apps on iOS devices for researchers who familiar with mathematical computations in Matlab.

After transformation to Xcode, the CNN model originally derived by MatConvNet could be tested online on iOS devices. Users handwrite digits through the touch component, evaluating online performance of the transformed CNN model. In chapter 4, the authors adopt a dataset, which consists of 280,000 handwritten digits, for training and testing the CNN model of the published handwriting multiplication App.

Chapter 5 moves toward solving the problem of handwritten English letter recognition for developing iOS Apps. The categories in number extend to fifty two due capitalization and lower case of letters. The authors created a dataset that contains 411,302 images of handwritten English letters. All images are randomly partitioned to training and testing sets, respectively containing 86% and 14% images. For this example, early numerical experiments suffer from unacceptable performance for online testing. The improvement is not trivial and the details will be summarized in chapter 5 for further developing pattern recognition Apps on iOS based on the approach of learning in Matlab and executing on iOS devices. Data audition detects missed classification for distinguishing similar capital and small cases of some letters and confused labelling in the dataset. Performance improvement by data audition is required for developing handwritten letter recognition App on iOS devices. It is suggested to evaluate intermediate performances according to stages of transforming of the CNN model. When intermediate performances evaluated at frameworks of MatConNet, Caffe and Xcode are acceptable for testing, eventual performance of handwritten letter recognition App on iOS devices could be acceptable for testing. The pattern recognition CNNs model of each App is tested before being mounted on iOS devices. The accurate rates for model testing of the first two Apps are respectively 99.4% and 97.0%. Numerical experiments show reliable and effective online testing performance of handwritten letter recognition App on iOS devices. The CNN model of handwritten letter recognition in Xcode can be widely applied to developing more interesting Apps on iOS devices for English learning.

Chapter 6 introduces iOS pattern recognition App for breast cancer diagnosis directly using medical images. Microscopic images in the dataset are in size greater than patterns in the previous examples. Each labelled pattern is with 460x700 RGB color pixels. Experts play a role of pattern labelling instead of feature selection. For this App, the designer may be without backgrounds of breast cancer diagnosis using microscopic tumor images. Unlike the rule-based expert system, learning the CNN model is data driven and needs no feature extraction by human experts. Deep learning extracts CNN filters that represent spatial invariant features of labelled images for breast cancer diagnosis. The CNN filters for this example are no more planar, but with internal representations by 3-dimensional matrices. Two-class classification is explored for breast cancer diagnosis. Numerical experiments show encouraging results of two-class classification based on the proposed approach for breast cancer diagnosis. Diagnosing lobular carcinoma breast cancer against phyllodes tumor and papillary carcinoma against adenosis attains accuracy rates of 94.9% and 87.3% respectively. This chapter also presents the idea of recursive convolution. A convolutional neural network for classification derived subject to smaller training patterns serves as a CNN filter for organizing deep convolutional neural networks. A CNN filter convolutes over a larger image and indeed is a convolutional neural network. The convoluting results could be further processed by deep convolutional neural network for classification.

The contexts of Chapter 1 and Chapter 2 introduce intelligent pattern recognition iOS Apps, CNN architecture, deep learning theory and software frameworks, providing readers theoretical and practical foundation of MatConvNet learning in Matlab for building CNN classifiers. Learning in Matlab integrates mass training patterns to the CNN model and offline validating the model with testing patterns. Chapter 3 compensates for the absence of MatConvNet in the supporting list of Core ML, providing details of transforming portable CNN models to Caffe framework and further Xcode, accomplishing the goal of online executing on iOS devices. Numerical simulations in Chapters 4-6 show success of the presented total solution to learning in Matlab and executing in Xcode for developing intelligent pattern recognition iOS Apps based on CNN classifiers. Especially in the example of handwritten letter recognition, numerical simulations clearly show requirement of data audition for improving the unacceptable performance evaluated online on iOS devices. The authors checked more than half million patterns for data audition, achieving audited training and testing handwritten letter images for developing CNN classifiers on iOS devices. The success of two-class classification for breast cancer diagnosis using medical images illustrate the presented total solution feasible and potential for solving problems of complicate medical image recognition. The presented solution connects mathematical modeling and computations to users of iOS devices and future artificial intelligence.

Acknowledgment

Firstly, we would like to express sincere gratitude to Prof. Chang-Yuan Liou for providing us with scientific guidance. Thanks for his motivation and immense knowledge so that we can gain a foothold in the field of deep learning and complete this book.

We also acknowledge the Department of Applied Mathematics from National Dong Hwa University, Hualien, Taiwan for providing us with the research environment and equipment so that we can realize our research ideas and publish the latest research. In this book, we use mathematical knowledge to construct models. We sincerely thank all the professors of the Applied Mathematics Department of Dong Hwa University for providing us with professional knowledge of mathematics. Also, we thank all members of the IT Lab for participating in the discussions and sharing their views so that we can present the best results.

We sincerely thank all experts for the contributions in the field of deep learning. Their contributions have led to the development of deep learning field so that we can further research and realize applications. We thank the providers of the MNIST database, EMNIST database, and BreakHis databases, who respectively are LeCun, Cohen et al., and Spanhol et al. Additionally, we also acknowledge the MatConvNet team, the developers of the Caffe deep learning framework, and the Visual Geometry Group at the University of Oxford, who offer the open sources so that we can save time in constructing the models. With these databases and open sources, we complete the academic research and present the total solution to enable the application of deep learning models.

Last but not least, we would like to thank IGI Global for accepting our proposal and publishing this book and also sincerely thank the Assistant Development Editors for their offer assistance in the editing of this book.

Introduction

Deep learning is a hot issue nowadays in the field of artificial intelligence. By definition of Hinton (LeCun, Bengio, & Hinton, 2015), deep learning means training adaptive built-in parameters of a deep neural network or a deep convolutional neural network, where there exist more two hidden layers in additional to the input and output layers. A well trained deep neural network is totally defined by its layer organization and built-in parameters or weights of interconnections.

Deep learning has been widely applied to image analysis (Litjens, et al., 2017), audio analysis (Lee, Largman, Pham, & Ng, 2009), speech analysis (Wang & Chen, 2018), data analysis (Wang & Pei, 2017), classification (Krizhevsky, Sutskever, & Hinton, 2012), and pattern recognition (Gao, Zhang, & Wei, 2018). For past decades, researchers have proposed many methods for pattern recognition and prediction in the field of machine learning, such as k-nearest neighbor (K-NN) (Coomans & Massart, 1982), logistic regression (Peng, Lee, & Ingersoll, 2002), support vector machine (SVM) (Boser, Guyon, & Vapnik, 1992) (Cortes & Vapnik, 1995), radial basis function (RBF) network (Orr, 1996), multilayer neural networks (NN) (Charalambous, 1992), convolutional neural network (CNN) (LeCun, et al., 1989), etc. However, deep learning began demonstrating effectiveness and reliability of solving the problem of pattern recognition until the latest decade. Deep learning increasingly impacts on artificial intelligence and industrial applications.

Deep network architecture and parameter share is oriented from the idea of simulating the neural system in the mammalian brain. The deep network architecture means more than two hidden layers of neurons and synapses between successive hidden layers. The neurons in the model are connected by synapses. Once the data image is imported, the information flows across nerve bonds to neurons. As the deep network architecture model contains a lot of hidden layers, neural activation flows help resolve complex information in the image essential for classification, extracting internal representations for desired neural mappings. By the way, the output of the model will recognize the class of image input. The model of deep learning can recognize the image input in feed-forward mode. It can also self-learn by back-propagation (Rumelhart, Hinton, & Williams, 1986) of the approximating errors of desired outputs.

Filters are essential internal representations of convolutional neural networks, serving as spatial invariant features for pattern recognition. The architecture of convolutional neural networks has been extensively combined with fully connected multilayer neural networks for solving the problem of image classification. The operation of convolution replaces traditional hand-crafted textural descriptors and has been added to deep neural network architecture. The convolutional layers in CNN extracts important information of local image, and conveys to the next layer to process complex features. A convolution layer has multiple filters or kernels whose convolution over outputs of the previous layer attains stacked features for feed-forward processes. Also, kernel parameters of the convolutional layers in CNN can be modified by the error back-propagation and stochastic gradient descent method. Deep learning can gradually reduce the output error by iterative trainings. Eventually, the deep neural model with high training accuracy through performance evaluation is expected with high testing accuracy for further applications. This book presents a total solution for the purpose of deep learning in Matlab and performing the derived deep convolutional neural networks through Xcode on iOS devices. The goal aims to transform deep network architecture across software platforms, which are respectively supported by Mathworks and Apple. Of course, such transformation is not trivial and not directly supported by Xcode, but facilitating application of deep network architecture derived under the Matlab environment to iOS Apps. Mathematical modeling and computing have been recognized fundamental for developing deep learning and deep network architecture. Researchers familiar with mathematical modeling and computing under the Matlab environment could accomplish deep network architecture for pattern recognition and publish it to Apple's App store once the transformation of the deep CNN across platforms of Matlab and Xcode is feasible. On the basis, mathematical modeling and computing in Matlab that improves deep learning in the future is extensible for deriving advanced deep network architecture and mounting to pattern recognition Apps on iOS devices. Advanced deep learning software can be developed in Matlab beyond Xcode for mounting to pattern recognition Apps on iOS devices.

Toward applying the highly accurate trained deep model to iOS Apps and developing the pattern recognition App for iOS devices, the total solution presented in this book is on scope of data audition, data pre-processes, constructing deep learning model, model training, model evaluation, the appropriate model selection for application, model cross-platform conversion, and the real-life application of the model on iOS devices.

In addition to the presented total solution, the contexts of this book also introduce mathematical foundations of deep learning. The technique of deep learning is with solid mathematical foundations, combining a lot of mathematical operations and methodologies to deal with complex linear or non-linear problems. In the past, mathematics played a fundamental and indispensable role in developing deep learning. Mathematics has been described as a science or an art. Mathematical modeling and computing are an engine for developing deep learning in the future. The deep learning models implement computing stages of feedforward and backpropagation based on linear algebra and calculus. No matter the Turing machine and the Von Neumann architecture are all high relevant to mathematics. Mathematics promotes the development of science. Furthermore, the combination of mathematics and computer science has developed Artificial Intelligence (AI). Being different from Turing machines, the parameters in the model of AI deep learning are no longer only 0 or 1 but contain the real number by implementation of analog integrated circuits. Additionally, the numerical-analysis software integrates knowledge of mathematics and computations. Researchers can analyze the large-scale dataset, solve complex mathematical problems and develop deep learning model with reliable and effective numerical-analysis software. The strong connection between mathematics, numerical-analysis software and AI has significantly contributed to the successful development of deep learning. The presented total solution will use Matlab numerical-analysis software to derive the deep learning model, convert the well trained deep network architecture to the Caffe framework, and apply the deep learning to develop pattern recognition Apps on iOS devices.

Under Matlab software environment, this book primarily introduces MatConvNet deep learning to build the CNN Model by supervised analysis of the given dataset. MatConvNet (Vedaldi & Lenc, 2015) is an open source from the Oxford Visual Geometry Group. It implements the deep learning method and integrates the blocks of CNNs as a toolbox in Matlab environment. It allows users to design a deep CNN model and train it subject to a dataset, and supports the use of one or multiple GPUs on learning large and deep convolutional neural networks. It has been widely used as an educational and research platform for rapid design of CNN models. The Matlab environment provides reliable mathematical toolboxes for preprocesses, including independent component analysis, clustering analysis, image and signal analysis, unsupervised learning, dimensionality reduction and data visualization, and numerical solvers toward nonlinear system solving, integer programming solving and multivariate nonlinear regression solving, which are potential for further improvement of deep learning methodologies. A lot of numerical computations, such as dimension reduction, numerical differentiation, symbolic and numerical gradient calculations, have been employed in CNNs training. These pre-processes and numerical computations can be easily handled by developers familiar with Matlab environment for quickly building the CNN model using MatConvNet, directly training and testing the CNN Model by parallel and distributed processes. After evaluating the model, the process of mounting to Apps on iOS devices will select the well trained model that most suitable for solving the real-life problem.

The Xcode software environment, supported by Apple Inc., equipped with latest Swift programming language, is the most suitable selection for developing iOS Apps. Pattern recognition Apps in this book employs Swift in the Xcode environment to build the user interface and develop classifiers. Swift is an emerging programming language also developed by Apple Inc. On June 2, 2014, at the Apple Worldwide Developers Conference (WWDC), Apple announced the Swift 1.2. Easier to learn than Objective-C, the programming language is more efficient in developing iOS App in Xcode.

However, the well trained CNN models in MatConvNet cannot be directly integrated into the Xcode environment. The mathematical modeling and computing in the mathematical software environment faces a barrier for applications to iOS Apps. Numerical-analysis software provides an excellent environment for developing mathematical modeling and computing, but the developed models cannot be transferred to the Integrated Development Environment (IDE). Although we developed the valuable deep learning models in the Matlab environment, for the trend of applying well trained models on iOS Apps, we are unable to directly integrate the deep network models derived by MatConvNet into the Xcode development environment. This barrier causes developers necessary for re-constructing a mathematical network model in the IDE. The presented total solution overcomes this difficulty through the third-party deep learning framework. The deep learning framework is a toolbox that works in particular software environment. Developers can use the deep learning framework to develop deep network models. The deep network models are portable. The well trained models will retain the architecture and built-in parameters. The total solution uses MatCaffe, provided by the Caffe deep learning framework, to convert the model architecture and built-in parameters of the well trained model in MatConvNet to the Caffe model in the Caffe deep learning framework. After that, the Core ML method provided by Apple can integrate the Caffe network model into the Core ML model. Developers can import the AI image recognizer of MatConvNet to iOS App through the Core ML model and complete the design of an iOS App finally.

The total solution eventually mounts the well trained network model to iOS devices. The deep CNN model can execute independently on the user's mobile device, which is different from the pattern recognition system on the remote host and clouds. The pattern recognition system of iOS Apps will online identify the object as soon as the user gets the data information through mobile camera or touch components. The stand-alone App protects users from data leakage, improving privacy and security. The user's data object does not need to be sent to the cloud or remote host for recognition. The mechanism of the object recognition App can prevent data leakage from data delivery. The stand-alone App can still import the data image from the iOS device to complete pattern recognition, even if the iOS device is not connected to the cellular network of Wi-Fi. Further, the stand-alone recognition App can be hit to the shelves of App Store for sale or provide users for free. Users can easily download or update the App from the App Store. The presented total solution can help researchers who are familiar with the mathematical software, Matlab, develop intelligent pattern recognition Apps on iOS devices to assist solving the human real-life problem.

The second part, from chapter four to six, of this book demonstrates our latest research results based on the approach of learning deep CNNs in Matlab and performing derived deep CNNs on iOS devices. The last three chapters respectively give image recognition examples to illustrate how to use the total solution to solve the problem we interested and mount the trained network model on the iOS device. On variant levels of difficulty, the three examples for image recognition are separately for handwritten digit recognition, handwritten English letter recognition, and medical image recognition of breast cancer. The handwritten digit recognition is a basic problem in the field of machine learning. It is also considered as the Hello World in the field of deep learning after the paper, "Gradient-based Learning Applied to Document Recognition", was published by LeCun in 1998. Chapter four presents the example of developing the handwritten digit recognition App on iOS devices. The total solution starts at the process of learning a deep CNN classifier subject to a training dataset that contains 240,000 handwritten digit images from 0 to 9 and verifying the classifier with 40,000 test images. The training dataset and the testing dataset are mutually exclusive. The training and test images are equally distributed over ten categories. Numerical experiments employ MatConvNet in Matlab to construct a deep CNN model subject to the training dataset of handwritten digit images. Numerical experiments obtained a deep CNN model with 99.4% accuracy rate for 40,000 test images. For iOS pattern recognition App design, the deep CNN model derived by MatConvNet serves as a handwritten digit classifier that is transformed through the Caffe deep learning framework as well as the CoreML method to the Xcode environment. Chapter four describes details of the transforming process. Intermediate forms of the deep CNN model should be respectively verified under the platforms of Caffe and CoreML. Fortunately, the verification for the handwritten digit recognition example succeeds. The original deep CNN model including its organization and built-in parameters are exactly transformed to the Xcode environment and the high accurate testing rate illustrates reliable and effective generalization from deep learning subject to the training and validation datasets. The last step is to verify the online performance of the handwritten digit classifier that has been embedded within the pattern recognition App on iOS devices, termed as Handwriting 99 Multiplication. The App directly gets handwritten digits of users by the touch component of iOS devices, performing online classification for 9 by 9 multiplication and playing speeches of multiplication answer. Eventually, we developed the Handwriting 99 Multiplication App based on the MatConvNet trained deep CNN model and successfully published it on Apple's App Store. Acceptable online performance shows effective and reliable generalization of deep learning subject to the training dataset for recognizing handwritten digits on the touch component of iOS devices.

After introducing the Hello World problem of deep learning, in chapter five, this book further develops handwritten letter recognition by the strategy of deep learning in Matlab and performing CNN models on iOS devices. Handwritten letters are with more classes than handwritten digits, also possessing wider applications to real-life problem solving. Handwritten letter recognition in chapter five also depicts the significance of data audition for data-driven deep learning. Different from other classification methods, deep learning is a data-driven learning technique. The CNN model recognize objects based on adaptable built-in parameters derived by supervised learning subject to the given training dataset. Therefore, ability of the CNN model for recognizing objects in real-life highly depends on reliability and accuracy of paired training data. Designing handwritten letter recognition in chapter five faces the problem of uncertain reliability and inaccuracy among paired training data. Numerical experiments clearly show evidence for the requirement of data audition toward improving online performance. With careful data audition, chapter five attains a CNN model that recognizes handwritten letters with 97.4% accuracy for 58,405 testing images and acceptable online performance.

Nowadays, it has always been a hot topic for whether AI systems can assist our daily. For the aging of the population and the demand rising for healthcare resources, the AI systems assisted medical diagnosis will reduce the burden for medical staff. In chapter six, we use the state-of-the-art CNN model to develop the mobile-aided breast cancer diagnosis. The developed aided diagnosis system of the breast cancer embeds the pre-trained recognition model and accepts the 460x700 pixels microscope images of the 40X magnification factor. We illustrate effectiveness of problem solving by demonstrating two examples respectively for diagnosing lobular carcinoma breast cancer against phyllodes tumor and papillary carcinoma against adenosis, which attain the testing accuracy rate of 94.9% and 87.3%. Three examples we presented demonstrate how to use the total solution to solve the problem of interest and import the pre-trained model to the iOS device for real-life applications. With the presented total solution, developers not only develop deep learning models but also can package pre-trained models into products and publish the products through the App Store. We highly recommend this book to you, no matter you are beginner or expert in the field of deep learning. This book starts from the deep learning architecture and the mathematical theory of deep learning. Next, we present how to integrate deep learning models of MatConvNet into the iOS App. In this book, we also introduce how to use Caffe third-party deep learning framework and Core ML Tools to help us convert deep learning models. Finally, we can develop and publish iOS mobile App for pattern recognition.

The remaining of this book is organized as follows: Chapter 1 briefly introduces the convolutional neural networks. Convolutional neural networks are currently advanced technology for solving pattern recognition problems. The development of image recognition Apps on iOS devices has become a trend for further application of the deep learning model. Section 1.1 will discuss the iOS image recognition App based on the convolutional neural network. The deep CNN model is composed of many different types of hidden layers. Section 1.2 will explore the hidden layers commonly used in the CNN architecture. Today, in the industry and academia, there have been proposed a lot of CNN models to solve the classification problem of the large-scale image database. We will explore these well-known CNN models in Section 1.3 and study how to construct a deep CNN model.

Chapter 2 will explain deep learning theory and software. Mathematical science is the engine that drives the development of deep learning. Section 2.1 will explain the connection between mathematical science and artificial intelligence. Deep learning is a data-driven learning technique. The deep learning model can accurately recognize image classes after self-learning. Backpropagation is a technique that promotes self-learning of deep learning models. We will introduce how the deep learning model implements supervised learning and execute backpropagation in Section 2.2. After studying the architecture of the deep learning model and the self-learning technique of deep learning, we will introduce the MatConvNet and Caffe deep learning frameworks in Section 2.3. The presented total solution will use these two deep learning frameworks to construct the deep learning model. Further, Section 2.4 introduce how to import the Caffe model into the Matlab numerical analysis software. In Section 2.5 of this chapter, we introduce the mobile deep learning frameworks. This section compares the performance of different deep learning frameworks.

Chapter 3 introduces how to use Core ML and MatCaffe to achieve CNN transformation across platforms. This chapter details our presented total solution and implements the cross-platform transformation of the portable deep learning model. Section 3.1 describes the iOS device that realizes the total solution and the Core ML method of integrating the model of the third-party deep learning framework into the iOS App. In addition to integrating the model of third-party deep learning framework into the Core ML model, Apple's Core ML also allows developers to create Core ML model with image recognition on macOS. Section 3.2 will describe how to use Create ML to develop a Core ML model for recognizing images. After introducing the Core ML method, we will introduce the Caffe deep learning framework and the MatCaffe interface in Section3.3. Caffe framework is a bridge between Matlab numerical software and the Xcode development environment. Caffe is not easy to install and compile. Therefore, we provide detailed installation guide in Section 3.3 and briefly introduce the prototxt file and caffemodel file in Caffe. Next, we present the flow of total solution and use the MNIST example to implement the total solution in Section 3.4. Finally, we will use the same example as in Section 2.4 to introduce the conversion of the deep learning model from Matlab to Caffe model in Section 3.5. This section work in concert with the 2.4 section of the second chapter.

Chapter 4 will explain the Handwriting 99 Multiplication that has already hit the App Store shelves as an example. Handwriting 99 Multiplication is an iOS App that has been successfully published on the Apple App Store.

In this chapter, we will present the extension and application of the MNIST example. MNIST handwritten digits recognition problem has been regarded as the Hello World of deep learning. We will analyze past research methods and results for the MNIST example in Section 4.1. Although we use the example of recognizing handwritten digits as the chapter, we are not using the MNIST database to train the deep learning model. Section 4.2 will introduce the Extended-MNIST database used to train the recognition model of handwritten digits. Section 4.3 presents the CNN architecture constructed to recognize handwritten digits. Section 4.4 describes the training strategy for numerical experiments. Section 4.5 presents the results of the research using the CNN model to solve the problem of handwritten digits recognition. At the end of this chapter, Section 4.6, we integrate the handwritten digits recognition model from Matlab into the Xcode environment to develop iOS App. This handwritten digits recognition App completely present the total solution and successfully publish on Apple's App Store.

Chapter 5 introduces using CNN model recognition of handwritten English characters as second example. After solving the problem of handwritten digits recognition, the handwritten English characters recognition is another interesting topic. This chapter presents the importance of data audition for data-driven deep learning. We introduce the dataset of handwritten English letters in Section 5.1 and audit this large-scale dataset before training the deep learning model. Section 5.2 describes the CNN architecture we constructed for handwritten letters recognition. After that, Section 5.3 explains the training strategy of the CNN model and Section 5.4 presents the experimental results of handwritten letters recognition. At last, we import the recognition model of handwritten letters into the iOS App in Section 5.5 and online test the accuracy of the recognition model.

Chapter 6 introduces using CNN model diagnose Breast Cancers as a final example and conclusions the work and present some insights. In this chapter, we develop a mobile-aid diagnostic system for recognizing breast cancer image. This diagnostic system is a binary classifier that can directly accept a breast cancer image and diagnose it as benign or malignant. The research of breast cancer image recognition can be traced back to the Breast Cancer Wisconsin Data Set in the 1990s. Different from the traditional classification methods, we use the state-of-the-art CNN model in this chapter to recognize breast cancer images. Section 6.1 will describe the differences between CNNs techniques for breast cancer image recognition and traditional machine learning methods. Section 6.2 describes the BreakHis database we use for the research in this chapter. Section 6.3 presents the large deep learning model we construct for recognizing breast cancer image. Section 6.4 shows how we pre-processed high-resolution images of breast cancer before training the deep learning model. Section 6.5 presents the experimental results of the CNNs model for breast cancer imaging diagnosis. Further, we present the conclusions and future development of using CNNs technology to recognize breast cancer image. Finally, we introduce the medical-related experiment of the heart sound detection.

REFERENCES

Boser, B. E., Guyon, I. M., & Vapnik, V. N. (1992). A training algorithm for optimal margin classifiers. In *COLT '92 Proceedings of the fifth annual workshop on Computational learning theory* (pp. 144-152). Pittsburgh, PA: ACM.

Charalambous, C. (1992, June). Conjugate gradient algorithm for efficient training of artificial neural networks. *IEE Proceedings. Part G. Circuits, Devices and Systems, 139*(3), 301–310. doi:10.1049/ip-g-2.1992.0050

Coomans, D., & Massart, D. (1982). Alternative k-nearest neighbour rules in supervised pattern recognition: Part 1. k-Nearest neighbour classification by using alternative voting rules. *Elsevier, 136*, 15-27.

Cortes, C., & Vapnik, V. (1995, February 20). Support-Vector Networks. *Machine Learning, 20*(3), 273–297. doi:10.1007/BF00994018

Gao, X., Zhang, J., & Wei, Z. (2018). Deep learning for sequence pattern recognition. In *2018 IEEE 15th International Conference on Networking, Sensing and Control (ICNSC)*. Zhuhai, China: IEEE.

Kim, Y. (2014). Convolutional Neural Networks for Sentence Classification. In *Proceedings of the 2014 Conference on Empirical Methods in Natural Language Processing (EMNLP)* (pp. 1746-1751). Doha, Qatar: Association for Computational Linguistics. 10.3115/v1/D14-1181

Krizhevsky, A., Sutskever, I., & Hinton, G. E. (2012). ImageNet classification with deep convolutional neural networks. In *NIPS'12 Proceedings of the 25th International Conference on Neural Information Processing Systems* (vol. 1, pp. 1097-1105). Lake Tahoe, NV: Curran Associates Inc.

LeCun, Y., Bengio, Y., & Hinton, G. (2015, May 28). Deep Learning. *Nature, 521*(7553), 436–444. doi:10.1038/nature14539 PMID:26017442

LeCun, Y., Boser, B., Denker, J. S., Henderson, D., Howard, R. E., Hubbard, W., & Jackel, L. D. (1989, December). Backpropagation Applied to Handwritten Zip Code Recognition. *Neural Computation, 1*(4), 541–551. doi:10.1162/neco.1989.1.4.541

Lee, H., Largman, Y., Pham, P., & Ng, A. Y. (2009). Unsupervised feature learning for audio classification using convolutional deep belief networks. In *NIPS'09 Proceedings of the 22nd International Conference on Neural Information Processing Systems* (pp. 1096-1104). Vancouver, Canada: Curran Associates Inc.

Litjens, G., Kooi, T., Bejnordi, B. E., Setio, A. A., Ciompi, F., Ghafoorian, M., . . . Sanchez, C. I. (2017, Dec). A survey on deep learning in medical image analysis. *Elsevier, 42*, 60-80.

Orr, M. J. (1996). *Introduction to Radial Basis Function Networks.* Academic Press.

Peng, C.-Y. J., Lee, K. L., & Ingersoll, G. M. (2002). An Introduction to Logistic Regression Analysis and Reporting. *The Journal of Educational Research, 96*(1), 3–14. doi:10.1080/00220670209598786

Rumelhart, D. E., Hinton, G. E., & Williams, R. J. (1986). *Learning internal representations by error propagation* (D. E. Rumelhart & J. L. McClelland, Eds.; Vol. 1). MIT Press.

Vedaldi, A., & Lenc, K. (2015). MatConvNet: Convolutional Neural Networks for MATLAB. In *MM '15 Proceedings of the 23rd ACM international conference on Multimedia* (pp. 689-692). New York, NY: ACM.

Wang, D., & Chen, J. (2018, October). Supervised Speech Separation Based on Deep Learning: An Overview. *IEEE/ACM Transactions on Audio, Speech, and Language Processing, 26*(10), 1702–1726. doi:10.1109/TASLP.2018.2842159 PMID:31223631

Wang, J., & Pei, D. (2017). Kernel-based deep learning for intelligent data analysis. In *2017 First International Conference on Electronics Instrumentation & Information Systems (EIIS).* Harbin, China: IEEE. 10.1109/EIIS.2017.8298716

Chapter 1
iOS App and Architecture of Convolutional Neural Networks

ABSTRACT

Deep convolutional neural networks (CNN) have attracted many attentions of researchers in the field of artificial intelligence. Based on several well-known architectures, more researchers and designers have joined the field of applying deep learning and devising a large number of CNNs for processing datasets of interesting. Equipped with modern audio, video, screen-touching components, and other sensors for online pattern recognition, the iOS mobile devices provide developers and users friendly testing and powerful computing environments. This chapter introduces the trend of developing pattern recognition CNN Apps on iOS devices and the neural organization of convolutional neural networks. Deep learning in Matlab and executing CNN models on iOS devices are introduced following the motivation of combining mathematical modelling and computation with neural architectures for developing pattern recognition iOS apps. This chapter also gives contexts of discussing typical hidden layers in the CNN architecture.

CNN-BASED PATTERN RECOGNITION IOS APPS

Nowadays, artificial intelligence (AI) is a world-wide hot issue. Researchers make efforts for AI development, in order to let the AI system deal with some single job for humans, make life more convenient and reduce labour expenditure. The field of machine learning has been the focus of AI development. Machine

DOI: 10.4018/978-1-7998-1554-9.ch001

learning analyses large-scale datasets, constructing structured mathematical models for approximation, prediction, classification or visualization. In the past decade, deep learning of convolutional neural networks (CNNs) has a major breakthrough (LeCun, Bengio, & Hinton, 2015) and has been extensively applied for computer vision (Krizhevsky, Sutskever, & Hinton, 2012), image recognition (Simonyan & Zisserman, 2014), speech recognition (LeCun & Bengio, 1995), natural language (Kim, 2014), etc. Nowadays, the "data-driven" deep learning of CNNs directly extracts filters of convolutions for realizing classifiers or approximation formula subject to large-scaled training data, making use of advanced parallel and distributed processes in a way significantly different from constructing traditional expert systems. It no longer needs to define axioms and rules for resolving the problem of constructing classifiers or approximating formula. The designer can extract information or filters from the training dataset directly and classify patterns through convolutional neural networks derived by deep learning methods. Like human brain learning, deep learning adapts interconnections of neural networks subject to constraints proposed by labelled training patterns so that the neural network can correctly classify testing patterns properly to correspondent categories. The neural architecture for deep learning includes feed-forward multilayer neural network (Charalambous, 1992), deep feed-forward neural networks (Hagan & Menhaj, 1994), convolutional neural networks (LeCun, et al., 1989), and deep convolutional neural networks (LeCun, Bottou, Bengio, & Haffner, 1998), etc. Neural organization of deep feed-forward neural networks and deep convolutional neural networks will be discussed in this book.

In the era of the global village, the emergence of Internets, computers and smart phones has brought people closer together, and the App Store of the smart phones has also brought developers and users closer. In addition to developing software, developers can also hit the product to the shelves of App Store for sale or provide users for free, and users can instantly give feedback to developers. Finally, the products can be patched and updated based on the feedback of user.

Using Xcode environment to create app software, packaging the software into the product and finally hitting the App Store shelves, such a development process can be completed by a developer or a team of developers. The Xcode for developing apps is equipped with a good environment of designing user interface (UI) based on the latest Swift programming language. In addition, learning and writing of the Swift programming are friendly in the Xcode.

2

Figure 1. Every detail affects the growth of AI

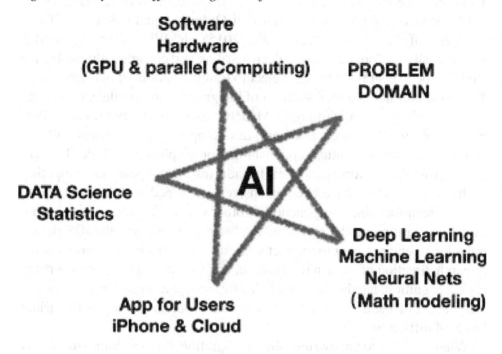

Even before the product is hit on the shelf, it can be easily tested and operated on iOS device by developers.

Deep learning arising in recent years has also begun to be applied to developing Apps of the smart phone, expanding applications of software and assisting operation of users. The combination of pattern recognition and video recognition with the App has becomed a trend. The new technology gradually affects and replaces the traditional App structure, making the App more user-friendly and increasing the processing speed of user requirement. As described in the article (Mrukwa, 2018), the App Store has announced many Apps that are equipped with the function of image pattern recognition and can be broadly classified into categories of Accessibility (Aipoly, 2019) (Cloudsight, TapTapSee, 2019), Shopping (Cloudsight, 2018) (Craze, 2018), Similarity Checks (Agarwa, 2018), Nature (Columbia University, Maryland University, & Smithsonian Institution, 2017), Food (Azumio, 2017), Fun (SeeFood Technologies, 2017), and so on. Obviously, the application of image recognition is extensive. Applying the function of image recognition to existing Apps or developing new Apps is a trend that cannot be ignored.

Today, in the industry and academia, there have been a lot of deep learning frameworks, such as TensorFlow of Google (Abadi, et al., 2016),

Torch of Facebook (Paszke, et al., 2017), Caffe of Berkeley (Jia, et al., 2014), MatCovnNet of the University of Oxford (Vedaldi & Lenc, 2015), and Keras of Francois Chollet (Chollet, 2015), etc. With these frameworks, we can easily explore the field of deep learning and conveniently establish a model of deep neural networks subject to training dataset of our interesting. This book introduces a total solution of integrating large-scale data sets and CNN models by deep learning in Matlab, mounting the pre-trained CNN models into the Xcode environment, designing a pattern recognition App on iOS devices and eventually publishing it on Apple's App Store. The iOS device provides developers and users friendly testing and powerful computing environments, which have been extensively equipped with modern audio, video, screen-touching components and other sensors for pattern recognition. The deep learning model simulates the brain learning, and the iOS device provides an environment to interact with the user. This book focuses on the research direction of pattern recognition, and uses examples of handwritten digit recognition, handwritten English letter recognition and medical image recognition of breast cancer to demonstrate problem solving with variant levels of difficulty.

When it comes to handwritten digit recognition, the first comes to mind is the Modified NIST(MNIST) database (LeCun, Bottou, Bengio, & Haffner, 1998). It contains 70,000 handwritten digit images from 0 to 9, in partition to 60,000 training patterns and 10,000 testing patterns, each of which is a 28x28 pixel grayscale image. After the LeNet CNNs model proposed by LeCun, researchers have regarded this example as *"Hello, World"* in the field of deep learning. This is a basic example for AI deep learning, like humans who also learn the digits 0, 1, 2, ..., 9 in childhood. We can find the MNIST example in well-known deep learning framework and track it. Here, we hope to expand the application of the MNIST example. We will pre-train the CNN model in Matlab for recognizing the handwritten digit image and install it on the iOS device. The user can directly write the digits on the touchscreen, and the smartphone instantly recognizes what they wrote. In order to allow more users to use this software, and hope that the model can adapt to more complex patterns of handwritten digits, we alternatively employ the Extension-MNIST(EMNIST) database (Cohen, Afshar, Tapson, & Schaik, 2017) from the MARCS Institute for Brain, Behaviour and Development of Western Sydney University to train our model. The pre-trained model subject to the EMNIST database with a test accuracy of 99.4% is derived under the Matlab environment and will be mounted into an iOS App, termed as *handwriting 99 multiplication*, and published on App Store finally.

After applying the total solution to handwriting 99 multiplication of deep learning, we hope to promote complexity of problem solving. In addition to handwritten digit datasets, the EMNIST database provides multiple balanced or unbalanced datasets. These datasets contain different combinations of handwritten digit and letter images. We believe that well trained deep CNNs can handle unbalanced datasets, so we chose the By_Class dataset of EMNIST database to increase the difficulty of problem solving. Here, we only consider classification of handwritten English characters, including uppercase and lowercase, and tests on iOS devices. After training in Matlab, we got the pre-trained CNN model. For 58,405 testing images, the recognition accuracy rate was as high as 97.0%. This recognition model of handwritten letter can be further developed and applied to the Apps of handwritten English translators, handwritten notes and handwritten English crossword, etc. The model of high-accuracy handwritten letter recognition can replace traditional touch-typing mode, increasing the convenience of application Apps and the diversity of the educational Apps. Besides, we can also combine the models of handwritten digits and letters to develop assistive apps for people with disabilities. The people with disabilities can communicate messages by writing on the mobile-screen or scanning text from the paper with camera.

After understanding the basic image recognition of deep learning, we increase the difficulty of the pattern recognition problem again. We hope that image recognition can be extended to medical-aided diagnosis. For humans around the world, cancer diagnosis has been the most important health problem, especially Breast Cancer, which is one of the most common cancers among women. The World Health Organization (WHO) has a section on breast cancer description:

Breast cancer is the most frequent cancer among women, impacting 2.1 million women each year, and also causes the greatest number of cancer-related deaths among women. In 2018, it is estimated that 627,000 women died from breast cancer – that is approximately 15% of all cancer deaths among women. While breast cancer rates are higher among women in more developed regions, rates are increasing in nearly every region globally. (World Health Organization, 2018)

We have observed that breast cancer has seriously threatened health of women around the world. For medical image recognition of breast cancer, our approach is no longer the same as the traditional. In our approach, there is no need to define axioms to distinguish between malignant and benign, and it is not necessary to invite a professional cytologist to help us circle the nuclei in breast cancer image before classification. In feature extraction of images, we no longer use hand-crafted textural descriptors, which can reduce the bias of machine learning due to manual extraction features. We hope to develop a mobile-aided diagnosis system that can directly process a raw image. It will automatically extract features, more precisely filters of a deep CNN for image recognition derived by deep learning subject to dataset collected in the past. This exactly illustrates the reason why CNNs are effective. Therefore, we will establish a CNN architecture to help diagnose breast cancer images, and illustrate effectiveness of problem solving by demonstrating two examples respectively for diagnosing lobular carcinoma breast cancer against phyllodes tumor and papillary carcinoma against adenosis, which attain the testing accuracy rate of 94.9% and 87.3%.

CNN ARCHITECTURE

Deep learning addresses on learning the deep neural network that is equipped with more than two hidden layers. In the past decade, the development of deep convolutional neural networks has attracted much attention in the field of artificial intelligence for image pattern recognition of industrial applications. Deep learning of the convolutional neural network can automatically extract spatial invariant features, and the convolutional capability of dealing with pattern recognition problems had been extensively demonstrated. LeNet is the basic CNN architecture proposed by LeCun. In the previous work (LeCun, et al., 1989) (LeCun, Bottou, Bengio, & Haffner, 1998), the operation of spatial convolution through filters has been recruited to hidden layers of the deep neural network, where the visual features need no more hand-craft. Especially significant features in the training images for classification can be self-learned by the Back-Propagation (BP) training method and related to convolutional filters of LeNet. Deep convolutional neural networks have significant breakthroughs in pattern recognition, audio analysis, speech analysis and natural language etc. CNNs are getting attention. In recent years, there have been some famous CNN architectures, such as AlexNet (Krizhevsky, Sutskever, & Hinton, 2012), VGG (Simonyan & Zisserman, 2014), GoogLeNet (Szegedy, et al., 2015), ResNet (He, Zhang, Ren, & Sun, 2015), RCNN (Girshick, Donahue, Darrell, & Malik, 2014) (Girshick, Fast R-CNN, 2015), etc. These CNN architectures are designed to deal with the problem of classification subject to large-scale datasets. With these well-known architectures, more scholars and practitioners have joined the deep learning field, devising a large number of CNNs for processing datasets of interest. The deep learning paper (LeCun, Bengio, & Hinton, 2015) published in 2015, give comprehensive understanding of the architecture, training methods and application of deep convolutional neural networks. The CNN consists of one or more convolutional layers as well as multiple fully connected hidden layers into a deep neural network. Convolution is usually designed to extract the spatial invariant characteristics of the visual image (LeCun, Kavukcuoglu, & Farabet, 2010), and BP is used to make the deep neural networks self-learning. In this book, we hope to use the deep CNN architecture to deal with basic pattern recognition and diagnosis of medical images.

In deep learning, except for the basic input layer and output layer, the other layer is called the hidden layer. For all hidden layers, we can combine arbitrarily, such as common using Convolutional layer, Pooling layer, ReLU and BatchNorm, etc. as a hidden layer. The output layer get used to using Softmax or Softmaxloss that makes the output of CNNs a probability value, facilitating calculation of the derivative of the output or deviation. The following is a summary of several types of hidden layers common in CNN architecture, which provide a basic discussion of CNN architecture.

- **Input Layer:** Input data to this layer maybe a grayscale image, color image (RGB 3-channels), video, speech and audio. A 28x28 color image says the input image is a 28x28x3 three-dimensional (3D) matrix.
- **Convolution layer (LeCun, et al., 1989):** The convolution layer contains a lot of kernels. The kernel is sometimes called the filter or channel. Each kernel in the same convolution layer has the same size. This type of layer will convolve the input map with each kernel according to a fixed stride. After the convolution, the output of the layer is called feature map, and the size of the feature map depends on the size of the input map and kernels. The weight of kernel will be updated continuously during the training phase. Suppose the size of input map is NxN, and the size of kernel is KxK, and stride is S. The size of feature map will be $\left(\frac{N-K+1}{S}\right) \times \left(\frac{N-K+1}{S}\right)$ Figure 2 shows the feedforward process of the convolution layer, with a kernel and stride = 1, where the size of the input map is 5x5 and the size of the kernel is 2x2. The size of the feature map after convolution is 4x4.

Figure 2. A convolution layer with a 5x5 input map and a 2x2 kernel

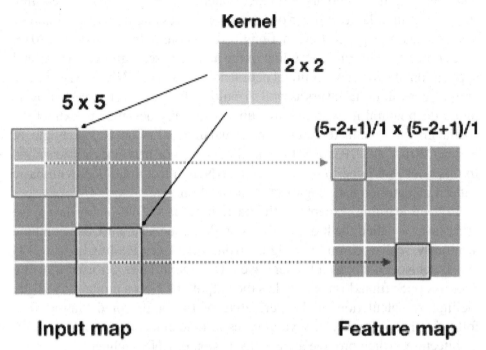

After convolution, the size of feature map will be reduced. If you want the feature map to have same size as the input map, one can set the size of padding. It will add 0 around the input map so that you can get the feature map of same size after the convolution. If there are multiple 2D input maps, the kernel could be extended and represented by a 3D array.

- **Pooling Layer (Scherer, Müller, & Behnke, 2010):** Pooling layer is a subsampling mechanism. The pooling has two types: maximum pooling (Max pooling) and average pooling (Avg pooling). The feature map of the previous layer will be downsampling through the pooling layer, reducing the dimension of feature map. A pooling layer can greatly reduce the parameters required by the next layer, speed up the calculation, and retain important information Figure 3 show two types of pooling, respectively employing filters of downsampling by taking the maximum or average values.

Figure 3. Max-pooling and avg-pooling.

Max Pooling

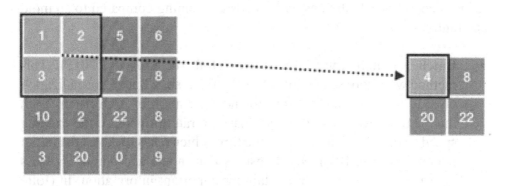

Avg Pooling

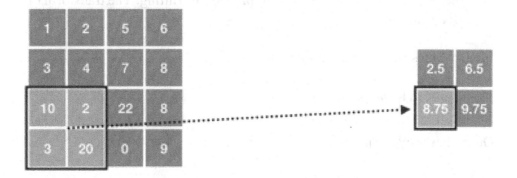

- **ReLU Layer (Nair & Hinton, 2010):** Rectified Linear Unit (ReLU) is an activation function like sigmoid and tanh (Agostinelli, Hoffman, Sadowski, & Baldi, 2014) (Nwankpa, Ijomah, Gachagan, & Marshall, 2018). Adding a nonlinear activation function to the hidden layer, can increase the complexity of the neural network, avoiding the output of a deep network simply a linear combination of inputs. In the ReLU layer, all the negative numbers will be forced to zero, and the positive numbers will be retained, as follows:

Input: $x = \{x_{1...m}\}$

Outputs: $f(x) = \max(0, x)$

ReLU is used in many well-known CNN architectures because ReLU reduces complex calculations and speeds up training compared to sigmoid and tanh.

- **Batch Normalization (BN) Layer (Ioffe & Szegedy, 2015):** This method was proposed by Ioffe & Szegedy. It adds Batch Normalization layer to the CNN architecture for normalization of each batch. With this method, we can use higher learning rate to increase the training speed of the model, and reduce the time which takes to adjust the initial parameters. The BN method ensures that inputs and outputs possess the same distribution while retaining important information. In (Ioffe & Szegedy, 2015), it is mentioned that BN can act as a regularizer. The training dataset is decomposed to batches of equal sizes. In some cases, there is no need to use dropout to prevent overfitting. The transform of BN as follows:

Input: Values of x over a mini-batch: $B = \{x_{1...m}\}$;

Parameters to be learned: γ, β

Output: $\{y_i = BN_{\gamma,\beta}(x_i)\}$

mini-batch mean: $\mu_\beta \leftarrow \dfrac{1}{m}\sum_{i=1}^{m} x_i$

mini-batch variance: $\sigma_\beta^2 \leftarrow \dfrac{1}{m}\sum_{i=1}^{m}(x_i - \mu_\beta)^2$

normalize: $\hat{x}_i \leftarrow \dfrac{x_i - \mu_\beta}{\sqrt{\sigma_\beta^2 + \varepsilon}}$

scale and shift: $y_i \leftarrow \gamma \hat{x}_i + \beta \equiv BN_{\gamma,\beta}(x_i)$

- **Fully Connected Layer:** The fully connected layer is a component of the multilayer perceptron (MLP). In the deep learning architecture, the fully connected layer maps an input vector to an output vector. The neurons in the hidden layer will be fully connected to the neurons in the next layer. In the Caffe deep learning framework, the fully connected layer also be called the Inner Product Layer. Additionally, the fully connected layer is a special case of the convolutional layer. When the filter size of the convolutional layer amounts to the input size of the fully connected layer, the convolutional layer can replace the fully connected layer. The paper published by LeCun in 1998 (LeCun, Bottou, Bengio, & Haffner, 1998), the network architecture of LeNet-5 also used a convolutional layer to replace the first fully connected layer.

- **Output Layer:** When we use CNNs to deal with the problem of classification, we want to output a probability value for each category. This allows the neural network to automatically select the maximum value as the output, and compare with the correct category afterwards. Thus we are usually using Softmax as the output layer, and even conveniently to get the gradient in the training phase, we will use the Softmaxloss in the last layer of which the principle is the same as Softmax. The formulas are as follows:

  1.   Softmax layer (Bridle, 1990) –

Suppose input of softmax layer have m components: $x = \{x_{1..m}\}$

then $\sigma(x)_i = \dfrac{e^{x_i}}{\sum_{j=1}^{m} e^{x_j}}$ for $i = 1, \dots, m$

The output label is $i^* = argMax_{\{i\}}(\sigma(x)_i)$

  2.   Softmaxloss layer (Liu, Wen, Yu, & Yang, 2016) –

In the softmaxloss layer except for computing softmax of input the output unit will compute loss for the correct label. $Loss = -log\sigma(x)_i$, where i denotes the correct label. The gradient is easy to compute after loss of the correct label is given.

INTRODUCTION TO THE CELEBRATED
CNN ARCHITECTURES

As mentioned in the previous section, there have been many well-known convolutional neural network architectures in the last decade. These network architectures are constructed to solve the classification of large-scale databases. We will review these well-known deep learning models in this section, such as LeNet, AlexNet, VGG, GoogLeNet, ResNet, and so on.

LeNet

First of all, LeNet is recognized as the earliest ancestor of the convolutional neural networks with self-learning. LeCun proposed the LeNet-5 architecture in the 1998 paper (LeCun, Bottou, Bengio, & Haffner, 1998). The deep learning architecture of LeNet-5 consists of an input layer, two convolutional layers, two subsampling layers, two fully connected layers, and a Gaussian connected output layer. It is a typical deep CNN model. The input layer will receive a 32x32 pixel image and recognize the image label through the deep CNN model. The first hidden layer in the LeNet-5 deep network architecture is the convolutional layer, which has six filters each with 5x5 size and the stride with one. After convolving the 32x32 pixel image, the first hidden layer will output six feature maps each with 28x28 size. The second hidden layer is the subsampling layer. It downsamples the feature maps of the previous layer output to six feature maps each with 14x14 size. Next, the third hidden layer is a convolutional layer, which has sixteen filters each with 5x5 size and the stride with one. This convolutional layer will output sixteen feature maps, each with 10x10 size. The fourth hidden layer is the subsampling layer, which will downsample the feature map of the previous layer to sixteen feature maps, each of which has a 5x5 size. The last three layers of LeNet architecture are two fully connected layers and a Gaussian connected output layer. Although the fifth hidden layer is a fully connected layer, the fifth hidden layer is implemented by a convolutional layer rather than a fully connected layer. This layer consists of one hundred twenty filters and each filter size is equal to the feature map of the fourth hidden layer output. The fully connected layer can be considered as a special case of the convolutional layer. Therefore, we can obtain one hundred twenty feature maps at the output of the fifth hidden layer. The sixth hidden layer is a fully connected layer. The fifth hidden layer of neurons is fully connected to the sixth hidden layer of neurons. The sixth hidden layer consists of eighty-four neurons. The final layer of the LeNet architecture is the output layer of network, which contains ten neurons each neuron represents a recognition class. The architecture of the output layer is the same as Radial Basis Function Network model. Each unit in the output layer is not only fully connected to the eighty-four units of the sixth hidden layer but also calculates the Gaussian function. The LeNet-5 model can achieve a test error of 0.95% for the MNIST handwritten database. The achievement of LeNet-5 prompted people to believe in the effectiveness of CNNs and use CNNs to solve other large-scale databases.

AlexNet

AlexNet was designed by Alex Krizhevsky and published in 2012 with Ilya Sutskever and Geoffrey E. Hinton (Krizhevsky, Sutskever, & Hinton, 2012). AlexNet is a deep convolutional neural network consisting of multiple hidden layers. The model was designed to classify into 1000 different classes for the 1.2 million high-resolution color images in the 2010 ImageNet Large-Scale Visual Recognition Challenge (LSVRC) competition. For 150,000 test images, the top-1 and top-5 error rates of AlexNet were 37.5% and 17.0%, respectively. Further, the variant of the AlexNet model achieved a top-5 test error of 15.3% and won the championship in the ImageNet LSVRC 2012 competition. The architecture of AlexNet is similar to LeNet-5. The model consists of five convolutional layers and three fully connected layers. It was constructed to solve the recognition of large databases. The input layer of the AlexNet model will receive 256x256 pixel color images. The model can recognize 1000 classes, such as goldfish, great white shark, airliner and ambulance, etc. In addition, several new technologies have been added to the AlexNet architecture to enhance the recognition performance of the model, such as ReLU (Nair & Hinton, 2010) (Glorot, Bordes, & Bengio, 2011), Dropout (Hinton, Srivastava, Krizhevsky, Sutskever, & Salakhutdinov, 2012) (Srivastava, Hinton, Krizhevsky, Sutskever, & Salakhutdinov, 2014), and Local Response Normalization (Jarrett, Kavukcuoglu, Ranzato, & LeCun, 2009). ReLU is an activation function like sigmoid function and hyperbolic tangent (tanh), but the paper of AlexNet clearly points out that using ReLU in a deep neural network architecture can make the model converge faster than using tanh or sigmoid function. In the architecture of AlexNet, there is a ReLU layer after each convolutional layer. The paper also presents the addition of the dropout method to the behind of the first and second fully connected layers in AlexNet architecture. The dropout mechanism is used to reduce the over-fitting of the fully connected layer during training. In the fully connected layer, each neuron will fully connect to the neurons of the next layer. Dropout can set a probability value p such that each neuron in the fully connected layer has a probability that does not participate in the transmission of the next layer during the training process. The AlexNet architecture also adds the Local Response Normalization hidden layer behind the first two ReLU layers. According to experiments in the AlexNet paper, normalization in the network architecture can reduce the test error of the model. However, the local response normalization method in deep CNNs has gradually been replaced by Batch Normalization in recent years. In addition to using these techniques to improve the convergence speed and recognition performance of the model, AlexNet also uses GPU parallel operations to accelerate the efficiency of CNN model training. AlexNet has made many contributions to the field of deep learning and presented the power of combining GPU of the computer hardware and 2D convolution of the deep learning model.

VGGNet

After AlexNet in 2012, what deserves our attention is the 2014 VGGNet (Simonyan & Zisserman, 2014). The VGG deep convolutional neural network was developed by the Visual Geometry Group, Department of Engineering Science, University of Oxford. VGGNet won the second place in the classification competition of the ImageNet LSVRC 2014. VGGNet is a very deep convolutional neural network. The input layer of the model receives 224x224 fixed-size color images and the output layer recognizes one thousand different classes. The network architecture of VGG contains a large number of convolutional layers and three fully connected layers. VGGNet follows the advantages of AlexNet, using the convolutional layer plus the ReLU layer to construct a deep CNN model. The model advocates the use of 3x3 sized filters in the convolutional layer and pushes forward the depth of the convolutional neural network to 16-19 layers. The model uses a lot of small receptive fields to replace a large filter in the convolutional layer. Specifically, the VGG model replaces a 5x5 size filter with two 3x3 size filters in the convolutional layer and replaces a 7x7 size filter with three 3x3 size filters. This mechanism not only reduces the number of training parameters but also enhances the recognition performance of the model by increasing the depth of the network. VGGNet presents six very deep CNN models, namely VGG-

11, VGG-11 with LRN, VGG-13, VGG-16 with 1x1 filters convolution, VGG-16, and VGG-19. The VGG network architecture most commonly used by researchers is VGG-16 and VGG-19. VGG-16 contains thirteen convolutional layers and three fully connected layers. VGG-19 expands the convolutional layer of VGG-16 from thirteen to sixteen layers. Since these two models are very deep CNN models, the network training process is time-consuming. Therefore, the VGG network first trained an eleven-layer of convolutional neural networks containing eight layers of convolutional layers and three layers of fully connected layers. For deeper architecture models, they used an eleven-layer pre-trained network to initialize the first four convolutional layers and the last three fully connected layers to enable the model to converge quickly. The uninitialized layers in the model are randomly initialized by a normal distribution $N(0,10^2)$ and self-learned through model training. This approach leads the deep network model to train from a well starting point. Also, the paper of the VGG network presents their experiments that local response normalization cannot effectively improve the recognition accuracy of the model. For the deeper network models, they no longer add the LRN method. The contribution of the VGGNet is that increasing the depth of the CNN can improve the recognition accuracy of the model and provide an efficient training approach for the deep CNN models.

GoogLeNet

GoogLeNet (Szegedy, et al., 2015) was the first in the 2014 ImageNet LSVRC classification competition. GoogLeNet is also named Inception by the Google team. Inception is a deep and wide convolutional neural network. The concept of Inception model is from the Network in Network paper published by Lin et al. in 2013 (Lin, Chen, & Yan, 2013). Google released a total of four versions of the Inception model between 2014 and 2016. Inception v1 (Szegedy, et al., 2015) improves the problems that are likely to occur with many deep neural networks. For example, the built-in parameters are too large, the gradient disappears in the deep network during the training process, and the fully connected layer is easily over-fitting. Different than other well-known CNN models, the deep network architecture of GoogLeNet is a combination of many Inception modules. The Inception module integrates four hidden layers, a convolutional layer with 1x1 sized filters, a convolutional layer with 3x3 sized filters, a convolutional layer with 5x5 sized filters, and a maximum pooling with 3x3 receptive fields. Figure 4 shows the naïve version of the

Inception module proposed by GoogLeNet in Inception v1. At the same time, GoogLeNet proposes a big problem for the naïve version of the Inception module. Since the convolutional layer implements feature extraction for the feature map of the previous layer, even if an appropriate amount of 5x5 convolutions are used in the model, the calculation in a convolution layer with a large number of filters is very expensive. GoogLeNet proposes an Inception module with dimension reductions for solving this problem, as shown in Figure 5. This Inception module will merge the feature map of the previous layer before executing 3x3 convolutions or 5x5 convolutions. This Inception module can effectively prevent computational blow-up. For Inception v1 of very deep CNN, the Google group added two auxiliary classifiers to the model architecture during the model training process. Two auxiliary classifiers are used to prevent the gradient disappears when the backpropagation realized to the foremost hidden layer in the network architecture. In 2015, the Google launched the Inception v2 (Ioffe & Szegedy, 2015) and Inception v3 (Szegedy, Vanhoucke, Ioffe, Shlens, & Wojna, 2015) deep CNN models. The Inception v2 model references the method in VGGNet to replace the 5x5 filter in convolutional layer of Inception v1 with two 3x3 filters. Further, GoogLeNet uses asymmetric convolutions to replace the 3x3 filter in the Inception module. In the both papers, the team also questioned the necessity of auxiliary classifiers in Inception model and added the Batch Normalization approach to the network architecture of Inception v2. In 2016, the Google team added the residual network architecture proposed by He et al. (He, Zhang, Ren, & Sun, 2015) to the Inception model and published the Inception v4 deep CNN (Szegedy, Ioffe, Vanhoucke, & Alemi, 2016). The Inception v4 model can achieve a top 5 error of 3.08% on the test images of the ImageNet classification challenge.

ResNet

Finally, ResNet (He, Zhang, Ren, & Sun, 2015) is also a well-known deep convolutional neural network. ResNet is a deep CNN model developed by the Microsft teams. ResNet follows the concept of the deep network architecture of VGGNet (Simonyan & Zisserman, 2014) to enhance the recognition accuracy of the CNN model. It is a deep residual network with the depth of one hundred fifty-two layers. We know that the training of deep CNNs becomes more complex as the network architecture grows deeper. At present, all deep learning models realize self-learning through gradient descent. For very deep

Figure 4. The Inception module of the naïve version proposed by Google

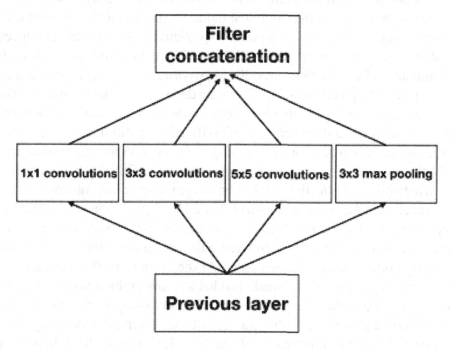

Figure 5. The Inception module with dimension reductions has been improved for problems encountered with the naïve version of the Inception module

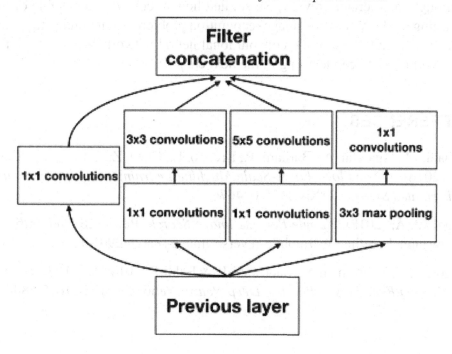

network architectures, the gradient of the output error easily disappears in backpropagation so that the frontmost hidden layers cannot implement self-learning. ResNet proposed a method of residual learning and referenced the shortcut connection method of Highway Network (Srivastava, Greff, & Schmidhuber, Highway Networks, 2015) (Srivastava, Greff, & Schmidhuber, Training very deep networks, 2015) to train deep CNNs. The combination of residual learning units and shortcut connections has made ResNet's network architecture deeper and deeper. In the classification task of ImageNet LSVRC 2015, ResNet achieved a top-5 error of 3.57% and won the championship.

With these well-known deep learning models, we find that convolutional neural networks can effectively solve the image recognition problem of large-scale databases. The state-of-the-art CNN technology has made the field of deep learning a breakthrough in the past decade. Scholars have found that increasing the depth of the hidden layer in the model can effectively improve the recognition accuracy of the model. At the same time, the deepening of deep convolutional neural networks has led to many problems in the training process. For example, a large number of the built-in parameter cause the computational explosion or the gradient of the frontmost hidden layers to disappear during backpropagation. Experts and scholars in the field of deep learning have gradually overcome problems and proposed new techniques to improve the effectiveness of the model in dealing with real-life problems. Through the literature review, we studied how to construct a suitable deep learning model for custom image recognition problems. After understanding the basic architecture of the convolutional neural network, we will explore the workings of deep learning in the next chapter.

REFERENCES

Abadi, M., Agarwal, A., Barham, P., Brevdo, E., Chen, Z., Citro, C., . . . Jia, Y. (2016). *TensorFlow: Large-Scale Machine Learning on Heterogeneous Distributed Systems.* arXiv:1603.04467

Agarwa, A. (2018). *Google Reverse Image Search.* Retrieved from https://www.labnol.org/internet/mobile-reverse-image-search/29014/

Agostinelli, F., Hoffman, M., Sadowski, P., & Baldi, P. (2014, Dec 21). *Learning Activation Functions to Improve Deep Neural Networks.* arXiv:1412.6830

Aipoly. (2019). *Aipoly Vision: Sight for Blind & Visually Impaired.* Retrieved from App Store Preview: https://itunes.apple.com/us/app/aipoly-vision-sight-for-blind-visually-impaired/id1069166437?mt=8

Azumio, I. (2017). *Calorie Mama AI: Diet Counter.* Retrieved from App Store: https://itunes.apple.com/app/apple-store/id1121789860?mt=8

Bridle, J. S. (1990). *Probabilistic Interpretation of Feedforward Classification Network Outputs, with Relationships to Statistical Pattern Recognition* (F. F. Soulié & J. Hérault, Eds.; Vol. 68). Berlin: Springer. doi:10.1007/978-3-642-76153-9_28

Charalambous, C. (1992, June). Conjugate gradient algorithm for efficient training of artificial neural networks. *IEE Proceedings. Part G. Circuits, Devices and Systems, 139*(3), 301–310. doi:10.1049/ip-g-2.1992.0050

Chollet, F. (2015). *Keras.* Retrieved from GitHub: https://github.com/keras-team/keras

Cloudsight, I. (2018). *CamFind.* Retrieved from App Store Preview: https://itunes.apple.com/app/camfind-visual-search-powered-by-cloudsight-ai/id595857716

Cloudsight, I. (2019). *TapTapSee.* Retrieved from App Store Preview: https://itunes.apple.com/us/app/taptapsee/id567635020

Cohen, G., Afshar, S., Tapson, J., & Schaik, A. V. (2017). *EMNIST: an extension of MNIST to handwritten letters.* arXiv:1702.05373

Columbia University, Maryland University, & Smithsonian Institution. (2017). *Leafsnap.* Retrieved from App Store: https://itunes.apple.com/us/app/leafsnap/id430649829?mt=8

Craze, I. (2018). *Screenshop by Craze.* Retrieved from App Store Preview: https://itunes.apple.com/us/app/screenshop-by-craze/id1254964391?mt=8

Girshick, R. (2015). Fast R-CNN. In *2015 IEEE International Conference on Computer Vision (ICCV).* Santiago, Chile: IEEE. 10.1109/ICCV.2015.169

Girshick, R., Donahue, J., Darrell, T., & Malik, J. (2014, Sep 25). Rich Feature Hierarchies for Accurate Object Detection and Semantic Segmentation. In *2014 IEEE Conference on Computer Vision and Pattern Recognition.* Columbus, OH: IEEE. 10.1109/CVPR.2014.81

Glorot, X., Bordes, A., & Bengio, Y. (2011). Deep Sparse Rectifier Neural Networks. In *Proceedings of the Fourteenth International Conference on Artificial Intelligence and Statistics* (pp. 315-323). Fort Lauderdale, FL: Proceedings of Machine Learning Research.

Hagan, M. T., & Menhaj, M. B. (1994, November). Training feedforward networks with the Marquardt algorithm. *IEEE Transactions on Neural Networks, 5*(6), 989–993. doi:10.1109/72.329697 PMID:18267874

He, K., Zhang, X., Ren, S., & Sun, J. (2015). *Deep Residual Learning for Image Recognition.* arXiv:1512.03385

Hinton, G. E., Srivastava, N., Krizhevsky, A., Sutskever, I., & Salakhutdinov, R. R. (2012, Jul 3). *Improving neural networks by preventing co-adaptation of feature detectors.* arXiv.

Ioffe, S., & Szegedy, C. (2015). *Batch Normalization: Accelerating Deep Network Training by Reducing Internal Covariate Shift.* arXiv:1502.03167

Jarrett, K., Kavukcuoglu, K., Ranzato, M. A., & LeCun, Y. (2009, Sep). What is the best multi-stage architecture for object recognition? In *2009 IEEE 12th International Conference on Computer Vision.* Kyoto, Japan: IEEE.

Jia, Y., Shelhamer, E., Donahue, J., Karayev, S., Long, J., Girshick, R., . . . Darrell, T. (2014). Caffe: Convolutional Architecture for Fast Feature Embedding. In *MM '14 Proceedings of the 22nd ACM international conference on Multimedia* (pp. 675-678). Orlando, FL: ACM.

Kim, Y. (2014). Convolutional Neural Networks for Sentence Classification. In *Proceedings of the 2014 Conference on Empirical Methods in Natural Language Processing (EMNLP)* (pp. 1746-1751). Doha, Qatar: Association for Computational Linguistics. 10.3115/v1/D14-1181

Krizhevsky, A., Sutskever, I., & Hinton, G. E. (2012). ImageNet classification with deep convolutional neural networks. In *NIPS'12 Proceedings of the 25th International Conference on Neural Information Processing Systems* (vol. 1, pp. 1097-1105). Lake Tahoe, NV: Curran Associates Inc.

LeCun, Y., & Bengio, Y. (1995). Convolutional Networks For Images Speech and Time Series. In M. A. Arbib (Ed.), *The handbook of brain theory and neural networks* (pp. 255–258). Cambridge, MA: MIT Press.

LeCun, Y., Bengio, Y., & Hinton, G. (2015, May 28). Deep Learning. *Nature, 521*(7553), 436–444. doi:10.1038/nature14539 PMID:26017442

LeCun, Y., Boser, B., Denker, J. S., Henderson, D., Howard, R. E., Hubbard, W., & Jackel, L. D. (1989, December). Backpropagation Applied to Handwritten Zip Code Recognition. *Neural Computation, 1*(4), 541–551. doi:10.1162/ neco.1989.1.4.541

LeCun, Y., Bottou, L., Bengio, Y., & Haffner, P. (1998, November). Gradient-based learning applied to document recognition. *Proceedings of the IEEE, 86*(11), 2278–2324. doi:10.1109/5.726791

LeCun, Y., Kavukcuoglu, K., & Farabet, C. (2010). Convolutional networks and applications in vision. In *Proceedings of 2010 IEEE International Symposium on Circuits and Systems*. Paris, France: IEEE. 10.1109/ISCAS.2010.5537907

Lin, M., Chen, Q., & Yan, S. (2013, Dec 16). *Network In Network*. arXiv.

Liu, W., Wen, Y., Yu, Z., & Yang, M. (2016). Large-margin softmax loss for convolutional neural networks. In *ICML'16 Proceedings of the 33rd International Conference on International Conference on Machine Learning* (vol. 48, pp. 507-516). New York, NY: JMLR.org.

Mrukwa, G. (2018, Oct 8). *11 Top Image Recognition Apps to Watch in 2019*. Retrieved from https://www.netguru.com/blog/11-top-image-recognition-apps-to-watch-in-2019

Nair, V., & Hinton, G. (2010). Rectified Linear Units Improve Restricted Boltzmann Machines. ICML 2010, Haifa, Israel.

Nwankpa, C., Ijomah, W., Gachagan, A., & Marshall, S. (2018, Nov 8). *Activation Functions: Comparison of trends in Practice and Research for Deep Learning*. arXiv:1811.03378

Paszke, A., Gross, S., Chintala, S., Chanan, G., Yang, E., DeVito, Z., . . . Lerer, A. (2017). Automatic differentiation in PyTorch. The future of gradient-based machine learning software and techniques in 2017 Autodiff Workshop, Long Beach, CA.

Scherer, D., Müller, A., & Behnke, S. (2010). Evaluation of Pooling Operations in Convolutional Architectures for Object Recognition. In K. I. Diamantaras, W. Duch, & L. S. Iliadis (Ed.), ICANN (vol. 3, pp. 92-101). Springer. doi:10.1007/978-3-642-15825-4_10

SeeFood Technologies. I. (2017). *Not Hotdog*. Retrieved from App Store: https://itunes.apple.com/us/app/not-hotdog/id1212457521?mt=8

Simonyan, K., & Zisserman, A. (2014). *Very Deep Convolutional Networks for Large-Scale Image Recognition.* arXiv:1409.1556

Srivastava, N., Hinton, G., Krizhevsky, A., Sutskever, I., & Salakhutdinov, R. (2014, June 15). Dropout: A Simple Way to Prevent Neural Networks from Overfitting. *Journal of Machine Learning Research.*

Srivastava, R. K., Greff, K., & Schmidhuber, J. (2015, May 3). *Highway Networks.* arXiv:1505.00387

Srivastava, R. K., Greff, K., & Schmidhuber, J. (2015). Training very deep networks. In *NIPS'15 Proceedings of the 28th International Conference on Neural Information Processing Systems* (vol. 2, pp. 2377-2385). Montreal, Canada: MIT Press.

Szegedy, C., Ioffe, S., Vanhoucke, V., & Alemi, A. (2016, Feb 23). *Inception-v4, Inception-ResNet and the Impact of Residual Connections on Learning.* arXiv.

Szegedy, C., Liu, W., Jia, Y., Sermanet, P., Reed, S., Anguelov, D., . . . Rabinovich, A. (2015, October 15). Going deeper with convolutions. In *2015 IEEE Conference on Computer Vision and Pattern Recognition (CVPR).* Boston, MA: IEEE.

Szegedy, C., Vanhoucke, V., Ioffe, S., Shlens, J., & Wojna, Z. (2015, Dec 2). *Rethinking the Inception Architecture for Computer Vision.* arXiv.

Turing, A. M. (1937). On Computable Numbers, with an Application to the Entscheidungsproblem. *Proceedings of the London Mathematical Society,* 2(1), 230–265. doi:10.1112/plms2-42.1.230

Vedaldi, A., & Lenc, K. (2015). MatConvNet: Convolutional Neural Networks for MATLAB. In *MM '15 Proceedings of the 23rd ACM international conference on Multimedia* (pp. 689-692). New York, NY: ACM.

World Health Organization. (2018). *Breast cancer.* Retrieved from World Health Organization: https://www.who.int/cancer/prevention/diagnosis-screening/breast-cancer/en/

Chapter 2
Deep Learning Theory and Software

ABSTRACT

In the past decade, deep learning has achieved a significant breakthrough in development. In addition to the emergence of convolution, the most important is self-learning of deep neural networks. By self-learning methods, adaptive weights of kernels and built-in parameters or interconnections are automatically modified such that the error rate is reduced along the learning process, and the recognition rate is improved. Emulating mechanism of the brain, it can have accurate recognition ability after learning. One of the most important self-learning methods is back-propagation (BP). The current BP method is indeed a systematic way of calculating the gradient of the loss with respect to adaptive interconnections. The main core of the gradient descent method addresses on modifying the weights negatively proportional to the determined gradient of the loss function, subsequently reducing the error of the network response in comparison with the standard answer. The basic assumption for this type of the gradient-based self-learning is that the loss function is the first-order differential.

DOI: 10.4018/978-1-7998-1554-9.ch002

INTEGRATING DATA AND CNNS BASED ON MATHEMATICAL DEEP LEARNING

Mathematics is the principal core of the development of artificial intelligence. Both machine learning and current deep learning are based on mathematical science. The mathematics is an "engine" for deep learning. Basic mathematics, including calculus, linear algebra and applied linear statistical models, etc., has been applied to deal with identification and classification problems. Deep learning based on the mathematical model induces variant mathematical approaches to discriminant analysis, derivation and calculation of the gradient of the cost function with respect to built-in parameters, the conversion of high-dimensional data to internal representations, and the approximation of the objective function by reducing the error, etc. The importance of mathematics is increasing for the development of AI in the future. The mathematics subjects that developers have studied in the past have great opportunities to enhance recognition accuracy of deep learning or create novel training methods for future AI.

The mathematical software that operates mathematical approaches using computers is critical for deep learning development. Turing machine of Alan Turing in 1936 (Turing, 1937), the Von Neumann architecture in 1945 (Von Neuman, 1993), and the first computer made in accordance with the Von Neumann architecture in the 1950s all tried to expand mathematical knowledge and methods to deal with the huge amount of computations for problem solving. With contributions of Alan Turing and Von Neumann, there is a clear and close connection among mathematics, high performance computing, and artificial intelligence. Today, with the improvement of computing efficiency, we can construct mathematical models on the computer to solve real-world problems which involve extremely high complexity of computations, large-scale data analysis, essential high-dimensional nonlinearity, information uncertainty and data loss. Most of them cannot be easily reduced to an existing mathematical problem. The numerical-analysis software developed by realizing mathematical approaches on high-performance computers helps to develop complex mathematical models. The numerical-analysis software relies on mathematical knowledge and methods that approach problem solving based on solidity of mathematical definitions, theorems and calculations.

The strong connection between mathematics, numerical-analysis software and AI has contributed to the successful development of deep learning. Developers can rely on learned mathematical mapping and use trusted numerical-analysis software to construct deep learning models on high-performance computers to realize the application of AI. Finally, the model of deep learning is used to deal with real-world problems such as image recognition, natural language, and speech analysis in various languages, etc.

How Does Deep Learning Work?

In the past decade, deep learning has achieved a significant breakthrough in development. In addition to the emergence of convolution, the most important is that deep neural networks can self-learning. Through self-learning methods, the weights of kernels and parameters are automatically modified, the error rate is reduced, and the recognition rate is improved. Emulating the mechanism of the brain, it can have accurate recognition ability after learning. This self-learning method is called Back-Propagation (BP) (Rumelhart, Hinton, & Williams, 1986) (LeCun Y., 1988). The current BP method is a systematic approach for calculating the gradient of the loss with respect to adaptive interconnections. The principal core of the gradient descent is to modify the weight of parameters negatively proportional to the gradient of the loss function which is the first-order differential, thereby reducing the error with the standard answer.

Before the experiment, we will construct a suitable model of deep learning based on the dataset of interested, and divide the dataset into a training dataset and test dataset which are assumed independent of each other. In training of deep learning model, including one phase of training and one phase of testing. During the training phase, we use the training dataset to train the model and execute feedforward and backpropagation. However, the testing dataset is merely feedforward executed during the testing phase. Sometimes the dataset obtained is too large, we will use the batch size mechanism to bundle multiple pieces of data into the one batch. During the training and testing of the model, the data will be in batches. For example, the data obtained contains 60,000 training data and 10,000 test data. We can set 100 batch size in the training and test data to reduce the time for model learning. In other words, the per batch contains 100 data, and the dataset simplified to 600 batches of training data and 100 batches of test data. It will perform the feedforward and backpropagation in a per batch during each training and testing phase. Next, we will explore the mathematical theory of feedforward and backpropagation in neural networks and convolutional neural networks. In the process of explanation, use one piece of data in the one batch to introduce.

Suppose a single data is an n-dimensional vector and has a standard answer in the m outputs of the neural network. We construct a suitable architecture of deep neural network as shown in Figure 1. It contains an input layer, two hidden layers and one output layer, which respectively contain n input neurons, n_1 hidden neurons, n_2 hidden neurons and m output neurons. Further, the upper and lower hidden layers are connected by neural bonds. The feedforward process of the neural network receives an input data ξ_1, ξ_2, ξ_3. We will get the stimulating value of the first hidden layer $H1\zeta_j$ (2.1) and the output value of $H1\delta_j$ (2.2). Similarly, the stimulating value and the output value of $H2$ and *Output* are expressed by equations (2.3)(2.4) and (2.5)(2.6), respectively.

$$\zeta_j = \sum_{i \in Input} \omega_{ij} \xi_i \qquad (2.1)$$

$$\delta_j = f\left(\zeta_j\right) \qquad (2.2)$$

$$\zeta_k = \sum_{j \in H1} \omega_{jk} \delta_j \qquad (2.3)$$

$$\delta_k = f\left(\zeta_k\right) \qquad (2.4)$$

$$\zeta_l = \sum_{k \in H2} \omega_{kl} \delta_k \qquad (2.5)$$

$$\delta_l = f\left(\zeta_l\right) \qquad (2.6)$$

In the output units, the neural network output value, δ_1 and δ_2, is obtained. After the error is calculated by comparing with the correct answer, the gradient is executed shown in Figure 2. The weight is modified by an updating rule that sets the change negatively proportional to the gradient of each layer, so that the error of the neural network output is gradually reduced. We can easily calculate the output gradient and stimulus gradient for each layer of neurons through chain rule of calculus. For example: Supposes E (2.7) is half the square error of a single data and the error gradient of neural network with respect to the output of neuron l is $\frac{\partial E}{\partial \delta_l}$ (2.8). We can calculate $\frac{\partial E}{\partial \delta_l} \frac{\partial \delta_l}{\partial \zeta_l}$ to get the stimulus gradient of neuron l which is $\frac{\partial E}{\partial \zeta_l}$ REF_Ref6834025\h (2.9). However, the error gradient of neural network with respect to the output of neuron k is $\frac{\partial E}{\partial \delta_k}$ (2.10). We also can obtain through calculation $\sum \omega_{kl} \frac{\partial E}{\partial \zeta_l}$. We can obtain the remaining gradients through calculation (2.11), (2.12), and (2.13), respectively.

$$E = \frac{1}{2}(\delta_l - \delta)^2 \tag{2.7}$$

$$\frac{\partial E}{\partial \delta_l} = \delta_l - \delta \tag{2.8}$$

$$\frac{\partial E}{\partial \zeta_l} = \frac{\partial E}{\partial \delta_l} \frac{\partial \delta_l}{\partial \zeta_l} \tag{2.9}$$

$$\frac{\partial E}{\partial \delta_k} = \sum_{l \in Output} \omega_{kl} \frac{\partial E}{\partial \zeta_l} \tag{2.10}$$

$$\frac{\partial E}{\partial \zeta_k} = \frac{\partial E}{\partial \delta_k} \frac{\partial \delta_k}{\partial \zeta_k} \tag{2.11}$$

$$\frac{\partial E}{\partial \delta_j} = \sum_{k \in H2} \omega_{jk} \frac{\partial E}{\partial \zeta_k} \tag{2.12}$$

$$\frac{\partial E}{\partial \zeta_j} = \frac{\partial E}{\partial \delta_j} \frac{\partial \delta_j}{\partial \zeta_j} \tag{2.13}$$

With each layer of stimulus gradient, the gradient of the error of the neural network output with respect to the weight of each layer $\frac{\partial E}{\partial \omega_{kl}}$ (2.14), $\frac{\partial E}{\partial \omega_{jk}}$ (2.15), $\frac{\partial E}{\partial \omega_{ij}}$ (2.16) also can be easily calculated, and the internal parameter ω of each layer is corrected one by one afterward.

When the feedforward and backpropagation are completed once, the single data in a single batch has been trained. In addition, this process can execute a batch to save time in the training phase. After the neural network learns all the batches in the training dataset, it will execute the testing phase with the feedforward. Finally, the model continuous execute the training and testing phases based on the number epoch set by developer.

$$\frac{\partial E}{\partial \omega_{kl}} = \frac{\partial E}{\partial \zeta_l}\frac{\partial \zeta_l}{\partial \omega_{kl}} = \frac{\partial E}{\partial \zeta_l}\delta_k \tag{2.14}$$

$$\frac{\partial E}{\partial \omega_{jk}} = \frac{\partial E}{\partial \zeta_k}\frac{\partial \zeta_k}{\partial \omega_{jk}} = \frac{\partial E}{\partial \zeta_k}\delta_j \tag{2.15}$$

$$\frac{\partial E}{\partial \omega_{ij}} = \frac{\partial E}{\partial \zeta_j}\frac{\partial \zeta_j}{\partial \omega_{ij}} = \frac{\partial E}{\partial \zeta_j}\delta_i \tag{2.16}$$

Figure 1. The feedforward process of neural networks

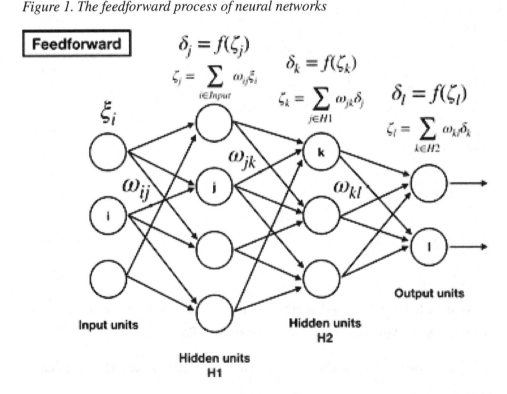

Figure 2. The backpropagation process of neural networks

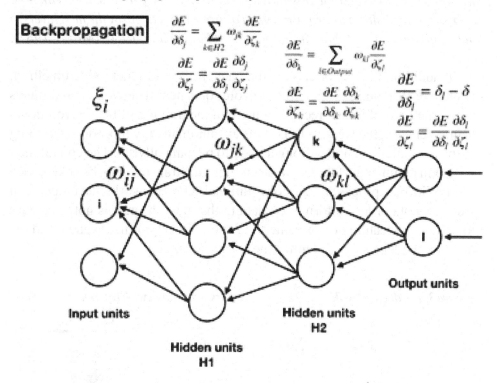

In addition to the basic deep learning architecture, BP is also used in the most popular CNN architecture. From the past to today, we always expect a method to make the neural network like a human being able to recognize. The convolution gives the neural network an automatic extraction of image features, enabling the convolutional neural network to simulate the mammalian visual nervous system. We introduced in the first chapter that convolutional layer contains multiple kernels. These specific size kernels inner product the input map in a fixed stride and extract the features of the local area. Finally, the feature map is transmitted to the next hidden layer and deal with higher order and more complex features. In 1989, LeCun described the feature map in the paper Backpropagation Applied to Handwritten Zip Code Recognition (LeCun, et al., 1989).

Distinctive features of an object can appear at various locations on the input image. Therefore it seems judicious to have a set of feature detectors that can detect a particular instance of a feature anywhere on the input plane. Since the precise location of a feature is not relevant to the classification, we can afford to lose some position information in the process. Nevertheless, approximate position information must be preserved, to allow the next levels to detect higher order, more complex features (Fukushima, 1980) (Mozer, 1987).

In addition, this paper applies the backpropagation method (Rumelhart, Hinton, & Williams, 1986) to the convolutional neural network, and it stands out in the field of image recognition. With the training of the convolutional neural network, the weights of kernels are automatically modified according to the error gradient and no longer need to be manually set. The convolution layer will retain important feature accurately and transmit it to the next hidden layer. With backpropagation in convolutional neural networks, developers can feed raw data or low-information data to the input layer. It is not necessary to extract the feature vector using the feature descriptor in advance, and the network model also can identify the image accurately.

Figure 3. The deep convolutional neural network was drawn with reference to LeNet-5

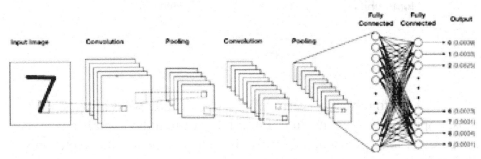

The convolutional neural network generally consists of multiple convolutional layers, pooling layers, nonlinear layers, fully connected layers, etc., as shown in Figure 3. Moreover, the calculation of feedforward and backpropagation are different for the type of each layer. The fully connected layer is an original architecture of the deep neural network and has discussed. We are going to discuss the feedforward and backpropagation of convolutional and pooling layers.

In the feedforward of the convolutional layer, the kernel will convolve the input map according to the set stride, and the resulting output map will be called the feature map. In the first chapter, we give a formula for calculating the size of the feature map based on the size of the input map, kernel, and stride. This formula allows us to build the next hidden layer after convolutional layer. In

Figure 4. A 2x2 kernel is convolving a 5x5 input map in the feedforward process of the convolutional layer

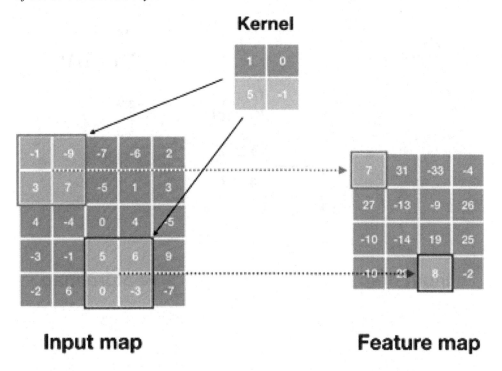

the Figure 4 gives an example of the convolutional layer, a 2x2 kernel with stride equal to 1 is convolving a 5x5 input map and will obtain a 4x4 feature map. This approach can extend to high-dimensional kernel and input map.

Moreover, for the convenience of explaining the backpropagation of convolution, we mark the 2x2 kernel(ω_{conv}) of convolution in Figure 5 in order of 1 to 4, which are represented by kernel(1), kernel(2), kernel(3), and kernel(4), respectively.

We can understand from the Figure 5 that the marked element of input map $\delta_{conv}(1,1)$ only contributes to Feature map $\zeta_{conv}(1,1)$ by multiplying the kernel(1). For the marked element in $\delta_{conv}(1,2)$, in addition to multiplying the kernel(2) contribution to $\zeta_{conv}(1,1)$, it is multiplied by the kernel(1) and contributes to $\zeta_{conv}(1,2)$.

For Figure 6, we can know the marked $\delta_{conv}(2,2)$ which is multiplied by kernel(4), kernel(3), kernel(2), and kernel(1) respectively and contributes to $\zeta_{conv}(1,1)$, $\zeta_{conv}(1,2)$, $\zeta_{conv}(2,1)$, and $\zeta_{conv}(2,2)$.

Figure 5. The feedforward of the convolution layer

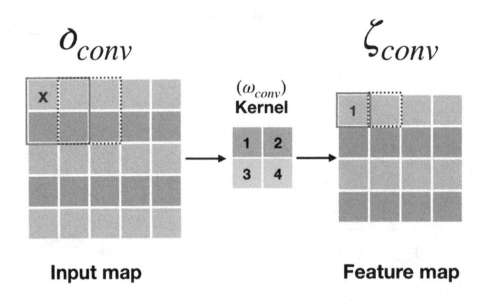

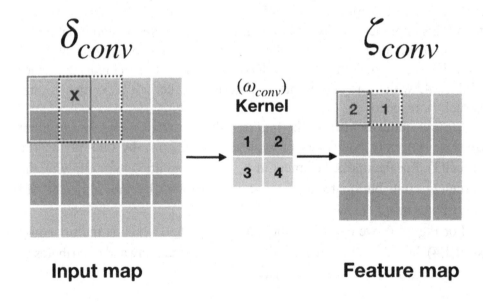

Figure 6. The feedforward and backpropagation of the convolutional layer

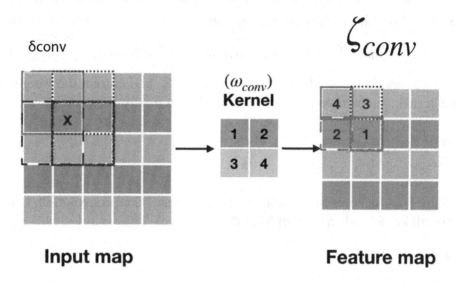

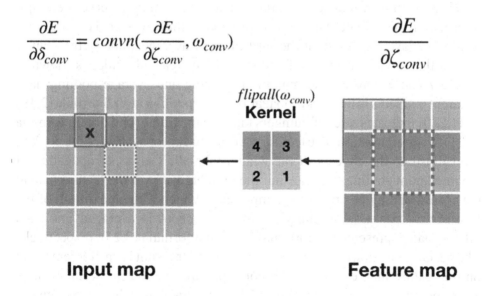

Assume that we have calculated that the error gradient of neural network output with respect to the neuron stimulus is $\frac{\partial E}{\partial \zeta_{conv}}$. We can get the gradient of the Input map $\frac{\partial E}{\partial \delta_{conv}}$ (2.17) by convoluting $\frac{\partial E}{\partial \zeta_{conv}}$ through $flipall(\omega_{conv})$. We also can obtain the gradient of the kernel (2.18) and correct the weight of the kernel, and complete the BP of convolution finally.

$$\frac{\partial E}{\partial \delta_{conv}} = convn\left(\frac{\partial E}{\partial \zeta_{conv}}, \omega_{conv}\right) \tag{2.17}$$

Where *convn* denotes the operation of high-dimensional convolution, which flips all kernels when used in Matlab.

$$\frac{\partial E}{\partial \omega_{conv}} = \frac{\partial E}{\partial \zeta_{conv}} \frac{\partial \zeta_{conv}}{\partial \omega_{conv}} = \frac{\partial E}{\partial \zeta_{conv}} \delta_{conv} \tag{2.18}$$

After introducing the feedforward and backpropagation of the convolution, we mentioned in the first chapter that the pooling layer has two types of maximum pooling and average pooling. The pooling layer in the convolutional neural network can reduce the training parameters and preserve the major information in the feature map of the previously hidden layer. The two types of pooling layers will output the maximum or average value in the feature map of the previous layer in a fixed size of the area and stride, as shown in Figure 7 and Figure 8. The maximum pooling and average pooling have different gradients in the backpropagation of the pooling layer. Formula (2.19) and (2.20) indicates a set of numbers take the maximum and obtain formula (2.21) by differentiation. The feedforward and backpropagation of the pooling layer illustrate the concept of the winner-take-all. The backpropagation of the maximum pooling will transmit the gradient value of the feature map to the corresponding position of the input map, which is the maximum of the feedforward process. Similarly, a set of numbers is averaged and then differentiated, presented in formula (2.22) and formula (2.23), respectively. The backpropagation of the average pooling will transmit each gradient value on the feature map equally to the corresponding region in the input map. Therefore, suppose we have calculated the error gradient of the neural network output with respect to the neuron stimulus is $\frac{\partial E}{\partial \zeta_{pooling}}$. Figure 9 and Figure 10 presents the gradients of the input map for maximum pooling and average pooling, respectively.

Figure 7. The feedforward of the maximum pooling layer

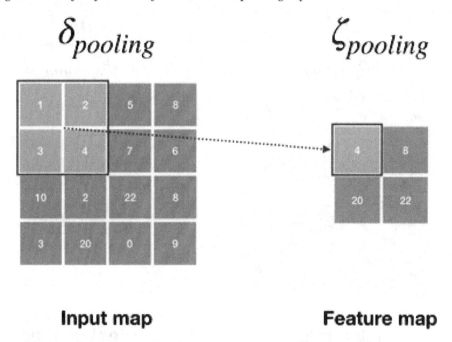

Input map   Feature map

Figure 8. The feedforward of the average pooling layer

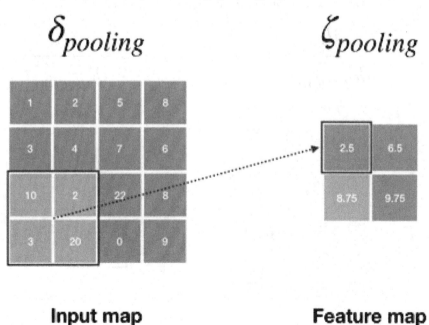

Input map   Feature map

Figure 9. The backpropagation of the maximum pooling layer

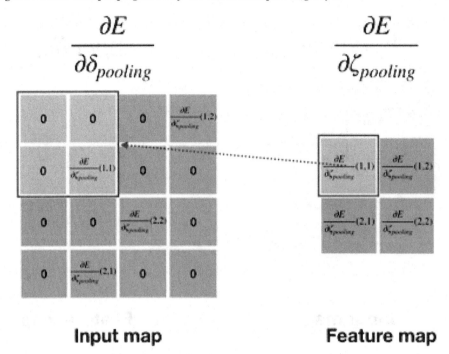

Figure 10. The backpropagation of the average pooling layer

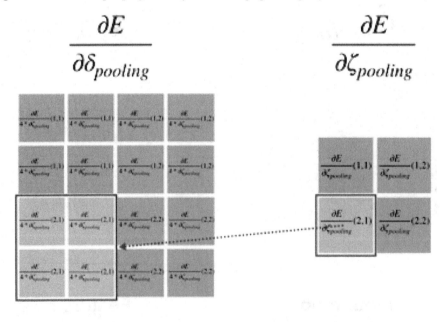

$$x^* = \max\{x_1, x_2, x_3, \ldots, x_{n-1}, x_n\}, n > 0 \tag{2.19}$$

$$k = argmax\{x_1, x_2, x_3, \ldots, x_{n-1}, x_n\}, \text{n} > 0 \tag{2.20}$$

$$\frac{\partial E}{\partial x_i} = \begin{cases} \frac{\partial E}{\partial x^*}, if \ i = k \\ 0, others \end{cases}, \text{for all } i = 1, 2, \ldots, n \tag{2.21}$$

$$y^* = \frac{1}{n}(y_1 + y_2 + y_3 \ldots + y_{n-1} + y_n), n > 0 \tag{2.22}$$

$$\frac{\partial E}{\partial y_j} = \frac{1}{n}\frac{\partial E}{\partial y^*} \text{ for all } j = 1, 2, \ldots, n \tag{2.23}$$

The deep learning with backpropagation enables it to achieve self-learning by gradient descent. Each weight of the hidden layer can be gradually modified based on the error gradient of the output. After the training phase, we will arrange a set of test data to validate the accuracy rate of the model. In the phase of the test, the model only executes feedforward. Finally, the output of the neural network will compare with the correct answer for calculating the accuracy rate of the model.

Deep Learning Frameworks of MatConvNet and Caffe

Today there are currently a lot of deep learning frameworks. In other words, the toolbox implements the gradient-based BP method, which can quickly build deep learning architecture, such as TensorFlow of Google (Abadi, et al., 2016), Torch of Facebook (Paszke, et al., 2017), Caffe of Berkeley (Jia, et al., 2014), MatCovnNet of the University of Oxford (Vedaldi & Lenc, 2015), and Keras of Francois Chollet (Chollet, 2015), etc. These deep learning frameworks significantly reduce the time for research and development, and lower threshold in the field of deep learning. The developer can according to interested dataset rewrite deep network architecture or create a new architecture for training easily when understanding deep learning theory comprehensively. This book will employ two deep learning frameworks MatConvNet and Caffe as our research tools.

MatConvNet (Vedaldi & Lenc, 2015) (Vedaldi, Lux, & Bertini, 2018) is a toolbox that works on Matlab. Matlab was published by MathWorks company which is over 30 years of history in the market. In view of Matlab reliability in the field of mathematics and support by MathWorks company, we can trust it and process our data conveniently on Matlab. The deep learning model is composed of many hidden layers. For state-of-the-art CNN models, the MatConvNet toolbox compiles various types of hidden layers into the calculational blocks. Developers can take these blocks to construct the CNN model on Matlab without having to re-define the function for each hidden layer. The deep learning model is portable. We can use the model to recognize objects at any time via retaining the deep learning architecture and built-in parameters after training the model. MatConvNet provides two model wrappers for developers, one called SimpleNN and the other DagNN. We can choose one of the wrappers to package the model architecture, built-in parameters, and training parameters before training the deep learning model. SimpleNN is simpler and easier to use than the DagNN wrapper. SimpleNN is suitable for smaller deep learning models, and the blocks in the architecture of the model present as a linear chain. The feedforward and backpropagation of deep learning model in SimpleNN wrapper is implemented by the vl_simplenn function in MatConvNet. We can execute the CIFAR-10 example provided by MatConvNet to demonstrate the deep learning model with SimpleNN wrapper. Before the demo, let's introduce the CIFAR-10 example.

CIFAR-10 is an image database created by Alex Krizhevsky, Vinod Nair and Geoffrey Hinton (Krizhevsky, Nair, & Hinton, CIFAR-10 and CIFAR-100 datasets, 2009). The database contains 60,000 color images each with 32x32 pixel. These images are distributed in 10 classes. The 10 classes are airplane, automobile, bird, cat, deer, dog, frog, horse, ship and truck. The color images in each class do not overlap in the other classes. The authors of the database have placed special emphasis on automobile class that include sedans, sport utility vehicles and sports cars, etc. However, the truck class include large vehicles such as big lorries. The images in these two classes are not overlapping. For 60,000 color images, they have been randomly divided into a training dataset with 50,000 images and a test dataset with 10,000 images. MatConvNet provides two CNN architectures for the CIFAR example, one is the LeNet architecture (LeCun, Bottou, Bengio, & Haffner, 1998) and the other is the Network in Network architecture referred to as the NIN (Lin, Chen, & Yan, 2013). We are using the LeNet architecture to demonstrate the CIFAR-10 model with SimpleNN wrapper. The default CIFAR-10 example has chosen SimpleNN network type to package the model architecture and built-in parameters. After forty-five iterations of training, we will obtain Figure 11. The best training result for the CIFAR-10 model in the figure is the forty-fifth number epoch. The top-1 error and top-5 error of the forty-fifth number epoch model can reach 19.68% and 1.16%, respectively. A pre-trained deep learning model is valuable and portable. The model can recognize unlabeled images by receiving images and performing feedforward process. We will demonstrate the feedforward of SimpleNN via Table 1. First, we must import the architecture and pre-trained parameters of the model on Matlab. Here we select the pre-trained model of the forty-fifth number epoch to recognition unlabeled images. After importing the model, we can observe the model's architecture and built-in parameters from the "cifar10_model.net.layers" variable. The architecture of the model consists of five convolutional layers, three pooling layers, four ReLU layers, and an output layer with softmaxloss. When the model receives the image and executes feedforward, we will obtain the predicted result of the model at the output layer. As we explained in the first chapter, the deep learning model uses softmaxloss as the output layer during the training phase for calculating gradient conveniently. Therefore, when the model only executes the feedforward for recognizing an image, we need to modify the type of the last hidden layer to softmax. After preparing the pre-trained model, we import the CIFAR-10 database that has been deducted the mean of the training dataset and store it as the "imdb" variable. The imdb. mat file stores the CIFAR-10 database that has been pre-processed during the model training phase. These pre-processing includes deducting mean of the training data, reshaping the images of the database, conversion of the image format, and so on. The "test_images" and "test_labels" variables store 10000 images of the CIFAR-10 test data set and labels of the relative classes for each image in the test data set, respectively. Here, we assign the "im" variable as the first image in the test data set and the "im_label" variable as the correct label for the first image. The correct label is invisible to the recognition model. In other words, the model dose not receive the correct label when it executes the feedforward for recognizing object. The correct label is used to compare the correctness of the model's recognition result. After preparing the pre-trained model and the data to be tested, we use the vl_simplenn function to implement the feedforward of the model. The vl_simplenn function must input four fixed variables, net, x, dzdy, and res. The net variable stores the network architecture and built-in parameters. The x variable stroes the data received by the input layer of the model. The dzdy variable stores the gradient information of the backpropagation. The res variable records the feedforward and backpropagation of each hidden layer. The remaining option variables can be input to the vl_simplenn function by variable-length input argument list (varargin) provided by Matlab, such as the information of the CuDNN, specifying the model's mode of operation, the restriction of backpropagation, and so on. Since we only execute feedforward to recognize the input image, we specify the mode of operation as "test" and store it in the "eval" variable. Finally, we sort the ten probability values in the output layer for descending order. The first sorted label is the predicted result of the model for the input image. Since we have referred top-5 error when training the model, the end of the code shows the top five classes of the model's predictions.

After demonstrating the feedforward of the CNN model wrapped by the SimpleNN, we will demo the feedforward process of the model with the DagNN. Although the DagNN wrapper is more complex and less understandable than SimpleNN, DagNN is more flexible than SimpleNN.

Figure 11. This figure presents the line graph of top-1 error and top-5 error for CIFAR-10 model with SimpleNN wrapper

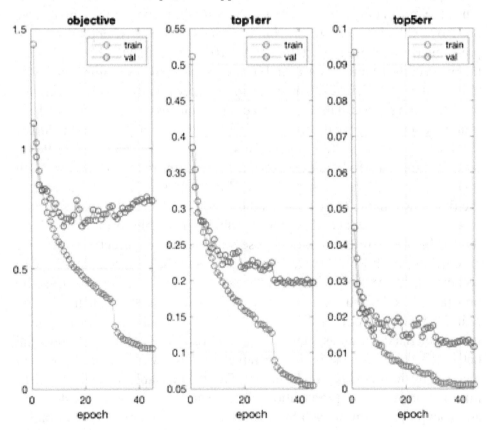

Table 1. This code implements the feedforward of the CIFAR-10 model in Matlab

```
% Select and import the SimpleNN pre-trained CIFAR-10 model.
% Here, we import the pre-trained parameters of the forty-fifth number epoch.
cifar10_model = load('./data/cifar-lenet/net-epoch-45.mat') ;
cifar10_model.net.layers{end}.type = 'softmax' ;
% Import CIFAR-10 test dataset, which has deducted the data mean of the training data.
imdb = load('./data/cifar-lenet/imdb.mat') ;
test_images = imdb.images.data(:,:,:, imdb.images.set == 3) ;
test_labels = imdb.images.labels(imdb.images.set == 3) ;
classes = imdb.meta.classes(:) ;
% Select a test image for realizing feedforward of the pre-trained. CIFAR-10 model.
% The "number" variable ranges from 1 to 10000.
number = 1 ;
im = test_images(:,:,:,number) ;
im_label = test_labels(number) ;
% Executing feedforward of the pre-trained model to recognize the selected test image.
dzdy = [] ;
res = [] ;
% 'test' is the test mode and 'normal' is the training model.
evalMode = 'test' ;
% Use the vl_simplenn function to implement feedforward and backpropagation.
res = vl_simplenn(cifar10_model.net, im, dzdy, res,...
'mode', evalMode) ;
% The presentation of the recognition result after the feedforward is executed.
[prob recognizing_label] = sort(res(14).x, 'descend') ;
% The correct label of the test image.
fprintf('The labeled class of the test image is: "%s"\n',classes{im_label}) ;
% The top-1 label and top-5 labels predicted by the model.
fprintf('The top-1 recognition result predicted by the model is: "%s"\n', classes{recognizing_label(1)}) ;
fprintf('The top-5 recognition result predicted by the model are:') ;
fprintf(1,' "%s"', classes{recognizing_label(1:5)}) ;
```

DagNN is suitable for constructing large and complex network structures like GoogLeNet or ResNet. SimpleNN uses the struct format to store the CNN model in the Matlab environment. The building blocks of CNNs in the SimpleNN wrapper are constructed by the function methods of traditional programming, but the building blocks in DagNN are implemented by object-oriented programming. Object-oriented programming has many advantages, such as modularity, flexibility, and maintainability. We know that the CNN architecture is made up of many building blocks. These building blocks are modularized into separate classes in the DagNN wrapper. Although these building blocks appear to be independent, they can work in concert with each other. Object-oriented programming enhances the flexibility of deep learning models. Developers can avoid modifying the code to add a custom hidden layer to the CNN model. Developers can create a new file with the class format in Matlab to develop the building blocks needed for the CNN model. Object-oriented programming reduces the risk of mistake when modifying the code. Object-oriented programming is more flexible and less risky than traditional methods of function construction. Developers are also more convenient when building the architecture of deep learning models.

For the demonstration of DagNN, we also use the CIFAR-10 example. Different from the LeNet architecture of SimpleNN, we use the Network in Network (NIN) structure as the architecture for the deep learning model. The authors of NIN paper (Lin, Chen, & Yan, 2013) believe that the fully connected layers of the deep network are prone to overfitting during model training. Therefore, they proposed a strategy called Global Average Pooling in the NIN paper to replace the fully connected layer of CNN. The NIN structure does not only use a large number of convolutional layers but also incorporates the dropout method proposed by Srivastave et al. (Srivastava, Hinton, Krizhevsky, Sutskever, & Salakhutdinov, 2014) to prevent over-fitting of the model. NIN paper presents that they can achieve a test error of 8.81% for the CIFAR-10 example. Now, we use the CIFAR-10 example with NIN architecture to demonstrate the feedforward of DagNN network type.

We need to slightly modify the cnn_cifar.m file provided by MatConvNet before training the CIFAR-10 model. The default of the CIFAR-10 example is using LeNet as the model type and SimpleNN as the network type. Therefore, we need to modify the model type and the network type to NIN and DagNN, respectively, as shown in Table 2. The NIN architecture for the CIFAR-10 problem includes nine convolutional layers, eight ReLU layers, three pooling layers, two dropout layers, and an output layer with softmaxloss type. Since the architecture of NIN is more complex than LeNet, it is time-consuming in the model training. Figure 12 shows the training error and test error of the CIFAR-10 model of the NIN architecture after forty-five iterations of training. We can find that the best model of the pre-trained parameters after forty-five iterations of training is the forty-first number epoch. The model can achieve a test error of 14.75% for 1000 test images. For the same of CIFAR-10 example and number epochs, we can observe that the NIN architecture converges faster than the LeNet. After training the CIFAR-10 model of the NIN architecture, we can execute the feedforward of the model to recognize customized images. Table 3 presents the code of the DagNN network type

Table 2. We need to slightly modify the variables in the cnn_cifar.m file before training the CIFAR-10 model

```
opts.modelType = nin' ;
opts.networkType = 'dagnn' ;
```

to execute feedforward. We chose the model of the forty-first number epoch with the highest test accuracy to implement the feedforward process. First, we load the pre-trained DagNN model via "dagnn.DagNN.loadobj". After loading the pre-trained model, we must modify the network mode to "test". The test mode causes the DagNN network to execute the feedforward only. Next, we select a test image to detect the recognition performance of the model, just like the demonstrate of SimpleNN. We can use the net.eval object and assign the input as a test image to implement the complex feedforward process. Since we did not give the correct label of the test image for the model, the feedforward of the network will stop at the output of the last hidden layer. We calculate the softmax function for the output of the last hidden layer and sort the probability values of the ten classes for descending order. Finally, the code will present the top one and top five labels predicted by the CIFAR-10 model.

Figure 12. This line graph presents the training error and test error of the CIFAR-10 model trained with DagNN and NIN architecture

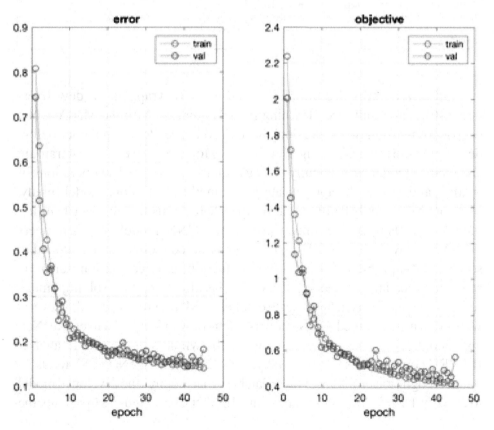

Table 3. We implement the feeforward of DagNN by pre-trained CIFAR-10 model

```
% Select and import the DagNN pre-trained CIFAR-10 model.
% Here, we import the pre-trained parameters of the forty-first number epoch.
% Use the dagnn.DagNN.loadobj command to activate a pre-trained deep learning model with DagNN network type.
load('./data/cifar-nin/net-epoch-41.mat') ;
net = dagnn.DagNN.loadobj(net) ;
% Select test mode.
% 'test' is the test mode and 'normal' is the training model.
net.mode = 'test' ;
% Import CIFAR-10 test dataset, which has deducted the data mean of the training data.
imdb = load('./data/cifar-nin/imdb.mat') ;
test_images = imdb.images.data(:,:,:, imdb.images.set == 3) ;
test_labels = imdb.images.labels(imdb.images.set == 3) ;
classes = imdb.meta.classes(:) ;
% Select a test image for realizing feedforward of the pre-trained CIFAR-10 model.
% The "number" variable ranges from 1 to 10000.
number = 1 ;
im = test_images(:,:,:, number) ;
im_label = test_labels(number) ;
% Executing feedforward of the pre-trained model to recognize the selected test image.
net.eval({'input', im}) ;
% Calculate the output of Softmax.
softmaxOutput = exp(net.vars(23).value) / sum(exp(net.vars(23).value)) ;
% The presentation of the recognition result after the feedforward is executed.
[prob recognizing_label] = sort(softmaxOutput, 'descend') ;
% The correct label of the test image.
fprintf('The labeled class of the test image is: "%s"\n', classes{im_label}) ;
% The top-1 label and top-5 labels predicted by the model.
fprintf('The top 1 recognition result predicted by the model is: "%s"\n', classes{recognizing_label(1)}) ;
fprintf('The top 5 recognition result predicted by the model are:') ;
fprintf(1,' "%s"', classes{recognizing_label(1:5)}) ;
```

MatConvNet provides SimpleNN and DagNN wrappers for developers to construct and train deep learning models quickly. With the MatConvNet deep learning framework, we don't have to code deep learning theory before developing the models, saving a lot of time. Moreover, we can repeat training and modify model conveniently through reliable mathematical operations of Matlab, and choose the appropriate pre-trained model as our model finally. MatConvNet not only facilitates developers to train customized deep learning models but also provides many pre-trained CNN models for developers (The MatConvNet Team, 2014). These pre-trained models are developed to solve specific problems such as object detection, face recognition, semantic segmentation, and ImageNet ILSVRC classification. For solving image recognition problems in large-scale databases, MatConvNet provides several well-known pre-trained CNN models such as AlexNet, VGGNet, ResNet, and GoogLeNet. These CNN models are the winners of the past ImageNet ILSVRC competitions (Russakovsky, et al., 2015). ImageNet ILSVRC is an image recognition problem for large database that requires the developed model to classify 1.2 million color images into 1000 classes. Figure 13 presents the well-known deep learning models developed for the large database of the ImageNet ILSVRC competitions from 2012 to 2015 (The MatConvNet Team, 2014). MatConvNet has provided these pre-trained models on the official website and stored them in the DagNN format. We can demonstrate these pre-trained models with the ImageNet example provded by MatConvNet toolbox. In the ImageNet example of MatConvNet, we can not only retrain these well-known CNN architectures but also directly use a pre-trained model to recognize images. We use the cnn_imagenet_googlenet.m file in MatConvNet to implement image recognition. The file uses the pre-trained GoogLeNet as the recognition model. MatConvNet has packaged the pre-trained GoogLeNet into the DagNN format so that we can easily import the model into the Matlab environment for application. The default input image for this example is an image of peppers. We can modify it to a custom image and input it input the GoogLeNet model for recognizing. The custom image must be pre-processed before inputting the model. The pre-processing stage includes image resizing, image digitization and deduction the average of the training dataset. Figure 14 presents the recognition result of the GoogLeNet model for a flowerpot with a planting cactus. The model accurately recognizes the flowerpot in the image and present a recognition score of 0.882.

In addition to the application of the pre-trained model by manually inputting the image, the object can be recognized directly by the webcam. The cnn_imagenet_camdemo function in the imagenet folder implements the combination of the pre-trained deep learning model and the webcam. Before the demonstration, we must first import the pre-trained model in Matlab and install the webcam support package (MathWorks Image Acquisition Toolbox Team, 2019). During the demonstration, the webcam will continuously snapshot the specific area and import an image into the Matlab environment for executing pre-process and recognition. Figure 15 presents the recognition results of the GoogLeNet receive a beer glass image via the webcam. Through the demonstration of the above two examples, we can implement the application of the image recognition model in Matlab. Matlab provides a good development and testing environment for mathematical models. MatCovNet integrates the blocks of CNN technology into Matlab for quickly constructing the deep learning models. Therefore, we chose to use the MatConvNet deep learning framework of Matlab to develop a customized model.

Caffe (Jia, et al., 2014) is one of popular deep learning frameworks (Techlabs, 2018). Despite the flexibility of Caffe is not as good as TensorFlow and need to write in a high-level language if you want to build a complex layer type, Caffe can be said to be a deep learning library, though. It has provided Caffe

Figure 13. The deep learning models developed for the ImageNet large database from 2012 to 2015

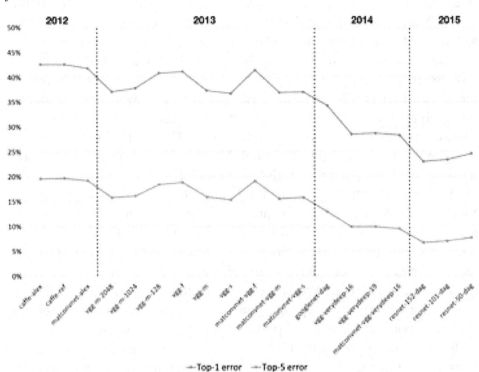

Model Zoo which contains many pre-trained neural network models. We can use and track it directly. The most important was Caffe support C, C++, Python, and Matlab interface that we can construct deep learning architecture of Caffe in our familiar environment of Matlab or Python. That's what we need, we need a third-party framework to help us transfer a pre-trained model of Matlab to iOS device, and Caffe offers this opportunity.

In this book, we use MatConvNet deep learning to build the CNN Model according to the given dataset. MatConvNet (Vedaldi & Lenc, 2015) is an open source from the Oxford Visual Geometry Group. It implements the deep learning method and integrates the blocks of CNNs as a toolbox in Matlab environment. It allows users to design a deep CNN model and train it subject to a dataset, and supports the use of one or multiple GPUs on training large neural networks. It has been widely used as an educational and research platform for rapid design of CNN models. The Matlab environment provides reliable mathematical toolboxes for pre-processes, such as independent component analysis, dimensionality reduction, and solvers, such as nonlinear system

Figure 14. We use pre-trained GoogLeNet to recognize customized images

pot, flowerpot (739), score 0.822

solving, integer programming solving, multivariate nonlinear regression solving, which are potential for further improvement of deep learning methodologies. A lot of numerical calculations are used in CNNs training, such as dimension reduction, numerical differentiation, reduced-gradient, etc. These can be easily handled on Matlab.

Developers familiar with Matlab environment can quickly build the CNN model based on the dataset using MatConvNet, and directly train and test the CNN Model by parallel and distributed processes, and finally determine the CNN Model that is the most suitable for this dataset. However, the pre-trained CNNs wrapper in MatConvNet cannot be integrated into the Xcode environment. So this book explain how to use MatConvNet of Matlab to train the deep neural network, and transform a CNN model between MatConvNet and Caffe through MatCaffe of Caffe, and use the Core ML provided by Apple to import the Caffe model into the Xcode environment and eventually complete the design of an iOS App which has been embedded with an artificial intelligence image recognition system.

Figure 15. We snap the physical object via the webcam and import the image into the GoogLeNet to recognize the object label

beer glass, score 0.850

Import Caffe Model into Matlab Environment

Nowadays, convolutional neural networks are widely used in the field of AI research. We can find a lot of pre-trained CNN models on the website of each deep learning framework. These models have a good effect on object recognition or pattern recognition problems. However, the development of face recognition systems is also an issue of interest to many researchers.

Especially when convolutional neural networks have a significant impact on image recognition, people are also curious about the effects that CNNs use to recognize face images. There are many applications for the development of face recognition systems, such as smart unlocking, access control, personal information inquiry, etc. For the development of deep learning models, the most basic and indispensable is a large-scale database, but the large-scale public database is lacking in the field of face recognition. The collection of face data is time consuming and labor intensive. At present, the public face database of the Internet has VGG-Face (Parkhi, Vedaldi, & Zisserman, 2015), CelebFaces Attributes (CelebA) (Liu, Luo, Wang, & Tang, 2015) (Yang, Luo, Loy, & Tang, 2015), Labeled Faces in the Wild (LFW Face) (Learned-Miller, Huang, RoyChowdhury, Li, & Hua, 2016), etc. VGG-Face is a face database, which created by the Oxford University of Visual Geometry Group (VGG). VGG-Face is the database of the most face images in the currently released face database. The database collects 2D facial images of 2,622 public figures, each of whom has nearly 1000 face images in the database. The database has approximately 2.6 million face images. Many of the face images in VGG-Face are not repeated in other well-known face databases. Besides the VGG-Face database, VGG announced a new large-scale face database in 2018 and named it VGGFace2 (Cao, Shen, Xie, & Parkhi, 2018). The database collected 3.31 million face images from 9,131 public figures. The face images of VGGFace2 come from different ethnicities, genders, ages, and professions. The VGGFace2 large-scale database has gradually become the first choice database for developing face recognition systems. The behind of VGG-Face is the CelebA dataset. The CelebA dataset is provided by the Multimedia Laboratory of the Chinese University of Hong Kong. The database contains a total of 202,599 face images. These images include 10,177 celebrities. CelebA is a large dataset of celebrity face attributes. The data set provides 40 attribute annotations for each image, such as Wearing Necktie, Wavy Hair, Mustache, Chubby, etc. for developing a recognition system. In addition to the CelebA dataset, LFW Face is another well-known dataset in the field of face recognition. The LFW Face dataset collected 13,233 face images from the Internet. These images come from 5,749 public figures of different ethnicities and genders, and most public figures have only one photo in the database. The paper pointed out that only 1,680 people have more than two photos in the LFW Face dataset. This data set was created for solving the problem of unconstrained face recognition (Huang, Ramesh, Berg, & Learned-Miller, 2007) (Huang, Narayana, & Learned-Miller, 2008). Unconstrained face recognition (Zhou, Chellappa, & Zhao, 2006) has always been a big problem in the field of computer vision research. The unconstrained face recognition problem refers to the study of face recognition under unconstrained conditions. Unconstrained conditions include pose variations, illumination, aging, and so on. Although the LFW Face dataset is designed for unconstrained face recognition, the dataset is not suitable for developing CNN face recognition systems. For data-driven deep learning, we need a large-scale database to develop a face recognition model. In this section, we will use the VGG-Face pre-trained model to introduce the CNN face recognition system. Additionally, we also use the VGG-Face example to present the import of the Caffe model on the Matlab environment.

For the VGG-Face database, the Visual Geometry Group of Oxford University constructed a deep learning model in 2015 for developing a face recognition system (Parkhi, Vedaldi, & Zisserman, 2015). The VGG-Face deep learning model is constructed based on the VGGNet model proposed in 2014 (Simonyan & Zisserman, 2014). It is also a very deep convolutional neural network consisting of thirteen convolutional layers and three fully connected layers. The fully connected layers in the VGG-Face model mimics the operation of LeNet (LeCun, Bottou, Bengio, & Haffner, 1998), all implemented by convolutions. The model receives a 224x224 size average face image (has been deducted the average of the training data) for face recognition. The VGG-Face pre-trained model proposed by VGG can achieve an accuracy of 98.95% for the LFW dataset with 13,233 face images. We can find the VGG-Face pre-trained model in many deep learning frameworks. For the VGG-Face pre-trained model in the MatConvNet and Caffe deep learning frameworks, we can use it in Matlab to recognize face images of public figures.

MatConvNet offers many pre-trained deep learning models (The MatConvNet Team, 2014), such as VGG-Face, ResNet-152, GoogLeNet, VGG-16, AlexNet, and so on. MatConvNet allows us to download and import these pre-trained models into Matlab. We can find the VGG-Face example in the folder of the MatConvNet toolbox. The VGG-Face pre-trained model has been stored as a network type of SimpleNN. We can perform feedforward of the VGG-Face model to recognize celebrity facial images, as the CIFAR-10 example in the previous section. Similarly, the Caffe deep learning framework also provides the VGG-Face pre-trained model. The total solution proposed in this book needs to break the barrier between Matlab and Caffe. Before we installed the Caffe deep learning framework, MathWorks provided developers with a software support package to import Caffe models into the Matlab environment. We use the VGG-Face example to show how to import a Caffe model in Matlab. We provide the complete code for this example in Table 4. First, we need to download and install the software support package from MathWorks (MathWorks Deep Learning Toolbox Team, 2019) for importing the Caffe model in Matlab. The software support package is named Deep Learning Toolbox Import for Caffe Models. With the software support package, we can use the importCaffeNetwork, predict, classify, and other commands in the Matlab environment to import Caffe models and execute feedforward. We want to import the Caffe models in Matlab, so we need to download the VGG-Face pre-trained model of the Caffe version from the Caffe Model Zoo (Berkeley Vision and Learning Center, 2019) and set path of VGG-Face file in Matlab. We used the same photo of the VGG-Face example provided by MatConvNet in this example to facilitate the comparison of the models. In the Matlab environment, we first read the image of the famous Indian actor Aamir Khan from the Internet and store it as the "im" variable. After that, we import a list of 2,622 celebrity names provided by the Caffe model and store it as the "classes" variable. The Caffe software support package provided by MathWorks allows us to import the Caffe model using the importCaffeNetwork command. The importCaffeNetwork command requires two paths input, one is the path of the prototxt file, and the other is the path of the caffemodel file. The prototxt file stores the architecture of the deep learning model. The caffemodel file stores the pre-trained parameters of the model. The imported Caffe model is a network type of SeriesNetwork. After pre-processing the image, we use the predict command to perform the feedforward of SeriesNetwork. Finally, we use the same function as the VGG-Face example of MatConvNet to display the model's predictions in a figure.

MathWorks provides a deep learning toolbox importer for developers. Before we installed Caffe and MatCaffe, we can use this package to import the pre-trained model of Caffe to Matlab. However, this package does not support the storage of the Matlab deep learning model to the Caffe model. The total solution proposed in this book is to integrate the pre-training model of Matlab into the Xcode development environment via the Caffe deep learning framework. We will present the installation and compilation of the Caffe deep learning framework and MatCaffe of Matlab interface in the next chapter. We use MatCaffe to overcome the barrier between Matlab and Caffe. Also, we will discuss more details about the Caffe deep learning framework and the Caffe model in Chapter 3.

Table 4. We use the importer of deep learning provided by MathWorks to import the Caffe model into Matlab and execute feedforward

```
%% This code implements the import of the VGG-Face Caffe model in Matlab.
%% Before executing the code, you must first download and install the software support package provided by
MathWorks for importing the pre-trained Caffe model. (Please refer to the following website)
%% Package: Deep Learning Toolbox Importer for Caffe Models
%% URL: https://www.mathworks.com/matlabcentral/fileexchange/61735-deep-learning-toolbox-importer-for-caffe-
models
%% Additionally, you must first download the Caffe version of the VGG-Face pre-trained model from the VGG
website and add the path to the environment variables of Matlab.
%% VGG-Face (Caffemodel): https://www.robots.ox.ac.uk/~vgg/software/vgg_face/
%% load an image for test.
% The image is a photo of Aamir Khan, a famous Indian actor.
im = imread('https://upload.wikimedia.org/wikipedia/commons/4/4a/Aamir_Khan_March_2015.jpg') ;
%% load the names (classes) of 2622 well-known persons.
classes = textread('names.txt','%s') ;
%% Import the caffe model using the software support package provided by Matlab.
model = 'VGG_FACE_deploy.prototxt' ;
weights = 'VGG_FACE.caffemodel' ;
net = importCaffeNetwork(model,weights) ;
%% Pre-process for the test image.
% Resize the test image.
im = im(1:250,:,:) ; % crop image
img = single(im) ;
img = imresize(img, [224, 224]) ;
% Deducting the average value of training dataset.
averageImage = single([129.1863,104.7624,93.5940]) ;
averageImage = reshape(averageImage, 1, 1, 3) ;
img = bsxfun(@minus,img,averageImage) ;
%% Use the "predict" command to execute the feedforward of the SeriesNetwork
predict_result = predict(net, img) ;
%% Take out the recognition result of the model, and present the prediction class and prediction score via the figure.
[prob recognizing_label] = max(predict_result) ;
figure(1) ; clf ; imagesc(im) ; axis equal off ;
title(sprintf('%s (%d), score %.3f',...
classes{recognizing_label}, recognizing_label, prob), ...
'Interpreter', 'none') ;
```

Mobile Deep Learning Frameworks

In the talk, "**The Deep Learning Revolution,**" of the Turing Lecture (Hinton & LeCun, 2019) at FCRC 2019, Geoffrey Hinton stressed the success of representation AI against traditional symbolic AI. The representation based on deep neural networks is biologically inspired instead of logically inspired. The key for representation AI is deep learning through backpropagation.

Nowadays, existing deep learning frameworks for developing representation PR (pattern recognition) systems, including MatConvNet, Caffe, TensorFlow and PyTorch, all realize supervised learning of deep convolutional neural networks. Representation PR employs vectors for system tuning and possesses nice property for portability. Recently, in additional to Core ML, iOS mobile deep learning frameworks, including DeepLearningKit, Pytorch Mobile and TensorFlowLite, have been respectively developed and released for supporting Caffe, TensorFlow and PyTorch. All of them are able to deploy models derived by deep learning frameworks on mobile devices with iOS.

In (Tveit, Morland, & Røst, 2016), the authors presented an open source mobile deep learning framework, termed as DeepLearningKit, for developing mobile Apps on iOS devices, such as iPhone/iPad, and tvOS-based Apps for the big screen. DeepLearningKit is realized in Metal and Swift. It aims to utilize the GPU efficiently and integrate Metal convolutional neural network operators, including convolution, pooling, rectifier layer and soft-max, with iOS Apps. It supports models trained with popular frameworks such as Caffe, Torch, TensorFlow, Theano and so on. For example, it converts Caffe models to JSON (JavaScript Object Notation), then integrating into Swift/Metal for developing the iOS mobile app.

TensorFlow Lite (TensorFlow, Deploy machine learning models on mobile and IoT devices, 2019) is an open-source mobile deep learning framework that deploys a TensorFlow model on mobile devices with Android or iOS. The native iOS library, TensorFlowLiteSwift written in Swift has been released for developing iOS Apps. It is mainly composed of a converter and an interpreter. The converter transforms a TensorFlow model to a compressed .tflite file that is with small binary codes. The interpreter is designed to run a TensorFlow Lite model for inference. It performs inference with low latency and fast initialization. A typical inference consists of model loading, data transforming, inference executing and output interpreting.

As applications demands privacy-preserving and lower latency continuously, importance of deploying deep learning models on mobile devices is growing. The open-source mobile deep learning framework, PyTorch Mobile in (PyTorch, PyTorch Mobile, 2019), is an early, experimental release. It converts a model to TorchScript format (.pt) and deploys the converted model on mobile devices. The task is to integrate deep learning models in mobile applications. PyTorch Mobile supports deployment on both iOS and Android, including features of building optimization and selective compilation according to required operators.

The benchmark here is the CIFAR-10 dataset (Canada Institute for Advanced Research, CIFAR) (Krizhevsky, Learning Multiple Layers of Features from Tiny Images, 2009) (Krizhevsky, The CIFAR-10 dataset, 2009). It contains 60,000 32x32x3 tiny color images, 50,000 for training and 10,000 for testing. Each tiny image is with a label for classification of airplane, automobile, bird, cat, deer, dog, frog, horse, ship and truck. Subject to the CIFAR-10 dataset, quantitative performance evaluation for MatConvNet, Caffe, PyTorch

Table 5. Matlab codes of CNN design in MatConvNet

```
% Block
lr = [.1 2] ;
net.layers{end+1} = struct('type', 'conv', ...
'weights', {{0.01*randn(5,5,3,32, 'single'), zeros(1, 32, 'single')}}, ...
'learningRate', lr, ...
'stride', 1, ...
'pad', 2) ;
net.layers{end+1} = struct('type', 'pool', ...
'method', 'max', ...
'pool', [3 3], ...
'stride', 2, ...
'pad', [0 1 0 1]) ;
net.layers{end+1} = struct('type', 'relu') ;
% Block 2
net.layers{end+1} = struct('type', 'conv', ...
'weights', {{0.05*randn(5,5,32,32, 'single'), zeros(1,32,'single')}}, ...
'learningRate', lr, ...
'stride', 1, ...
'pad', 2) ;
net.layers{end+1} = struct('type', 'relu') ;
net.layers{end+1} = struct('type', 'pool', ...
'method', 'avg', ...
'pool', [3 3], ...
'stride', 2, ...
'pad', [0 1 0 1]) ; % Emulate caffe
% Block 3
net.layers{end+1} = struct('type', 'conv', ...
'weights', {{0.05*randn(5,5,32,64, 'single'), zeros(1,64,'single')}}, ...
'learningRate', lr, ...
'stride', 1, ...
'pad', 2) ;
net.layers{end+1} = struct('type', 'relu') ;
net.layers{end+1} = struct('type', 'pool', ...
'method', 'avg', ...
'pool', [3 3], ...
'stride', 2, ...
'pad', [0 1 0 1]) ; % Emulate caffe
% Block 4
net.layers{end+1} = struct('type', 'conv', ...
'weights', {{0.05*randn(4,4,64,64, 'single'), zeros(1,64,'single')}}, ...
'learningRate', lr, ...
'stride', 1, ...
'pad', 0) ;
net.layers{end+1} = struct('type', 'relu') ;
% Block 5
net.layers{end+1} = struct('type', 'conv', ...
'weights', {{0.05*randn(1,1,64,10, 'single'), zeros(1,10,'single')}}, ...
'learningRate', .1*lr, ...
'stride', 1, ...
'pad', 0) ;
% Loss layer
net.layers{end+1} = struct('type', 'softmaxloss') ;
```

(PyTorch, TRAINING A CLASSIFIER, 2017) and TensorFlow is given in the upcoming contexts. The models trained by these four deep learning frameworks can be deployed on devices with iOS for developing pattern recognition Apps by mobile deep learning frameworks introduced above.

Matlab codes in Table 6 describe a deep convolutional neural network for processing labeled training tiny images in CIFAR-10 dataset by MatConvNet. Let $u = [u_1,...,u_j,...,u_J]$ denote J external fields of the softmax operation. The probability of recognizing the correspondent image as class k is expressed as

$$q_j = \frac{e^{u_j}}{\sum_l e^{u_l}} \tag{2.24}$$

The output layer in Table 5 employs softmaxloss in MatConvNet. The loss of supervised learning is shown equivalent to the Kullback-Leibler divergence. Let e_j denote a unitary vector of binary elements with the j th element one and others zero. Let $\delta = [\delta_1, \delta_2,...,\delta_J]$ denote a unitary vector that represents the network output, where $\delta_j \in \{0,1\}$ and $\sum_l \delta_l = 1$. It follows consider δ as a random vector with the probability $Pr(\delta = e_j) = q_j$. Let $q = [q_1,...,q_J]$ collect J probabilities and $p = [p_1,...,p_J] \in \{e_1,...,e_J\}$ denote the desired output class. The following Kullback-Leibler divergence can be shown equivalent to the softmax loss in MatConvNet.

$$KL(p \| q) = -\sum_l p_l log \frac{p_l}{q_l} \tag{2.25}$$

Further assume $p = e_{k^*}$, where p_{k^*} represents the only active bit in p. The summation in the above equation reduces to a single term, $-p_{k^*} log \frac{p_{k^*}}{q_{k^*}}$. By setting $p_{k^*} = 1$, one attains $KL(p \| q) = log q_{k^*}$.

It is shown that the Kullback-Leibler divergence is equivalent to the maxsoft loss. The curve of learning the deep CNN by MatConvNet subject to labeled training patterns of CIFAR-10 without data augmentation is sown in Figure 16. The first plot in Figure 16 sketches the criteria of maxsoft loss for training and testing versus execution iteration. The blue learning curve monotonically decreases whereas the red curve for testing blocks after 20 epochs of execution. The second plot shows error rates for classification. The

Figure 16. Convergence of learning a deep CNN

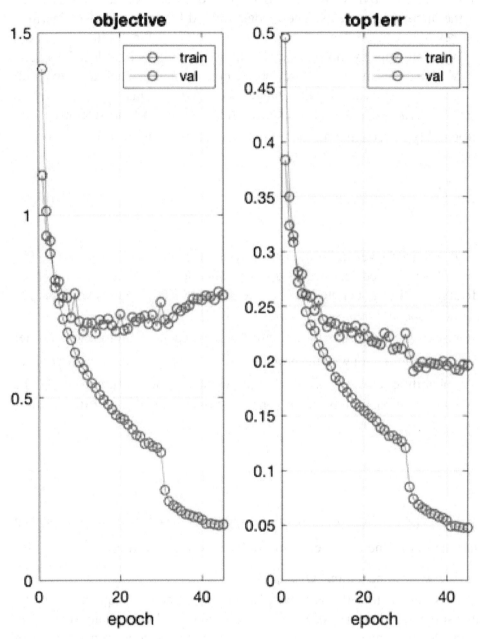

blue curve shows the training error rate near 1% after 40 epochs of execution. The stochastic gradient descent method based on back-propagation is effective for reducing softmax loss as well as the training error rate. Apparently deep learning is not trapped by local minima among the landscape of the objective function. It is notable that there is no square error in the Kullback-Leibler divergence and parameters of convolutional filters are optimized for reducing softmax loss significantly.

The other deep learning frameworks, including Caffe, PyTorch and TensorFlow, are compared for processing training tiny images of CIFAR-10. Subject to CIFAR-10, quantitative performance evaluation of deep learning frameworks proceeds without data augmentation. In (Jia, et al., 2014), CIFAR-10 tutorial reports success of reducing the training loss, summarizing the test accuracy near 75% by Caffe. In (PyTorch, TRAINING A CLASSIFIER, 2017), the experimental result of applying PyTorch for CIFAR-10 without data augmentation reports the test accuracy near 55%. Similar experiment in (Trencseni, 2019) reports an improved test accuracy by PyTorch near 74.5%. In (TensorFlow, Convolutional Neural Network (CNN), 2020), the experiment of applying TensorFlow for CIFAR-10 without data augmentation achieves the test accuracy near 70.7%.

Table 6. Quantitative performance evaluation of four deep learning frameworks for CIFAR-10 without data augmentation

CIFAR-10	Caffe	PyTorch	TensorFlow	MatConvNet
Test accuracy	75%	74.5%	70.7%	80.6%

As shown in Figure 16, without data augmentation, MatConvNet subject to labeled training patterns of CIFAR-10 achieves the test accuracy near 80.6%, which is better than those obtained by the other three deep learning frameworks in Table 6. Subject to training tiny images in CIFAR-10, models derived by all the four learning frameworks can be converted and deployed on devices with iOS. MatConvNet-oriented Apps on iOS mobile devices outperform the others for recognizing test tiny images of CIFAR-10 without data augmentation. High test accuracy means better generalization. Improving generalization still challenges researchers of deep learning for developing more reliable and effective Apps on mobile devices. Since trained MatConvNet model can be translated to Caffe models, the developer can select CoreML or DeepLearningKite to deploy translated Caffe models on mobile devices with iOS. CoreML is implemented by low level language. Compared with DeepLearningKite written in high level language, CoreML (Mohd Sanad

Zaki Rizvi, 2019) is more effective for optimizing on-device performance by seamlessly leveraging the CPU and GPU.

REFERENCES

Abadi, M., Barham, P., Chen, J., Chen, Z., Davis, A., Dean, J., . . . Steiner, B. (2016). TensorFlow: A system for large-scale machine learning. In *12th USENIX Symposium on Operating Systems Design and Implementation (OSDI 16)* (pp. 265-283). Savannah, GA: USENIX Association.

Berkeley Vision and Learning Center. (2019, Apr 25). *Model Zoo*. Retrieved from GitHub: https://github.com/BVLC/caffe/wiki/Model-Zoo

Cao, Q., Shen, L., Xie, W., & Parkhi, O. M. (2018). VGGFace2: A Dataset for Recognising Faces across Pose and Age. In *2018 13th IEEE International Conference on Automatic Face and Gesture Recognition (FG 2018)*. Xi'an, China: IEEE.

Chollet, F. (2015). *Keras*. Retrieved from GitHub: https://github.com/keras-team/keras

Fukushima, K. (1980, April). Neocognitron: A self-organizing neural network model for a mechanism of pattern recognition unaffected by shift in position. *Biological Cybernetics*, *36*(4), 193–202. doi:10.1007/BF00344251 PMID:7370364

Hinton, G., & LeCun, Y. (2019). The Deep Learning Revolution. In *Federated Computing Research Conference*. Phoenix, AZ: ACM FCRC 2019.

Huang, G. B., Narayana, M., & Learned-Miller, E. (2008). Towards unconstrained face recognition. In *2008 IEEE Computer Society Conference on Computer Vision and Pattern Recognition Workshops*. Anchorage, AK: IEEE. 10.1109/CVPRW.2008.4562973

Huang, G. B., Ramesh, M., Berg, T., & Learned-Miller, E. (2007). *Labeled faces in the wild: A database for studying face recognition in unconstrained environments. Technical Report*. Amherst, MA: University of Massachusetts.

Jia, Y., Shelhamer, E., Donahue, J., Karayev, S., Long, J., Girshick, R., . . . Darrell, T. (2014). Caffe: Convolutional Architecture for Fast Feature Embedding. In *MM '14 Proceedings of the 22nd ACM international conference on Multimedia* (pp. 675-678). Orlando, FL: ACM.

Krizhevsky, A. (2009). *Learning Multiple Layers of Features from Tiny Images*. Toronto: University of Toronto.

Krizhevsky, A. (2009). *The CIFAR-10 dataset*. Retrieved from The CIFAR-10 dataset: https://www.cs.toronto.edu/~kriz/cifar.html

Krizhevsky, A., Nair, V., & Hinton, G. (2009). *CIFAR-10 and CIFAR-100 datasets*. Retrieved from Alex Krizhevsky: https://www.cs.toronto.edu/~kriz/cifar.html

Learned-Miller, E., Huang, G. B., RoyChowdhury, A., Li, H., & Hua, G. (2016). Labeled Faces in the Wild: A Survey. Advances in Face Detection and Facial Image Analysis, 189-248.

LeCun, Y. (1988). A theoretical framework for back-propagation. In D. Touretzky, G. Hinton, & T. Sejnowski (Ed.), *Proceedings of the 1988 Connectionist Models Summer School* (pp. 21-28). Morgan Kaufmann.

LeCun, Y., Boser, B., Denker, J. S., Henderson, D., Howard, R. E., Hubbard, W., & Jackel, L. D. (1989, December). Backpropagation Applied to Handwritten Zip Code Recognition. *Neural Computation*, *1*(4), 541–551. doi:10.1162/neco.1989.1.4.541

LeCun, Y., Bottou, L., Bengio, Y., & Haffner, P. (1998, November). Gradient-Based Learning Applied to Document Recognition. *Proceedings of the IEEE*, *86*(11), 2278–2324. doi:10.1109/5.726791

Lin, M., Chen, Q., & Yan, S. (2013, Dec 16). *Network In Network*. arXiv.

Liu, Z., Luo, P., Wang, X., & Tang, X. (2015, Dec). Deep Learning Face Attributes in the Wild. *Proceedings of International Conference on Computer Vision (ICCV)*. 10.1109/ICCV.2015.425

MathWorks Deep Learning Toolbox Team. (2019, Mar 20). *Deep Learning Toolbox Importer for Caffe Models*. Retrieved from MathWorks: https://www.mathworks.com/matlabcentral/fileexchange/61735-deep-learning-toolbox-importer-for-caffe-models

MathWorks Image Acquisition Toolbox Team. (2019, Apr 19). *MATLAB Support Package for USB Webcams*. Retrieved from MathWorks: https://www.mathworks.com/matlabcentral/fileexchange/45182-matlab-support-package-for-usb-webcams

Mohd Sanad Zaki Rizvi. (2019, Nov 14). *Introduction to Apple's Core ML 3 – Build Deep Learning Models for the iPhone (with code)*. Retrieved from Analytics Vidhya: https://www.analyticsvidhya.com/blog/2019/11/introduction-apple-core-ml-3-deep-learning-models-iphone/

Mozer, M. C. (1987). Early parallel processing in reading: A connectionist approach. Attention and performance 12: The psychology of reading, 83-104.

Parkhi, O. M., Vedaldi, A., & Zisserman, A. (2015, Sep). Deep Face Recognition. *Proceedings of the British Machine Vision Conference (BMVC)*, 41.1-41.12.

Paszke, A., Gross, S., Chintala, S., Chanan, G., Yang, E., DeVito, Z., . . . Lerer, A. (2017). Automatic differentiation in PyTorch. In The future of gradient-based machine learning software and techniques in 2017 Autodiff Workshop, Long Beach, CA.

PyTorch. (2017). *Training a classifier*. Retrieved from PyTorch: https://pytorch.org/tutorials/beginner/blitz/cifar10_tutorial.html

PyTorch. (2019). *PyTorch Mobile*. Retrieved from PyTorch: https://pytorch.org/mobile/home/

Rumelhart, D. E., Hinton, G. E., & Williams, R. J. (1986). *Learning internal representations by error propagation* (D. E. Rumelhart & J. L. McClelland, Eds.; Vol. 1). MIT Press.

Russakovsky, O., Deng, J., Su, H., Krause, J., Satheesh, S., Ma, S., ... Fei-Fei, L. (2015, December). ImageNet Large Scale Visual Recognition Challenge. *International Journal of Computer Vision, 115*(3), 211–252. doi:10.100711263-015-0816-y

Simonyan, K., & Zisserman, A. (2014). *Very Deep Convolutional Networks for Large-Scale Image Recognition.* arXiv:1409.1556

Srivastava, N., Hinton, G., Krizhevsky, A., Sutskever, I., & Salakhutdinov, R. (2014, June 15). Dropout: A Simple Way to Prevent Neural Networks from Overfitting. *Journal of Machine Learning Research.*

Techlabs, M. (2018, Apr 5). *8 Best Deep Learning Frameworks for Data Science enthusiasts*. Retrieved from MISSION.ORG: https://medium.com/the-mission/8-best-deep-learning-frameworks-for-data-science-enthusiasts-d72714157761

TensorFlow. (2019). *Deploy machine learning models on mobile and IoT devices*. Retrieved from TensorFlow: https://www.tensorflow.org/lite

TensorFlow. (2020). *Convolutional Neural Network (CNN)*. Retrieved from TensorFlow: https://www.tensorflow.org/tutorials/images/cnn

The MatConvNet Team. (2014). *Pretrained models*. Retrieved from MatCovNet: https://www.vlfeat.org/matconvnet/pretrained/

Trencseni, M. (2019, May 14). *Solving CIFAR-10 with Pytorch and SKL*. Retrieved from http://bytepawn.com/solving-cifar-10-with-pytorch-and-skl.html

Turing, A. M. (1937). On Computable Numbers, with an Application to the Entscheidungsproblem. *Proceedings of the London Mathematical Society, 2*(1), 230–265. doi:10.1112/plms2-42.1.230

Tveit, A., Morland, T., & Røst, T. B. (2016, May 15). *DeepLearningKit - an GPU Optimized Deep Learning Framework for Apple's iOS, OS X and tvOS developed in Metal and Swift*. arXiv.org.

Vedaldi, A., & Lenc, K. (2015). MatConvNet: Convolutional Neural Networks for MATLAB. In *MM '15 Proceedings of the 23rd ACM international conference on Multimedia* (pp. 689-692). New York, NY: ACM.

Vedaldi, A., Lux, M., & Bertini, M. (2018, Apr 23). MatConvNet: CNNs are also for MATLAB users. *ACM SIGMultimedia Records, 10*(1).

Von Neuman, J. (1993, October 1). First Draft of a Report on the EDVAC. *IEEE Annals of the History of Computing, 15*(4), 27–75. doi:10.1109/85.238389

Yang, S., Luo, P., Loy, C.-C., & Tang, X. (2015). From Facial Parts Responses to Face Detection: A Deep Learning Approach. In *2015 IEEE International Conference on Computer Vision (ICCV)*. Santiago, Chile: IEEE. 10.1109/ICCV.2015.419

Zhou, S. K., Chellappa, R., & Zhao, W. (2006). *Unconstrained Face Recognition*. Springer.

Chapter 3
Transformation Across Deep Learning Frameworks

ABSTRACT

Since the presented approach uses MatConvNet of Matlab as a preliminary training platform, the pre-trained CNN model of MatConvNet cannot be directly integrated into the Xcode platform currently. Therefore, developers need a third-party platform as a bridge, so that developers can transfer the model of Matlab to the Xcode environment and finally mount the model to an app for executing and testing on the iOS device. Apple provides developers with Core ML Tools to support the Caffe framework. Therefore, developers can convert the Caffe model into the ML model through Core ML Tools. Moreover, the Caffe provides MatCaffe for connecting Matlab and Caffe. It is apparent that developers can achieve the goal through these two bridges.

IOS DEVICES AND CORE ML

iOS devices are the main reason for the company of Apple rapid growth in recent years (StatCounter, 2019). The unique appearance of iOS devices is also the object of mutual imitation and competition by other related companies. They are not only updated on hardware every year, but also pursuing new features in software. For all iOS devices, we are most familiar with is the iPhone. On June 29, 2007, Apple Inc. released the iPhone (1st generation) in the United States. It is equipped with the operating system of iPhone OS 1.0, the CPU of the 620 MHz Samsung 32-bit RISC ARM 1176JZ(F)-S

DOI: 10.4018/978-1-7998-1554-9.ch003

v1.0 (Patterson, 2008) and the Random Access Memory (RAM) of the 128 MB DRAM. For each subsequent year, Apple Inc. continued to release new iPhones. Both the hardware and the software, the iPhone is constantly improving. In particular, the iPhone 4 was first unveiled at Apples WWDC on June 7, 2010, its computing power was recognized compatible with the Cray-2 supercomputer. Today, the iPhone X and iPhone 11 are coming out one after another. Their computing power has improved the iPhone 4 more than twenty folds of the Cary-2 supercomputer. With the growth of the iPhone computing power, deep learning technology is more capable of realizing on mobile devices for pattern recognition.

In the past, we always pursued the breakthroughs and applications in deep learning technology on the Personal Computer (PC). We know that huge deep learning models must undergo a complex training process. Today, the computing power of an iPhone is on par with twenty Cary-2 supercomputers. It is no longer difficult for us to develop deep learning models on mobile devices. The well-known deep learning frameworks have also begun to extend from PC to mobile devices. The deep learning frameworks we are familiar with on PC are Caffe, Tensorflow, Pytorch, and Keras, etc. As with deep learning model training on PC, we can construct and train custom deep learning models with deep learning frameworks on mobile devices. In 2019, the mobile deep learning frameworks (Choudhury, 2019) most commonly used by developers are Caffe2, CoreML, DeepLearningKit, Mobile AI Compute Engine, Paddle Lite, Pythorch Mobile, Snapdragon Neural Processing Engine (SNPE) and TensorFlow Lite. The total solution of this book, we use Core ML to develop deep learning models for iOS devices.

At the 2017 Apple Worldwide Developers Conference (WWDC 2017), Apple officially announced Core ML, which allow developers to add machine learning model to their apps. This feature allows we to build and train machine learning or deep learning models on several specific platforms, and convert the model to ML model using Core ML afterwards, and import it into Xcode project finally. The following is an introduction of the Core ML on the official website (Apple, Machine Learning, 2018).

This new framework lets you easily build machine learning models, with no machine learning expertise required. Familiar and easy to use thanks to Swift, Create ML is integrated into playgrounds in Xcode 10 so you can view model creation workflows in real time. Just add a few lines of Swift code to leverage our Vision and Natural Language technologies and created models optimized for the Apple ecosystem for a variety of tasks, including regression, image classification, word tagging, and sentence classification. And you can use your Mac to train models from Apple with your custom data – no need for a dedicated server.

For the model developed in Matlab, we want to integrate it into the iOS device. At present, the most convenient way is to convert the model of third-party frameworks into the ML model using Core ML Tools. Core ML Tools is a package of Python that can import "coremltools" on the Python environment, and convert various deep learning models into ML models afterwards. Table 1 shows the model type and third-party frameworks supported by Core ML Tools, and Table 2 shows the code that will be used to convert the Caffe model to the Core ML (Apple, Converting Trained Models to Core ML, 2017). For example, the developer wants to convert the Caffe model of the third-party frameworks to Core ML model. We can use the Core ML converter to convert and save the model in the Python environment. Although we only provide several commands of the Core ML Tools converter, you can acquire more from the package documentation (Apple, coremltools, 2018). In addition to converting the neural network model of the third-party framework, developers can import the ready-to-use Core ML model into the App project. The official website of Apple offers many pre-trained Core ML models (Apple, Working with Core ML Models, 2017) such as MobileNet, SqueezeNet, Places205-

Table 1. The official of Apple provides support types and third-party platforms of Core ML Tools in WWDC2017

Model type	Supported models	Supported frameworks
Neural networks	Feedforward, convolutional, recurrent	Caffe v1 Keras 1.2.2+

Table 2. The code of the converter is used to convert the Caffe model

```
>> import coremltools
>> coreml_model = coremltools.converters.caffe.convert('my_caffe_model.caffemodel', 'my_caffe_model.
prototxt')
>> coreml_model.author = 'author_name' #optional
>> coreml_model.license = 'software_license' #optional
>> coreml_model.short_description = 'model_description' #optional
>> coreml_model.save('my_coreml_model.mlmodel')
```

GoogLeNet, ResNet50, Inception v3, and VGG16. Developers can use these pre-trained Core ML models to make the App's feature more plentiful.

As of now, Core ML has been updated to Core ML 3.0 version. Apple Inc. introduced the latest Core ML 3.0 at WWDC 2019 (Apple Inc., 2019). The biggest highlight of Core ML 3.0 is the function of On-device Training. Core ML 3.0 can not only integrate pre-trained models on the PC into iOS devices but also further train existing models on iOS devices. We know that training a deep learning model is complex and time-consuming. Core ML 3.0 seamlessly take advantage of the CPU, GPU and Neural Engine in iOS devices, so that developers and users can efficiently train and improve existing deep learning models on iOS devices. We can consider the On-devices training of Core ML 3.0 as a form of transfer learning or online learning. According to different users, existing deep learning models can be further adjusted and trained on iOS devices. We use Face ID of iOS devices as an example. The user's face will change over time, makeup and hairstyle, etc. Therefore, the developer provides the user with a face recognition model of the naïve version. The model will further improve the recognition rate of the user's face through on-device training. On-device training of Core ML 3.0 has three benefits (Mohd Sanad Zaki Rizvi, 2019) as follows:

1.   The model is further adjusted and trained on the personal device based on user data. It protects the user's data privacy. We no longer need to send personal data to developers over the Internet for improving the performance of the recognition model. Users will develop their recognition models through On-device training.
2.   Developers no longer need to set up huge servers to improve the performance of the recognition model for millions of app users.
3.   The feature of On-device training does not involve the Internet, so users can use the recognition model at any time.

Core ML not only protects the personal privacy of users but also improves the convenience for developers to develop recognition models. Developers can easily deploy deep learning models on iOS devices. We can consider the UI interface and deep learning model of the App as two modules. These can be improved and modified independently. We can also change the deep learning model of the app at any time. With the Core ML mobile deep learning framework, developers are more flexible in deploying deep learning models.

Apple provides us with a platform for conversion in software, allowing deep learning model to work on iOS devices. Through touch-screen, voice and microphone hardware of iOS devices, we can be more friendly input data and output data on iOS devices. The developers and users can easily perform functions of pattern recognition, voice analysis, and recognition of natural language on iOS devices. In the examples from the fourth to sixth chapters of this book, we will use Core ML to integrate model of Caffe into Core ML model, and import it to Xcode project afterwards to realize the deep learning across computational platforms.

CORE ML EXAMPLES ON XCODE ENVIRONMENT

The integration of the Core ML has made the App more plentiful. It is different from the recognition system of the remote host. Core ML model is bundled with the App project and runs independently on the customer's iOS devices. This advantage protects the privacy of the customer and prevents data theft during transportation. The privacy of users is always the first consideration for developers. We know that the stability of the stand-alone App is affected by the performance of the users' mobile devices. Especially for the deep neural network model, the size of the model is proportional to the output category increasing. Fortunately, Apple announced the Core ML 2.0 on WWDC 2018 (WWDC, 2018), which proposed ways to improve the problem and increase the speed of machine learning apps (Kambampati, 2018). On the other hand, what deserves our attention is the Create ML (Apple, Creating an Image Classifier Model, 2018). Developers can use Xcode playground to create a Core ML model for customized images, text and tabular data. In this section, we're going to demonstrate how to use Create ML tool to train image classifier for a customized dataset.

First, we need to prepare an image dataset for training and testing the model, and create a separate folder on the Apple Mac for the training dataset and testing dataset. They contain 80% and 20% of the images for each label, respectively. Also, it is necessary to ensure that the training images and the testing images are independent of each other. Figure 1 shows that the training data set and the test data set contain three types of fruits respectively (Buyukkinaci, 2018), including apple, banana, and orange. The names of the subfolders in the training data set or test data set represent the labels of the images. In other words, subfolders only have images with the same label. Apple officially describes that each label uses at least ten images as a training data set and balances the number of images. Furthermore, the official suggested that the images are at least 299x299 pixels, and can be a different size for each.

After the data ready, we need to create a new Xcode playground on the Mac and select macOS target, as shown in Figure 2. The developer can use the CreateMLUI in the playground to display the constructor of image classifier as shown in Table 3. After ensuring that the button of the Show the Assistant editor is turned on, the live view will present a constructor of the image classifier, as shown in Figure 3. Next, we need to drag the folder of the training data set into the specified area of the classifier constructor as shown in Figure 4. The visual constructor will start training the images inside the folder. We can observe the images processed, the elapsed time and the percent complete from the debug window, as shown in Figure 5.

During the training process, the constructor automatically and randomly decomposes the training dataset into a training and a validation. After training finishes, we can observe the accuracy rate of the training and validation, as shown in Figure 6. The result will be different for next time because the constructor decomposes randomly the training dataset into a training and a validation. We found that the model's performance has not been evaluated. Therefore, we give the testing data set to evaluate the accuracy of the classifier as shown in Figure 7. The visual constructor make is easy for developers to verify the accuracy of the model. In the occasion that the performance of testing is not acceptable, the developer can retrain the model by modifying the initial value or increasing training data (Apple, Improving Your Model's Accuracy, 2018). Otherwise we can save it for import into the App project, as shown in Figure 8 and Figure 9. The details of importing Core ML model into an App will be introduce in Chapter 4.

CAFFE AND MATCAFFE

Caffe is from Berkeley AI Research that is one of the most popular deep learning frameworks, now maintained and developed by Berkeley Vision and Learning Center (BVLC). It provides an environment that let developers easily construct deep learning architecture. It can train the model directly after constructing the deep learning architecture. Since it is an open source software, the internal code of software has been released to the user. Apparently, we can view it, track it, and even modify it. But we don't modify it generally. The official of Caffe (Jia, et al., 2014) provides methods for using Caffe in

Figure 1. The folders of the training and testing contain three types of fruit, respectively, and each subfolder is named the label of the fruit

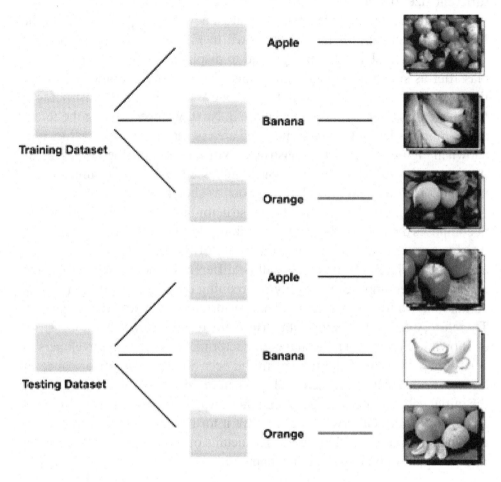

Table 3. The instructions are used to import CreateMLUI in the Xcode playground and display the visual constructor of the classifier

```
>> import CreateMLUI
>> let constructor = MLImageClassifierBuilder()
>> constructor.showInLiveView()
```

Python and Matlab, respectively PyCaffe and MatCaffe, so that we can choose a more beautiful compilation interface to build and train the Caffe model.

For the fourth to sixth chapters, we will use MatCaffe to convert the pre-trained model of Matlab to the Caffe model. However, compared with modern

Figure 2. The Create ML tool works on the playground of macOS target

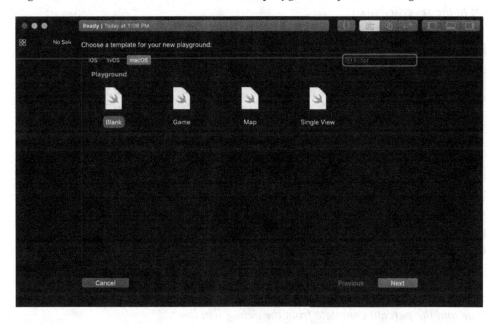

Figure 3. After executing the code, Live View will display the visual constructor

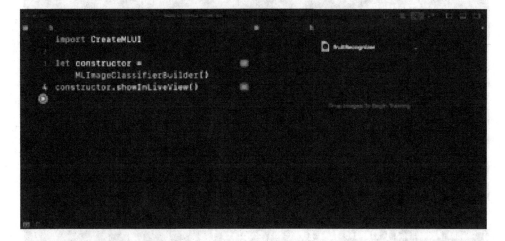

software, the installation of Caffe is not easy. It doesn't have a complete installation interface, so we can't install it by clicking Next. Caffe is compiled based on many dependencies, such as hdf5, opencv, openblas, protobuf, boost, etc. Although the official website provides installation guide (Jia & Shelhamer, Installation, 2014), the compilation of Caffe will be hindered after updating

Figure 4. The constructor will start training by dragging the folder of training data set to the specified area

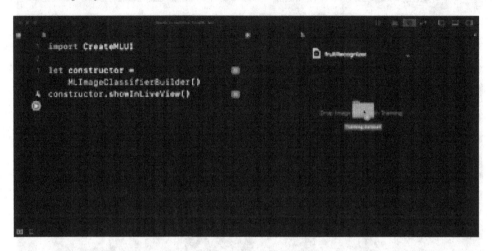

Figure 5. During the training, we can observe the processed image, the elapsed time and the percent complete from the debug window

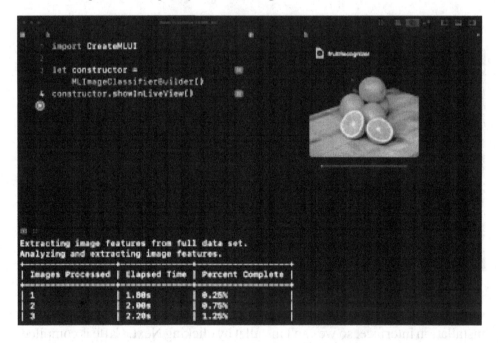

Figure 6. After completing the training, we can observe the accuracy rate of training and validation in the constructor of live view

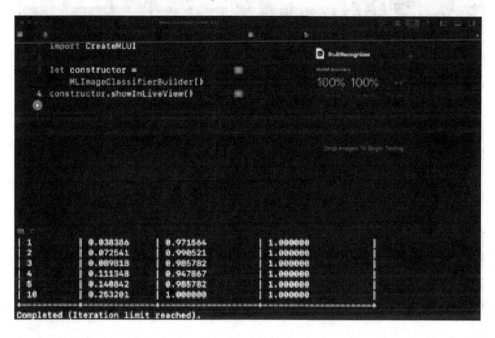

Figure 7. We need to prepare a set of testing data that are independent of the training data to evaluate the accuracy rate of the model

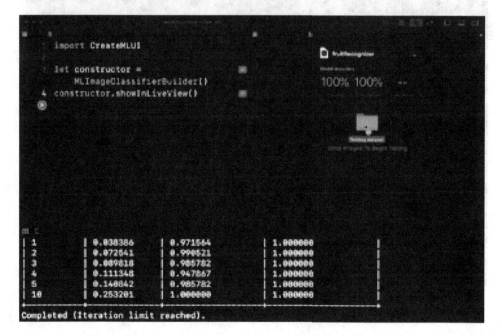

Figure 8. When the test performance of the model is acceptable, we will save it

Figure 9. We can import this Core ML model to create an app that recognizes fruits

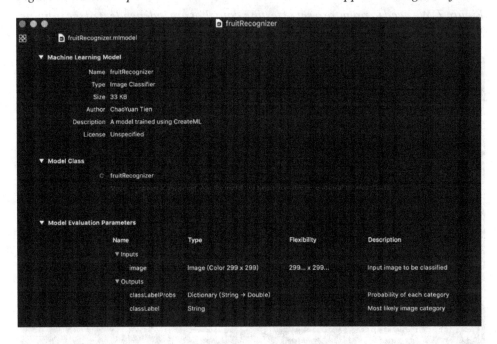

the operating system or dependencies. Since February 7th, 2019, Mac can be updated to macOS 10.14.3. Therefore, we will describe how to install Caffe on macOS 10.14.3 in this section. Besides, the author's website (Tien, 2019) also provides detailed installation guide. After installing Caffe, the reader will understand how to convert a pre-trained model into Caffe model in Matlab.

Before installing Caffe, we need to establish a good relationship with the terminal. We will use the terminal to install and compile Caffe framework. Further, we need to install Xcode and Homebrew on Mac. Xcode (Apple, Xcode, 2019) is a tool for developing iOS apps and compiling Caffe, that can download and install from the App Store. Homebrew (Howell, 2009) is a package manager for macOS. We can install the Homebrew and wget package by executing the code of Table 4 on the terminal. The "brew install" is a command that Homebrew provides us with the installation packages. For more commands of Homebrew on the terminal, we can refer to the list of frequently asked questions provided by Homebrew (Prévost, McQuaid,

Table 4. We can execute instructions on the terminal to install the Homebrew and wget package

```
$ /usr/bin/ruby -e "$(curl -fsSL https://raw.githubusercontent.com/Homebrew/install/master/install)"
$ brew install wget
```

& Lalonde, 2009). With Homebrew, we can easily install the dependencies needed to compile Caffe.

According to Caffe's official installation guide, we need to install the

Table 5. We need to install the general dependencies before compiling Caffe

```
$ brew install -vd snappy leveldb gflags glog szip lmdb
$ brew install hdf5 opencv
```

general dependencies, as shown in Table 5. The general dependencies include snappy, leveldb, gflags, glog, szip, lmdb, hdf5, and opencv packages.

Table 6. We will use the openblas package to compile the Caffe framework

```
$ brew install openblas
```

Then install the remaining dependencies, namely openblas, boost, and protobuf three packages.

After testing and research, we found that the protobuf 3.6.1 package and

Table 7. We install boost 1.59 to replace the latest version of boost so that Caffe compile successfully

```
$ brew install boost@1.59
$ brew link boost@1.59 --force
```

the boost 1.67 package were problematic during Caffe compilation. Therefore, we install the boost 1.59 and protobuf 3.5.1 to replace the latest version.

Here we need to download the protobuf-all-3.5.1 file from GitHub (Google, 2017) and unzip it (Wan, 2016). The following instructions need to execute

Table 8. We need to download and compile protobuf 3.5.1 from the Protocol Buffers of the GitHub to replace the latest version of protobuf

```
$ cd /user/XXXXX/protobuf-3.5.1
$ ./configure
$ make
$ make check
$ sudo make install
$ which protoc
$ protoc --version
```

under the directory of protobuf. we can use the "cd" plus "file path" on the terminal to enter the directory of protobuf.

After installing all the dependencies, we will install and compile Caffe framework. In advance, we ensure that the current directory of the terminal is in the home directory. Then download the Caffe framework from GitHub

Table 9. We use the terminal to download Caffe and copy the file of Makefile.config

```
$ cd ~
$ git clone https://github.com/BVLC/caffe.git
$ cd caffe
$ cp Makefile.config.example Makefile.config
```

via the terminal. As shown in Table 9, we download Caffe, enter the folder and copy the specified file.

Now we can find the Caffe folder under the home directory and the file of Makefile.config under the Caffe folder. The file of Makefile.config can be opened using Xcode. We can refer to the Table 10 to modify the contents of Makefile.config and specify the absolute path for certain variables.

Table 10. Caffe will compile according to the file of Makefile.config, so we need to specify the file path of the dependencies package to the relevant variable

```
# Cancel the annotations of CPU_ONLY and USE_OPENCV.
CPU_ONLY:= 1
USE_OPENCV:= 0
# Cancel the annotations of USE_LEVELDB and USE_LMDB.
USE_LEVELDB:= 0
USE_LMDB:= 0
# Cancel the annotation of CUSTOM_CXX and make sure the absolute path to clang++ is correct.
CUSTOM_CXX:= /usr/bin/clang++
# Annotate all variable of CUDA because we only need to use the CPU.
# Specify the BLAS variable to OpenBlas
BLAS:= open
# Cancel the annotations of BLAS_INCLUDE and BLAS_LIB and make sure the path can find the folders of include
and lib in openblas.
BLAS_INCLUDE:= /usr/local/Cellar/openblas/0.3.6_1/include
BLAS_LIB:= /usr/local/Cellar/openblas/0.3.6_1/lib
# Cancel the annotations for the following two lines.
BLAS_INCLUDE:= $(shell brew --prefix openblas)/include
BLAS_LIB:= $(shell brew --prefix openblas)/lib
# Cancel the annotations of MATLAB_DIR
MATLAB_DIR:= /Applications/MATLAB_R2017a.app
# Annotate all variable of python.
# Add the remaining paths to INCLUDE_DIRS and LIBRARY_DIRS variables.
INCLUDE_DIRS:= /usr/local/include $(BLAS_INCLUDE)
LIBRARY_DIRS:= /usr/local/lib $(MATLAB_DIR)/bin/maci64 $(BLAS_LIB)
```

Furthermore, we need to install Matlab 2017a beforehand so that we can compile Caffe and MatCaffe at the same time.

After modifying, save the file and back to the terminal. Start compiling Caffe and MatCaffe under the Caffe directory, as shown in Table 11. Since

Table 11. We can use the "make" command on the terminal to compile Caffe

```
$ make all
$ make runtest
$ make matcaffe
$ make mattest
```

Caffe deep learning framework was written by the C++ programming language, we need to use the make command when compiling it.

If there is an error during the compilation process, we can find the solution to the problem from Caffe-users group (caffe-users, 2014). Most of the errors that occur are strongly related to the update of the dependencies. After finding the solution to the problem, we need to use "make clean" in the Caffe directory to clear the previous compilation and recompile Caffe using the commands in Table 11. After successful compilation and testing, we can open the Caffe deep learning framework in the Matlab interface through the instructions in Table 13. Further, we need to set the path of

Table 12. We can use "make clean" to clear the previous compilation

```
$ make clean
```

Table 13. We can use this instruction on the terminal to open Matlab and execute the Caffe framework

```
$ export DYLD_INSERT_LIBRARIES=/usr/local/opt/libtiff/lib/libtiff.5.dylib & /Applications/MATLAB_R2017a.
app/bin/matlab
```

Caffe's matlab folder in Matlab. However, we can start using the Caffe deep learning framework in the Matlab interface.

For the deep learning model in the Matlab to Caffe framework conversion, there are two main files in the Caffe environment. The first one is the *.prototxt* file, as shown in Figure 10-13. This file can be made using Protocal Buffers and Matlab, which records the type and parameter structure of each layer of deep learning. Caffe will build a complete deep learning architecture based on this file. Here, we only want to convert the pre-trained model of Matlab to the Caffe model and perform feedforward, so we only introduce the prototxt file for testing.

Figure 10 presents the input layer and convolutional layer in the Caffe model. Apart from the input layer and output layer, there are four fixed variables in each hidden layer, namely **name**, **type**, **top**, and **boom**. The **name** variable can be arbitrarily named, but it is preferably related to the type of the hidden layer and is well distinguishable. The content of the **type** variable will depend on the type in which the hidden layer performs feedforward and

Figure 10. Quick description the input layer and convolution layer of my_net.prototxt

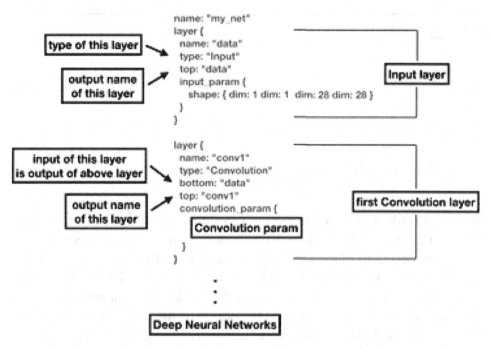

backpropagation. The commonly used type names in the Caffe model are Input (Input layer), Convolution (Convolutional layer), BatchNorm (Batch Normalization layer), Scale (Batch Normalization layer), Pooling (Pooling layer) and Softmax (Output layer). For more types of hidden layers in the Caffe model, we can refer to the Layer Catalogue provided by BAIR (Berkeley AI Research, Layer Catalogue, 2014). The content stored in the **top** variable is the output data name of the current hidden layer. Conversely, the **bottom** variable stores the name of the data received by the current hidden layer. Although the **top** and **bottom** variables can be arbitrarily named, they have a corresponding relationship in successive hidden layers. For example, the bottom variable of the first convolutional layer in Figure 10 corresponds to the top variable of the input layer. If they do not have correspondence, the model will not be able to perform the feedforward and backpropagation processes. Furthermore, Table 14 shows the format of the input layer of the Caffe model in the prototxt file. There are four dimensions in the input layer that need to be defined. The first dimension is the batch size of the input. The second dimension is the channel of the image, such as the grayscale image channel is 1, and the color image is 3. Finally, the third dimension and the fourth dimension respectively record the height and width of the image. Since

Table 14. The format of the Input layer in the prototxt file of the Caffe model

```
layer {
name: "data"
type: "Input"
top: "data"
input_param {
shape {
dim: 1
dim: 1
dim: 28
dim: 28
}
}
}
```

the prototxt file we created is used to recognize a 28x28 pixel handwritten pattern, the first two dimensions of the input layer are 1, and the others are 28.

For the next layer of the input layer, we call it the first hidden layer. Here, the first hidden layer we use is the convolutional layer. Table 15 presents the format of the convolutional layer in the Caffe's prototxt file. The input value of this convolutional layer is the output of the input layer, so we can observe that the **bottom** variable in the convolutional layer is equal to the **top** variable of the input layer. The convolutional layer needs to define five parameters in the prototxt file, namely num_output, kernel_h, kernel_w, stride, and pad. The num_output parameter is the number of filters included in the convolutional layer. The kernel_h and kernel_w parameters are the height and width of the filter. If the height and width of the filter are the same, we can use kernel_size instead of the kernel_h and kernel_w variables. The stride parameter of convolution is the stride of the filter movement. Finally,

Table 15. The format of the Convolutional layer in the prototxt file of the Caffe model

```
layer {
name: "conv1"
type: "Convolution"
bottom: "data"
top: "conv1"
convolution_param {
num_output: 20
kernel_h: 5
kernel_w: 5
stride: 1
pad: 0
}
}
```

the pad parameter in the convolutional layer records the number of padding around the filter.

After introducing the format of the convolutional layer, we will continue to explain Batch Normalization. Table 16 presents the format of the Batch Normalization layer in the prototxt file of Caffe. Batch Normalization is a method used by GoogLeNet to accelerate deep network training (Ioffe & Szegedy, 2015). The Batch Normalization method consists of two phases, the first one is to normalize the output of the previous layer, and the other one is to scale and shift the normalized result. These two phases are implemented in the architecture of the Caffe model by the BatchNorm layer and the Scale layer. There are two parameters in the BatchNorm layer of the Caffe architecture. The first is the use_global_stats parameter that records a Boolean value. Caffe left a message in the open source of the BatchNorm layer explaining the use of the use_global_stats parameter (Berkeley AI Research, Batch Norm Layer, 2014).

If false, normalization is performed over the current mini-batch and global statistics are accumulated (but not yet used) by a moving average. If true, those accumulated mean and variance values are used for the normalization.

Table 16. The format of the Batch Normalization layer in the prototxt file of the Caffe model

```
layer {
name: "bnorm1"
type: "BatchNorm"
bottom: "conv1"
top: "bnorm1"
batch_norm_param {
use_global_stats: true
eps: 0.000010
}
}

layer {
name: "bnorm1_scale"
type: "Scale"
bottom: "bnorm1"
top: "bnorm1_scale"
scale_param {
bias_term: true
}
}
```

By default, it is set to false when the network is in the training phase and true when network is in the testing phase.

We construct this prototxt file for executing the feedforward of the test phase, so we set the use_global_stats parameter to true. The other parameter in the BatchNorm layer of Caffe is eps. The eps is an abbreviation of Greek alphabet epsilon. In mathematics, epsilon usually represents an arbitrarily small positive quantity or an error term. The default value of epsilon in the Batch Normalization layer is 10^{-5} and is added to the variance of the normalization. After the BatchNorm layer normalizes the output of the previous layer, the Scale layer scales and shifts the normalized result. The bias_term variable in the Scale layer is true to say that the layer learned the multiplication scaling factor and the constant term during the training. Also, the feedforward of the model will scale and shift the normalized result by the multiplication scaling factor and the constant term.

For our example, the next layer of the Batch Normalization layer is a Pooling layer. Table 17 presents the format of the Pooling layer in the Caffe model. The method of performing feedforward and backpropagation in the Pooling layer depends on the pool variable. If the pool variable is MAX, it means that the layer is a maximum pooling layer. However, if the pool variable is AVG, it will be an average pooling layer. The pooling layer will down-sampling the output of the previous hidden layer. The kernel_size variable records the size of the square filter in the pooling layer. If the filter

Table 17. The format of the Pooling layer in the prototxt file of the Caffe model

```
layer {
name: "pool1"
type: "Pooling"
bottom: "bnorm1_scale"
top: "pool1"
pooling_param {
pool: MAX
kernel_size: 2
stride: 2
}
}
```

Figure 11. Quick description the batch normalization layer of my_net.prototxt

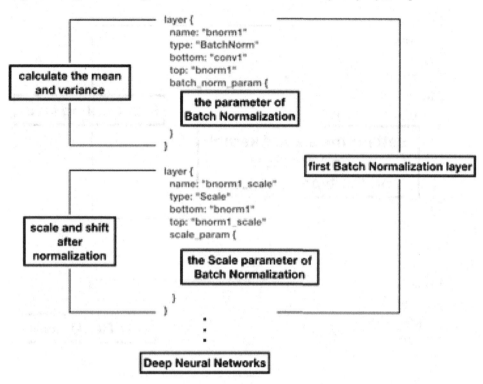

in the pooling layer is asymmetrical, we can use the kernel_h and kernel_w variables to record the height and width of the filter. Additionally, the stride variable in the pooling layer means the step size of the kernel.

In addition to the hidden layer described above, we also add the activation function in the successive hidden layer to avoid the output of the model is a linear combination of input. Table 18 presents the most commonly used ReLU activation functions in convolutional neural networks. The hidden layer uses the ReLU activation function to map the output of the previous layer to the input of the next layer. It has been proved in a lot of literature (Nair & Hinton,

Table 18. The format of the ReLU layer in the prototxt file of the Caffe model

```
layer {
name: "relu1"
type: "ReLU"
bottom: "pool1"
top: "relu1"
}
```

Figure 12. Quick description the pooling layer and ReLU layer of my_net.prototxt

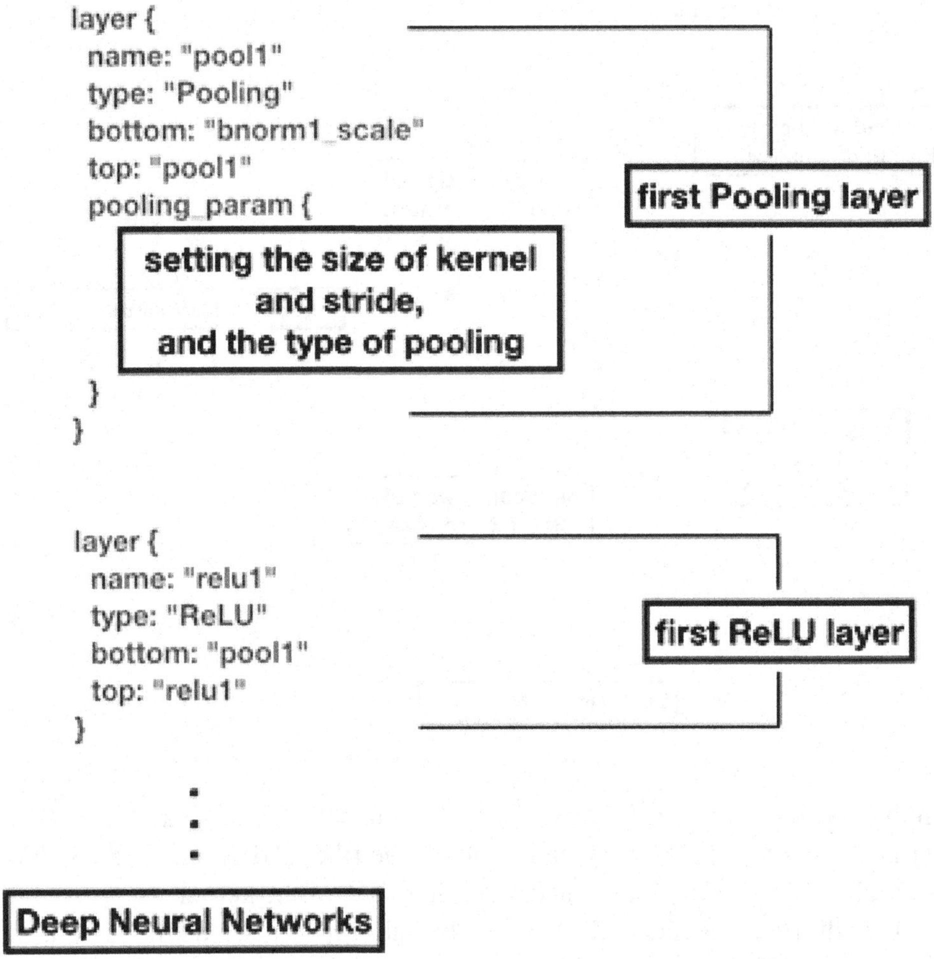

```
layer {
  name: "pool1"
  type: "Pooling"
  bottom: "bnorm1_scale"
  top: "pool1"
  pooling_param {
```

first Pooling layer

setting the size of kernel and stride, and the type of pooling

```
  }
}
```

```
layer {
  name: "relu1"
  type: "ReLU"
  bottom: "pool1"
  top: "relu1"
}
```

first ReLU layer

.
.
.

Deep Neural Networks

2010) (Glorot, Bordes, & Bengio, 2011) (Agarap, 2019) that ReLU is more suitable for deep CNNs than sigmoid function (Han & Moraga, 1995) and hyperbolic tangent (Weisstein, 2002).

In the architecture of the deep learning mode, we will use the output layer in the behind of the last hidden layer to make the output format of the model conform with our expectation. Table 19 presents the output layer with the softmax type in the architecture of the Caffe model. The output layer of the Softmax type will change the output of the last hidden layer to the probability value. Finally, the model will determine the label of the image based on the probability value of the classes.

Table 19. The format of the Softmax output layer in the prototxt file of the Caffe model

```
layer {
name: "prob"
type: "Softmax"
bottom: "conv5"
top: "prob"
}
```

The other main file in the Caffe environment is the *.caffemodel* file, which records the built-in parameters for each layer. Since we have completed the compilation of Caffe and MatCaffe, we can easily import the pre-trained parameters of the CNN model in Matlab to the caffemodel file of Caffe. For the CNN architecture we described above, the caffemodel file will record the built-in parameters of the convolutional layers and the Batch Normalization layers. Before importing the CNN built-in parameters of Matlab into the caffemodel file, we need to use the command of Table 13 to open MatCaffe in the terminal. We can use the Caffe deep learning framework in the familiar Matlab environment afterward.

For converting a deep learning model in Matlab to a Caffe model, we need to create a Caffe network using the pre-made prototxt file firstly. The Matlab code in Table 20 presents the creation of the Caffe network and the load of the SimpleNN pre-trained model in the Matlab environment. We select the CPU mode to implement the Caffe deep learning framework. The official website of Caffe emphasizes that we must specify one of the CPU or GPU models before we create a network or solver (Berkeley AI Research, Interfaces, 2014). Next, we use the caffe.Net command with the pre-made prototxt file

Table 20. Before we convert a pre-trained model in Matlab to the Caffe model, we need to create a Caffe network firstly (Berkeley AI Research, Interfaces, 2014)

```
% There is a prerequisite to executing the following code in Matlab.
% You must use the MatCaffe interface supported by Caffe to start the Matlab Software.
% We specify the CPU mode before creating the Caffe network.
caffe.set_mode_cpu() ;
% Specify a pre-made prototxt file for the Caffe model.
model = './my_net.prototxt' ;
% The caffe.net command will construct a Caffe network based on the specified model architecture.
net = caffe.Net(model,'test') ;
% Load the network architecture and pre-trained parameters of the SimpleNN model into Matlab.
matlab_CNN = load('./my_net.mat') ;
```

Figure 13. Quick description the output layer of my_net.prototxt

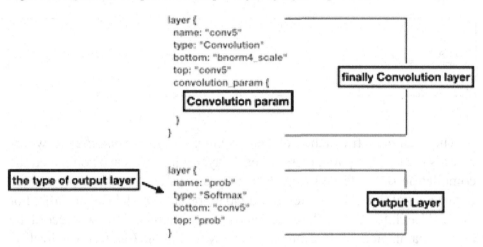

Table 21. We use the commands of MatCaffe (Berkeley AI Research, Interfaces, 2014) to import the pre-trained parameters of the SimpleNN model into the corresponding layers in the Caffe network

```
% Import the pre-trained built-in parameters of filters in the first convolutional layer into the first convolutional layer
of the Caffe network.
net.layers('conv1').params(1).set_data(matlab_CNN.layers{1,1}.weights{1}) ;
% If there have the bias values of filters in the convolutional layer, we import it into the convolutional layer of Caffe.
if ~isempty(matlab_CNN.layers{1,1}.weights{2})
    net.layers('conv1').params(2).set_data(matlab_CNN.layers{1,1}.weights{2}') ;
end
```

to create a Caffe network. The caffe.Net command builds the Caffe network based on the specified prototxt file. After constructing the Caffe network, we load the SimpleNN pre-trained model into the Matlab environment and feed the pre-trained built-in parameters into the Caffe network. Table 21 and Table 22 show how to import the pre-trained built-in parameters of the convolutional layer and Batch Normalization layer to the corresponding hidden layer in the Caffe network. The convolutional layer in the SimpleNN model has two weights. The first weight is the built-in parameters of all filters. The other one is the bias value of each filter. If the next layer of the convolutional

Table 22. We refer to the dagnn_caffe_deploy file provided by Ernesto Coto (Coto, 2017) to implement the conversion of parameters in the Batch Normalization layer

```
%% We create this code by referring to the dagnn_caffe_deploy.m file, an open source provided by Ernesto Coto on
GitHub (Coto, 2017).
%% The dagnn_caffe_deploy.m file is copyright (c) 2017 Ernesto Coto, Samuel Albanie. Visual Geometry Group,
University of Oxford. All rights reserved.
% The Batch Normalization layer of MatConvNet model contains three weights, the first two for Caffe's Scale layer
(scale and shift) and the third one for Caffe's BatchNorm layer (mean and variance).
moments = matlab_CNN.layers{1,2}.weights{3} ;
% Import the mean value to BatchNorm layer.
mean = moments(:,1) ;
net.layers('bnorm1').params(1).set_data(mean) ;
% Since the pre-trained variance contains the value of epsilon, we. must deduct the epsilon value before importing
into the BatchNorm layer.
variance_plus_eps = moments(:,2).^2 ;
variance = variance_plus_eps - 0.00005 ;
% Inport the pre-processed variance to the BatchNorm layer.
net.layers('bnorm1').params(2).set_data(variance) ;
% Since this model is used to execute feedforward and recognize images of input, the scale factor always equal to 1.
scale_factor = 1; net.layers('bnorm1').params(3).set_data(scale_factor) ;

% Import the scale and shift parameters into the Caffe's Scale layer.
% Set the scale parameters of the Scale layer.
mult = matlab_CNN.layers{1,2}.weights{1} ;
net.layers('bnorm1_scale').params(1).set_data(mult) ;
% Set the shift parameters of the Scale layer.
const = matlab_CNN.layers{1,2}.weights{2} ;
net.layers('bnorm1_scale').params(2).set_data(const) ;
```

layer is Batch Normalization layer, the built-in parameters of the layer will not contain the bias value.

Additionally, the Batch Normalization layer of the SimpleNN model includes three weights. The first weight stores the multiplication scaling factor for scaling. The second weight stores the constant terms for shifting. The last weight of the batch normalization layer corresponds to the moments in the probability distribution, the first moment is the mean, and the second moment is the variance. Normally, the size of the last weight in the Batch Normalization layer will be a Nx2 matrix. The N is a variable, depends on

Table 23. When we have imported all the parameters into the Caffe network, we can use the command to store the Caffe network as a caffemodel file

```
net.save('my_net.caffemodel');
```

the number of filters in the previous layer. After pre-processing, we can import the weights into the BatchNorm layer and Scale layer of the Caffe network, respectively. When the import of all built-in parameters is completed, we use the net.save command to store the Caffe model, as shown in Table 23.

There are other documents in Caffe that record different content, but in

Figure 14. Flow chart of CNN model transformation across platforms

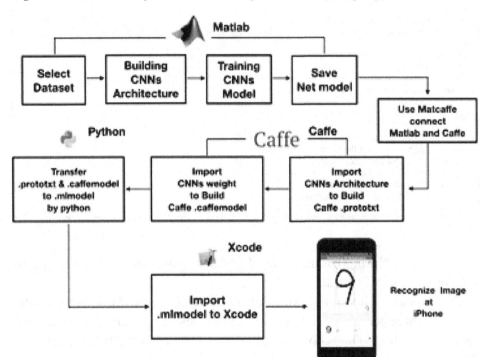

this book, only use the Caffe as a bridge of cross-platform instead of using Caffe to train the model. Therefore, we only need to prepare these two files, we can convert the pre-trained model into the model of Caffe to execute feedforward during the phase of testing.

LEARNING BY MATCONVNET AND
EXECUTING ON IOS DEVICES

Since we use MatConvNet of Matlab as a preliminary training platform, the pre-trained CNN model of MatConvNet cannot be directly integrated into the Xcode platform currently. Therefore, we need to rely on a third-party platform as a bridge, so that we can transfer the model of Matlab to the Xcode environment and finally make the model into an app to run and test on the iOS device.

Apple provides developers with Core ML to support the Caffe framework. Therefore, we can convert the Caffe model into ML model through Core

Figure 15. We can choose the model to be applied based on the evaluation error

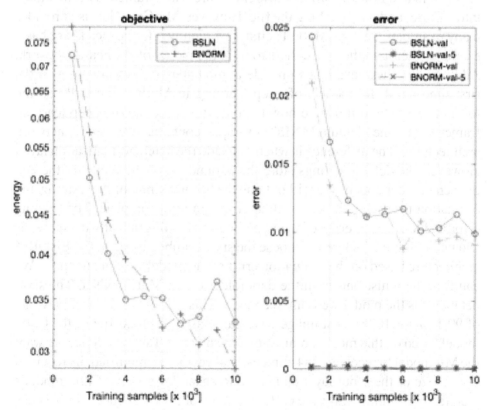

ML Tools. Moreover, the Caffe provides MatCaffe for connecting Matlab and Caffe. It is apparent that we can achieve the goal through these two bridges as shown in Figure 14. We first used MatConvNet to build a CNN architecture for the specified dataset in Matlab and trained it. After training, we selected the appropriate model, made it into *.prototxt* and *.caffemodel* through MatCaffe, converted Caffe model into *.mlmodel* by Core ML Tools of Python afterwards, and finally imported *.mlmodel* to Xcode environment to run and test on the iOS device. After the app is completed, it can be published on App Store of Apple.

MatConvNet provides the code to convert the pre-trained model of the SimpleNN network type into the files of the prototxt and caffemodel. We can find the file named "simplenn_caffe_deploy" from the "untils" subfolder (The MatConvNet Team, MatConvNet: CNNs for MATLAB, 2018). We can understand how to convert the architecture and parameters of the model into a Caffe model by tracking the file. However, MatConvNet also provides many examples, such as MNIST, cifar, fast rcnn, vggfaces, etc. These basic examples facilitate the researchers to train the model of the neural network. Additionally, these examples provide a good start for developers who the first time build the models of deep learning in Matlab. We will use the MNIST example to illustrate how to convert a model across deep learning frameworks. The default MNIST example contains two neural network architectures. The difference is whether to add the batch normalization layer. However, the default settings store the parameters of the model at the end of each number epoch. We will obtain the accuracy rate of the training and evaluation for each number epoch after the training complete. The training error and evaluation error of the neural network will gradually decrease, as shown in Figure 15. Here we choose the sixth number epoch of the BNORM architecture based on the evaluation error as the model we want to apply. We can find the mnist-bnorm in the data folder of the MatConvNet. The sixth net inside is the model we want to convert. This model has the accuracy rate of 99.12% for 10,000 test images. We can make a prototxt file of the Caffe model based on this model architecture, as shown in Table 24. Since we want the ML model to receive a 784-dimensional vector, we modified the received image size of the input layer and add a Reshape layer to the Caffe model's architecture. Additionally, the caffemodel file of the Caffe model only needs to record the parameters of the convolutional layers and batch normalization layers. It is cumbersome to always make the prototxt file and the caffemodel file during the experiment, so we refer to the simplenn_caffe_deploy.m file provided by MatConvNet (The MatConvNet Team, MatConvNet: CNNs for

MATLAB, 2018) and the dagnn_caffe_deploy.m file provided by Ernesto Coto (Coto, 2017) to create two conversion functions. The first one of conversion functions is named prototxtFile_creator, which will create a prototxt file of the Caffe model according to the architecture of the SimpleNN model, as shown in Table 27. The other one of the conversion functions is named caffemodelFile_creator, which will export the pre-trained parameters in the SimpleNN model to the corresponding hidden layer in the Caffe model and save the Caffe network as a caffemodel file, as shown in Table 28. With these two conversion functions, we can easily convert the MNIST and VGG-Face examples provided by MatConvNet to the Caffe model. The two functions are the naïve versions we used to demonstrate, so there are a lot of hidden layers and conditions that are not defined. If you encounter barriers in converting models other than MNIST and VGG-Face, you can refer to the files provided

Figure 16. We can execute the feedforward of the Caffe model in Matlab through MatCaffe

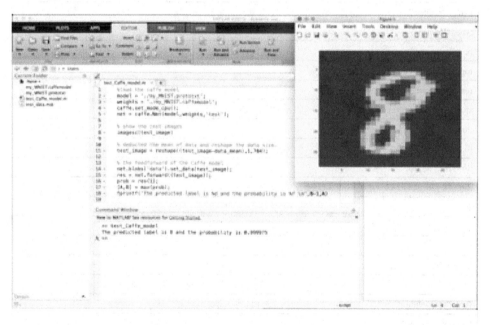

by MatConvNet (The MatConvNet Team, MatConvNet: CNNs for MATLAB, 2018) and Ernesto Coto (Coto, 2017) to help you debug.

Before converting to the Core ML model, we will execute the feedforward of the Caffe model to test whether the model live up to our expectations, as

Table 24. The file of my_MNIST.prototxt presents the architecture of the MNIST model

name: "my_MNIST"
layer {
name: "data"
type: "Input"
top: "data"
input_param {
shape {
dim: 1
dim: 1
dim: 784
dim: 1
}
}
}
layer {
name: "reshape"
type: "Reshape"
bottom: "data"
top: "reshape"
reshape_param {
shape {
dim: 0
dim: 1
dim: 28
dim: 28
}
}
}
layer {
name: "conv1"
type: "Convolution"
bottom: "reshape"
top: "conv1"
convolution_param {
num_output: 20
kernel_size: 5

continued on following page

Table 24. Continued

stride: 1
pad: 0
}
}
layer {
name: "bnorm1"
type: "BatchNorm"
bottom: "conv1"
top: "bnorm1"
batch_norm_param {
use_global_stats: true
eps: 0.00001
}
}
layer {
name: "bnorm1_scale"
type: "Scale"
bottom: "bnorm1"
top: "bnorm1_scale"
scale_param {
bias_term: true
}
}
layer {
name: "pool1"
type: "Pooling"
bottom: "bnorm1_scale"
top: "pool1"
pooling_param {
pool: MAX
kernel_size: 2
stride: 2
}
}
layer {

continued on following page

Table 24. Continued

name: "conv2"
type: "Convolution"
bottom: "pool1"
top: "conv2"
convolution_param {
num_output: 50
kernel_size: 5
stride: 1
pad: 0
}
}
layer {
name: "bnorm2"
type: "BatchNorm"
bottom: "conv2"
top: "bnorm2"
batch_norm_param {
use_global_stats: true
eps: 0.00001
}
}
layer {
name: "bnorm2_scale"
type: "Scale"
bottom: "bnorm2"
top: "bnorm2_scale"
scale_param {
bias_term: true
}
}
layer {
name: "pool2"
type: "Pooling"
bottom: "bnorm2_scale"
top: "pool2"
pooling_param {

continued on following page

Table 24. Continued

pool: MAX
kernel_size: 2
stride: 2
}
}
layer {
name: "conv3"
type: "Convolution"
bottom: "pool2"
top: "conv3"
convolution_param {
num_output: 500
kernel_size: 4
stride: 1
pad: 0
}
}
layer {
name: "bnorm3"
type: "BatchNorm"
bottom: "conv3"
top: "bnorm3"
batch_norm_param {
use_global_stats: true
eps: 0.00001
}
}
layer {
name: "bnorm3_scale"
type: "Scale"
bottom: "bnorm3"
top: "bnorm3_scale"
scale_param {
bias_term: true
}
}

continued on following page

Table 24. Continued

layer {
name: "relu1"
type: "ReLU"
bottom: "bnorm3_scale"
top: "relu1"
}
layer {
name: "conv4"
type: "Convolution"
bottom: "relu1"
top: "conv4"
convolution_param {
num_output: 10
kernel_size: 1
stride: 1
pad: 0
}
}
layer {
name: "prob"
type: "Softmax"
bottom: "conv4"
top: "prob"
}

Table 25. The code is used to convert the pre-trained VGG-Face model into a Caffe model

```
%% Please ensure the following prerequisites before executing this code.
% Downloaded and compiled MatConvNet toolbox
% Installed the Caffe deep learning framework and MatCaffe interface
% Started Matlab with the MatCaffe interface
% Check if the pre-trained VGG-Face model exists in the specified path.
% If true, the code starts to create the Caffe model.
% If it is false, the code will automatically download the vgg-face.mat file from the list of pre-trained models provided by
MatConvNet (The MatConvNet Team, 2016).
modelPath = fullfile(vl_rootnn,'data','models','vgg-face.mat') ;
if ~exist(modelPath)
fprintf('Downloading the VGG-Face model .... this may take a while\n') ;
mkdir(fileparts(modelPath)) ;
urlwrite(...
'http://www.vlfeat.org/matconvnet/models/vgg-face.mat', ...
modelPath) ;
end
% Load the pre-trained VGG-Face model into the Matlab environment.
load('./data/models/vgg-face.mat')
% We store the layers variable as net.layers for creating the Caffe model conveniently.
net.layers = layers;
% We use the prototxtFile_creator function to export the architecture of the VGG-Face model provided by MatConvNet to
the prototxt file of Caffe.
prototxtFile_creator(net, [224 224 3], 'vggfaces_proto_MatConvNet');
% After creating the prototxt file, we use the caffemodelFile_creator function to export the pre-trained parameters of the
VGG-Face model.
caffemodelFile_creator(net, 'vggfaces_proto_MatConvNet', 'vggfaces_caffemodel_MatConvNet');
```

Table 26 We used the Caffe model, which converted from MatConvNet's pre-trained VGG-Face model, to recognize the facial image of Aamir Khan

```
% We load a test image and feed it into the VGG-Face model for recognition.
% The image is a photo of Aamir Khan, a famous Indian actor.
im = imread('https://upload.wikimedia.org/wikipedia/commons/4/4a/Aamir_Khan_March_2015.jpg') ;
% Load the names (classes) of 2622 well-known persons.
classes = textread('names.txt', '%s') ;
% Assign the paths of the prototxt file and the caffemodel file to the model variable and weight variable.
% The prototxt file and the caffemodel file were created from the VGG-Face model provided by MatConvNet.
model = 'vggfaces_proto_MatConvNet.prototxt' ;
weights = 'vggfaces_caffemodel_MatConvNet.caffemodel' ;
% Import the Caffe model using the caffe.Net command provide by MatCaffe (Berkeley AI Research, Interfaces, 2014).
net = caffe.Net(model, weights, 'test') ;
% Resize the test image to the format allowed by the VGG-Face model.
im = im(1:250,:,:) ; % crop image
img = single(im) ;
img = imresize(img, [224, 224]) ;
% Deducting the average value of training dataset.
averageImage = single([129.1863, 104.7624, 93.5940]) ;
averageImage = reshape(averageImage, 1, 1, 3) ;
img = bsxfun(@minus, img, averageImage) ;
% Use the net.forward command provided by MatCaffe to execute feedforward of the Caffe network.
predict_result = net.forward({img}) ;
% Take out the recognition result of the model, and present the prediction class and prediction score via the figure.
[prob recognizing_label] = max(predict_result{1, 1}) ;
figure(1) ; clf ; imagesc(im) ; axis equal off ;
title(sprintf('%s (%d), score %.3f',...
classes{recognizing_label}, recognizing_label, prob), ...
    'Interpreter', 'none') ;
```

Table 27. With this prototxt creator, we can quickly create a prototxt file for the SimpleNN model

function prototxtFile_creator(simplenn_net, inputSize, output_filename)
% PROTOTXTFILE_CREATOR create a Caffe prototxt file based on the model of the SimpleNN network type.
% Inputs:
% simplenn_net: A struct of the SimpleNN network type.
% inputSize: A 3-dimansion vector means the image size received. by the model.
% For example, the input layer of the VGG-Face model receives an image of 224x224x3, so the inputSize variable is equal to [224 224 3].
% output_filename: A string for naming the prototxt file.
% Outputs: [output_filename, '.prototxt']
% Check if the inputSize variable in keeping with the format of the definition.
if isempty(inputSize) || (size(inputSize,2) ~= 3)
error('Please enter the size of the image received by the input layer.')
end
% Create and write a prototxt file.
[~, network_name] = fileparts(output_filename) ;
prototxtFile = [output_filename '.prototxt'] ;
file = fopen(prototxtFile, 'w') ;
% Network name of the Caffe model.
fprintf(file,'name: "%s"\n\n', network_name) ;
% Write the format of the input layer according to the inputSize variable.
fprintf(file,' layer { \n') ;
fprintf(file,' name: "data" \n') ;
fprintf(file,' type: "Input" \n') ;
fprintf(file,' top: "data" \n') ;
fprintf(file,' input_param { \n') ;
fprintf(file,' shape { \n') ;
fprintf(file,' dim: 1 \n') ;
fprintf(file,' dim: %d \n', inputSize(3)) ;
fprintf(file,' dim: %d \n', inputSize(1)) ;
fprintf(file,' dim: %d \n', inputSize(2)) ;
fprintf(file,' } \n') ;
fprintf(file,' } \n') ;
fprintf(file,' } \n\n') ;
bottom = 'data' ;
% Use for loop to write the format of the hidden layers to the prototxt file. The following four variables are used to name the hidden layers.

continued on following page

Table 27. Continued

conv_layers = 0 ;
relu_layers = 0 ;
bnorm_layers = 0 ;
pool_layers = 0 ;
for idx = 1:length(simplenn_net.layers)
% Determine the write format of the hidden layer according to the architecture of the SimpleNN model.
fprintf(file,' layer { \n') ;
switch simplenn_net.layers{1, idx}.type
case 'conv'
% Write the format of the Convolutional layer.
conv_layers = conv_layers+1 ;
name = ['conv' int2str(conv_layers)] ;
weights_size = size(simplenn_net.layers{1, idx}.weights{1}) ;
fprintf(file,' name: "%s" \n',name) ;
fprintf(file,' type: "Convolution" \n') ;
· fprintf(file,' bottom: "%s"\n', bottom) ;
fprintf(file,' top: "%s" \n', name) ;
fprintf(file,' convolution_param { \n') ;
fprintf(file,' num_output: %d \n', weights_size(end)) ;
fprintf(file,' kernel_h: %d \n', weights_size(1)) ;
fprintf(file,' kernel_w: %d \n', weights_size(2)) ;
fprintf(file,' stride: %d \n', simplenn_net.layers{1, idx}.stride) ;
fprintf(file,' pad: %d \n', simplenn_net.layers{1, idx}.pad) ;
fprintf(file,' } \n') ;
bottom = name ;
case 'relu'
% Write the format of the ReLU layer.
relu_layers = relu_layers+1 ;
name = ['relu' int2str(relu_layers)] ;
fprintf(file,' name: "%s" \n', name) ;
fprintf(file,' type: "ReLU" \n') ;
fprintf(file,' bottom: "%s" \n',bottom) ;
fprintf(file,' top: "%s" \n',name) ;
bottom = name ;
case 'bnorm'
% The Batch Normalization method in Caffe model is implemented by the BatchNorm layer and Scale layer.

continued on following page

Table 27. Continued

% Write the format of the BatchNorm layer.
bnorm_layers = bnorm_layers+1 ;
name = ['bnorm' int2str(bnorm_layers)] ;
fprintf(file,' name: "%s" \n', name) ;
fprintf(file,' type: "BatchNorm" \n') ;
fprintf(file,' bottom: "%s" \n', bottom) ;
fprintf(file,' top: "%s" \n', name) ;
fprintf(file,' batch_norm_param { \n') ;
fprintf(file,' use_global_stats: true \n') ;
fprintf(file,' eps: %f \n', simplenn_net.layers{1, idx}.epsilon) ;
fprintf(file,' } \n') ;
fprintf(file,' } \n\n') ;
bottom = name ;
% Write the format of the Scale layer.
name = [bottom,'_scale'] ;
fprintf(file,' layer { \n') ;
fprintf(file,' name: "%s" \n', name) ;
fprintf(file,' type: "Scale" \n') ;
fprintf(file,' bottom: "%s" \n', bottom) ;
fprintf(file,' top: "%s" \n', name) ;
fprintf(file,' scale_param { \n') ;
fprintf(file,' shift_term: true \n') ;
fprintf(file,' } \n') ;
bottom = name ;
case 'pool'
% Write the format of the Pooling layer.
pool_layers = pool_layers+1 ;
name = ['pool' int2str(pool_layers)] ;
fprintf(file,' name: "%s"\n', name) ;
fprintf(file,' type: "Pooling" \n') ;
fprintf(file,' bottom: "%s"\n', bottom) ;
fprintf(file,' top: "%s"\n', name) ;
fprintf(file,' pooling_param { \n') ;
% Select the type of the pooling layer.
switch (simplenn_net.layers{1, idx}.method)
case 'max'

continued on following page

Table 27. Continued

pool_type = 'MAX' ;
case 'avg'
pool_type = 'AVE' ;
otherwise
error('The method variable of %s has not been defined in the pooling layer of caffemodel_converter.',...
simplenn_net.layers{idx}.name);
end
fprintf(file,' pool: %s\n', pool_type) ;
fprintf(file,' kernel_size: %d\n',
simplenn_net.layers{1, idx}.pool(1)) ;
fprintf(file,' stride: %d\n', simplenn_net.layers{1, idx}.stride) ;
fprintf(file,' }\n') ;
bottom = name ;
case 'softmaxloss'
% Write the format of the Softmax layer.
% We create this. prototxt file for executing feedforward.
% Refardless of whether the ouput layer in the SimpleNN model is Softmaxloss or Softmax, we will use the Softmax output layer.
fprintf(file,' name: "%s"\n', 'prob') ;
fprintf(file,' type: "Softmax" \n') ;
fprintf(file,' bottom: "%s" \n', bottom) ;
fprintf(file,' top: "%s" \n', 'prob') ;
case 'softmax'
fprintf(file,' name: "%s"\n', 'prob') ;
fprintf(file,' type: "Softmax" \n') ;
fprintf(file,' bottom: "%s" \n', bottom) ;
fprintf(file,' top: "%s" \n', 'prob') ;
otherwise
error('The type of %s has not been defined in the. caffemodel_converter.',...
simplenn_net.layers{idx}.name)
end
fprintf(file,' } \n\n') ;
end
fclose(file) ;
end

Table 28. With this caffemodel creator, we can quickly create a caffemodel file for the SimpleNN model

function caffemodelFile_creator(simplenn_net, prototxt_filename, output_filename)
%% We create this code by referring to the dagnn_caffe_deploy.m file and simplenn_caffe_deploy.m file, which are open sources provided by Ernesto Coto on GitHub (Coto, 2017) and Zohar Bar-Yehud & Karel Lenc on MatConvNet toolbox (Vedaldi & Lenc, 2015), respectively.
%% The dagnn_caffe_deploy.m file is copyright (c) 2017 Ernesto Coto, Samuel Albanie. Visual Geometry Group, University of Oxford. All rights reserved.
%% The simplenn_caffe_deploy.m file is copyright (c) 2015-16 Zohar Bar-Yehuda, Karel Lenc. All reights reserved.
% CAFFEMODELFILE_CREATOR create a Caffe's caffemodel file based on the model of the SimpleNN network type.
% Inputs:
% simplenn_net: A struct of the SimpleNN network type.
% porotxt_filename: The name of the prototxt file.
% output_filename: A string for naming the caffemodel file.
% Outputs: [output_filename, '.caffemodel']
% Specify the CPU model and the path of the prototxt file to create a Caffe network.
model = ['./' prototxt_filename '.prototxt'] ;
caffe.set_mode_cpu() ;
net = caffe.Net(model,'test') ;
conv_layers = 0 ;
bnorm_layers = 0 ;
% Use for loop to import pre-trained parameters into the corresponding hidden layer in the Caffe network.
for idx = 1:length(simplenn_net.layers)
switch simplenn_net.layers{1, idx}.type
case 'conv'
% Specify the convolutional layer of the Caffe network.
conv_layers = conv_layers+1 ;
name = ['conv' int2str(conv_layers)] ;
% Import the pre-trained parameters of the filters to the first parameter position in the specified convolutional layer
conv_weight_1 = simplenn_net.layers{1, idx}.weights{1} ;
net.layers(name).params(1).set_data(conv_weight_1) ;
% If there is a bias of the filter, we need to import it into the second parameter position in the specified convolutional layer.
if ~isempty(simplenn_net.layers{1, idx}.weights{2})
conv_weight_2 = simplenn_net.layers{1, idx}.weights{2};
% The format of the bias value must be a column vector.
switch size(conv_weight_1, 4) == size(conv_weight_2, 2)
case 0

continued on following page

Table 28. Continued

net.layers(name).params(2).set_data(conv_weight_2);
case 1
net.layers(name).params(2).set_data(conv_weight_2');
end
end
case 'bnorm'
% Specify the Batch Norm layer of the Caffe network.
bnorm_layers = bnorm_layers+1 ;
name = ['bnorm' int2str(bnorm_layers)] ;
% Import the mean value to BatchNorm layer.
moments = simplenn_net.layers{1, idx}.weights{3} ;
mean = moments(:, 1) ;
net.layers(name).params(1).set_data(mean) ;
% Since the pre-trained variance contains the value of epsilon, we. must deduct the epsilon value before importing into the BatchNorm layer.
variance_plus_eps = moments(:, 2).^2 ;
variance = variance_plus_eps - simplenn_net.layers{1, idx}.epsilon ;
% Import the pre-processed variance to the BatchNorm layer.
net.layers(name).params(2).set_data(variance) ;
% Since this model is used to execute feedforward and recognize images of input, the scale factor always equal to 1.
scale_factor = 1 ;
net.layers(name).params(3).set_data(scale_factor) ;
% Import the scale and shift parameters into the Caffe network's Scale layer.
mult = simplenn_net.layers{1, idx}.weights{1} ;
net.layers([name '_scale']).params(1).set_data(mult) ;
const = simplenn_net.layers{1, idx}.weights{2} ;
net.layers([name '_scale']).params(2).set_data(const) ;
case 'relu'
case 'pool'
case 'softmaxloss'
case 'softmax'
otherwise

continued on following page

Table 28. Continued

error('The type of %s has not been defined in the. caffemodel_converter.', simplenn_net.layers{idx}.name')
end
end
%Store the Caffe network as a caffemodel file.
net.save([output_filename '.caffemodel']) ;
end

shown in Figure 16. Finally, we use the instructions in Table 2 to convert the Caffe model into the Core ML model. With the bridge of Caffe, we can realize the deep learning across computational platforms. In the fourth to sixth chapters, we will present our latest researches and use this total solution to apply the deep learning model.

CONVERT THE MATLAB PRE-TRAINED MODEL TO CAFFE MODEL WITH MATCAFFE

Matlab is a commercial numerical analysis software released by MathWorks. It is also a familiar platform for developing model to many scientists and researchers. Especially in Mathematical Science, many scientists and researchers use Matlab to develop mathematical model, and analyze a large amount of numerical data. The programming language of Matlab is a kind of interpreted language. The interpreted language makes developers more flexibly and quickly to develop models in Matlab. If we make a mistake while writing code, we can also use Matlab debug system to fix the error. For the beginner who do not know any programming languages, he still can learn quickly to use Matlab for developing software. Besides, Matlab provides a number of toolboxes to help scientists solve problem, such as Image Processing Toolbox, Signal Processing Toolbox, Parallel Computing Toolbox, Statistics and Machine Learning Toolbox, MATLAB Distributed Computing Server, and Deep Learning Toolbox, etc. The development of most toolbox is based on strict numerical proof and experimental results. We can not only use function to analyze big data, but also use these toolboxes to build mathematical models of artificial intelligence quickly in Matlab. In the field of artificial intelligence deep learning, Matlab is a good environment for developing models. We can pre-process and analyze large datasets in Matlab.

Even the datasets with high-dimensional, we can also use reliable numerical computing in Matlab to implement the dimension reduction. Convolutional Neural Networks have gradually become synonymous with Deep Learning in nowadays. There are many experiments show that the depth of convolutional neural network can effectively improve the performance of the recognition model. For the experiment of the large models, we can use the parallel and distributed process, and GPU to speed up the training of the mode in Matlab. In the past, when deep learning was not a hot issue, we have used a large amount of functions and object-oriented programming to construct the deep learning model for solving the mathematical problems, such as function approximation (Wu, Lin, & Hsu, 2006) (Wu, Multilayer Potts Perceptrons With Levenberg–Marquardt Learning, 2008) (Wu, Wu, & Huang, 2014) and classification (Wu, 2002). However, the growth of deep learning in recent years promotes many research teams to develop deep learning frameworks, such as Caffe, TensorFlow, Keras, Core ML, and so on. In recent year, Matlab also provide the Deep Learning toolbox and MatConvNet toolbox. We can use the building blocks provided by the MatConvNet toolbox and Caffe deep learning framework to construct the models quickly and solve the more mathematical problems. The effectiveness of deep learning has prompted researchers to focus on the application of models.

In this book, we use the MatConvNet toolbox to develop the deep learning model and expect to launch our pre-trained model in an iOS app to recognize the images. Since Matlab is a commercial numerical and symbolic analysis software, the pre-trained model of MatConvNet is limited apparently at the applied stage. Matlab supports the import of different programming language and the model of deep learning frameworks, but it is a challenge for us to export the Matlab model. In section 2.4 of the second Chapter, we introduce you about the import of Caffe pre-trained model in Matlab. Even if we don't install Caffe and MatCaffe, we can import the Caffe pre-trained model to Matlab by using the software support package provided by MathWorks. However, the pre-trained VGG-Face model provided by MatConvNet cannot be exported as a Caffe model. The total solution we presented can overcome this challenge and successfully published the iOS image recognition App on Apple's App Store. With the support of the Caffe deep learning framework and MatCaffe interface, we can save the MatConvNet pre-trained model as a Caffe model. Also, we can execute the feedforward of the Caffe model on Matlab to recognize images. In this section, we will present how to export the pre-trained VGG-Face model, which is provided by MatConvNet, as the Caffe model.

VGG-Faces is a large-scale database of facial images (Parkhi, Vedaldi, & Zisserman, Deep Face Recognition, 2015). The Visual Geometry Group of the Oxford University used VGGNet to develop a face recognition model for VGG-Faces database in 2015. The model can recognize 2D facial images of 2,622 public figures. We can find the pre-trained VGG-Face model from many examples of deep learning frameworks. The pre-trained VGG-Face model, which is composed of the prototxt file and the caffemodel file, is provided from Caffe deep learning framework. However, the pre-trained VGG-Face model provided from MatConvNet toolbox is a SimpleNN network type. We expect to export the SimpleNN model as the portotxt file and the caffemodel file of Caffe without modifying the network architecture and pre-trained parameters. Table 3.25 presents the process we use MatCaffe to export the SimpleNN model as the Caffe model. From the beginning of the code, we check whether the VGG-Face pre-trained model, which is provided by MatConvnNet, is in the **models** folder or not. If the **models** folder not includes the vgg-face.mat, the vgg-face.mat is automatically downloaded from the list of the pre-trained models which is provided from MatConvNet (The MatConvNet Team, 2016). Next, we load the pre-trained VGG-Face model into the Matlab environment. We can see there exist two variables in the Workspace of Matlab, one is the layer variable, the other is the meta variable. The layer variable stores the architecture and pre-trained parameters of the VGG-Face model. The meta variable stores the information of the training parameters. We can use the prototxtFile_creator function in Table 27 to quickly construct the prototxt file required by the Caffe model. We define three input variables for the protoxtFile_creator function. The first input variable is the pre-trained SimpleNN model, which includes the network architecture and pre-trained parameters. The second input variable is the size of the image received by the input layer of the model. The last input variable is used to name the prototxt file. After the prototxtFile_creator function created the prototxt file by the network architecture of SimpleNN, we use the caffemodelFile_creator function in Table 28 to export pre-trained parameters to the Caffe network and save it as the caffemodel file. We also define three input variables for the caffemodelFile_creator function. The first input variable is the pre-trained SimpleNN model. The second input value is the name of the prototxt file. The last input value is the name of the caffemodel file, which created from the caffemodelFile_creator function.

After successfully converting the VGG-Face model of MatConvNet into the Caffe model, we will find the prototxt file named vggfaces_proto_MatConvNet and the caffemodel file named vggfaces_caffemodel_MatConvNet at the current folder of Matlab. With these two files, we can use the code in Table 26 to execute the feedforward of the Caffe model. For example, we load a photo of Aamir Khan and import the txt file with 2,622 celebrities' names (Parkhi, Vedaldi, & Zisserman, 2015). Then, we assign the prototxt file and the caffemodel file of the VGG-Face model to create the Caffe network. Since the image size received by the input layer of the VGG-Face model is a 224x224 color image, we need to crop and resize the test image. After preprocessing the test image, we use net.forward to feed the test image into the VGG-Face model and execute the feed-forward. Finally, the model accurately recognizes the facial image of Amir Khan and show the prediction probability is 0.519.

When the Caffe deep learning framework and the MatCaffe interface are not installed, we can use the software support package, which is provided from Mathworks, to import the Caffe pre-trained model into the Matlab enironment. However, we cannot export the deep learning model, which structured by MatConvNet, to the Caffe model. Fortunately, MatCaffe, which is provided from Caffe, helps us to overcome the barrier between Matlab and Caffe. With the support of Caffe and MatCaffe, not matter import the Caffe model in Matlab or export the pre-trained model of SimpleNN as Caffe model, we all can easily do it. We also show that the pre-trained model of deep learning is portable with this example. We can preserve the network architecture and the pre-trained parameters after training model for further the application. In this section, we presented the standard operating procedure for importing the MatConvNet pre-trained model to the iOS app. Whether the developer is a beginner or an expert in the field of deep learning, developer can implement the application of deep learning model via the standard operating procedure. In the next chapter, we will solve the problem of handwritten digits recognition by the total solution we presented.

REFERENCES

Agarap, A. F. (2019, Feb 7). *Deep Learning using Rectified Linear Units (ReLU)*. arXiv:1803.08375

Apple. (2017, Jun). *Converting Trained Models to Core ML*. Retrieved from Apple Developer: https://developer.apple.com/documentation/coreml/converting_trained_models_to_core_ml

Apple. (2017). *Working with Core ML Models*. Retrieved from Apple Developer: https://developer.apple.com/machine-learning/build-run-models/

Apple. (2018). *coremltools*. Retrieved from coremltools: https://apple.github.io/coremltools/

Apple. (2018). *Creating an Image Classifier Model*. Retrieved from Apple Developer: https://developer.apple.com/documentation/createml/creating_an_image_classifier_model

Apple. (2018). *Improving Your Model's Accuracy*. Retrieved from Apple Developer: https://developer.apple.com/documentation/createml/improving_your_model_s_accuracy

Apple. (2018). *Machine Learning*. Retrieved from Apple Developer: https://developer.apple.com/machine-learning/

Apple. (2019). *Xcode*. Retrieved from Apple Developer: https://developer.apple.com/xcode/

Apple Inc. (2019). *Core ML 3 Framework*. Retrieved from Apple Developer: https://developer.apple.com/videos/play/wwdc2019/704/

Berkeley A. I. Research. (2014). *Batch Norm Layer*. Retrieved from Caffe: https://caffe.berkeleyvision.org/tutorial/layers/batchnorm.html

Berkeley A. I. Research. (2014). *Interfaces*. Retrieved from Caffe: http://caffe.berkeleyvision.org/tutorial/interfaces.html

Berkeley A. I. Research. (2014). *Layer Catalogue*. Retrieved from Caffe: https://caffe.berkeleyvision.org/tutorial/layers.html

Buyukkinaci, M. (2018). *Fruit Images for Object Detection*. Retrieved from kaggle: https://www.kaggle.com/mbkinaci/fruit-images-for-object-detection

caffe-users. (2014). *caffe-users*. Retrieved from Google Groups: https://groups.google.com/forum/#!forum/caffe-users

Choudhury, A. (2019). *8 platforms you can use to build mobile deep learning solutions*. Retrieved from Analytics India Magazine: https://analyticsindiamag.com/8-platforms-you-can-use-to-build-mobile-deep-learning-solutions/

Coto, E. (2017, Aug 1). *MatConvNet-DAGNN to Caffe converter*. Retrieved from GitHub: https://github.com/ecoto/dagnn_caffe_deploy

Glorot, X., Bordes, A., & Bengio, Y. (2011). Deep Sparse Rectifier Neural Networks. In *Proceedings of the Fourteenth International Conference on Artificial Intelligence and Statistics* (pp. 315-323). Fort Lauderdale, FL: Proceedings of Machine Learning Research.

Google. (2017, Dec 21). *Protocol Buffers v3.5.1.* Retrieved from GitHub: https://github.com/protocolbuffers/protobuf/releases/tag/v3.5.1

Han, J., & Moraga, C. (1995). The influence of the sigmoid function parameters on the speed of backpropagation learning. In J. Mira & F. Sandoval (Eds.), Lecture Notes in Computer Science: Vol. 930. *From Natural to Artificial Neural Computation. IWANN 1995* (pp. 195–201). Berlin: Springer. doi:10.1007/3-540-59497-3_175

Howell, M. (2009, May 21). *Homebrew.* Retrieved from Homebrew: https://brew.sh/

Ioffe, S., & Szegedy, C. (2015). *Batch Normalization: Accelerating Deep Network Training by Reducing Internal Covariate Shift.* arXiv:1502.03167

Jia, Y., & Shelhamer, E. (2014). *Installation.* Retrieved from Caffe: https://caffe.berkeleyvision.org/installation.html

Jia, Y., Shelhamer, E., Donahue, J., Karayev, S., Long, J., Girshick, R., . . . Darrell, T. (2014). Caffe: Convolutional Architecture for Fast Feature Embedding. In *MM '14 Proceedings of the 22nd ACM international conference on Multimedia* (pp. 675-678). Orlando, FL: ACM.

Kambampati, S. (2018, Jun 26). *What's New in Core ML 2.* Retrieved from Appcoda: https://www.appcoda.com/coreml2/

Mohd Sanad Zaki Rizvi. (2019, Nov 14). *Introduction to Apple's Core ML 3 – Build Deep Learning Models for the iPhone (with code).* Retrieved from Analytics Vidhya: https://www.analyticsvidhya.com/blog/2019/11/introduction-apple-core-ml-3-deep-learning-models-iphone/

Nair, V., & Hinton, G. (2010). Rectified Linear Units Improve Restricted Boltzmann Machines. ICML 2010, Haifa, Israel.

Parkhi, O. M., Vedaldi, A., & Zisserman, A. (2015). *VGG Face Descriptor.* Retrieved from Visual Geometry Group: http://www.robots.ox.ac.uk/~vgg/software/vgg_face/

Parkhi, O. M., Vedaldi, A., & Zisserman, A. (2015, Sep). Deep Face Recognition. *Proceedings of the British Machine Vision Conference (BMVC)*, 41.1-41.12.

Patterson, B. (2008). *Under the Hood: The iPhone's Gaming Mettle*. Retrieved from toucharcade: https://toucharcade.com/2008/07/07/under-the-hood-the-iphones-gaming-mettle/

Prévost, R., McQuaid, M., & Lalonde, D. (2009). *Homebrew Documentation*. Retrieved from Homebrew: https://docs.brew.sh/FAQ.html

StatCounter. (2019, Dec). *Mobile Vendor Market Share United States Of America*. Retrieved from Statcounter: https://gs.statcounter.com/vendor-market-share/mobile/united-states-of-america

The MatConvNet Team. (2016). *Index of /matconvnet/models*. Retrieved from MatConvNet: https://www.vlfeat.org/matconvnet/models/

The MatConvNet Team. (2018, Jul 29). *MatConvNet: CNNs for MATLAB*. Retrieved from GitHub: https://github.com/vlfeat/matconvnet

Tien, C. (2019, Mar 4). *Install Caffe and MatCaffe CPU-Only on MacOS 10.14.3*. Retrieved from CY's personal website: https://ctien2019.wordpress.com/

Vedaldi, A., & Lenc, K. (2015). MatConvNet: Convolutional Neural Networks for MATLAB. In *MM '15 Proceedings of the 23rd ACM international conference on Multimedia* (pp. 689-692). New York, NY: ACM.

Vedaldi, A., Lux, M., & Bertini, M. (2018, Apr 23). MatConvNet: CNNs are also for MATLAB users. *ACM SIGMultimedia Records, 10*(1).

Wan, S. (2016, Dec 15). *Mac OS X inatall protobuf*. Retrieved from JianShu: https://www.jianshu.com/p/f8b789280df4

Weisstein, E. W. (2002). *Hyperbolic Tangent*. Retrieved from MathWorld--A Wolfram Web Resource.: http://mathworld.wolfram.com/HyperbolicTangent.html

Wu, J.-M. (2002, March). Natural Discriminant Analysis Using Interactive Potts Models. *Neural Computation, 14*(3), 689–713. doi:10.1162/089976602317250951 PMID:11860688

Wu, J.-M. (2008, December). Multilayer Potts Perceptrons With Levenberg–Marquardt Learning. *IEEE Transactions on Neural Networks*, *19*(12), 2032–2043. doi:10.1109/TNN.2008.2003271 PMID:19054728

Wu, J.-M., Lin, Z.-H., & Hsu, P.-H. (2006, May). Function approximation using generalized adalines. *IEEE Transactions on Neural Networks*, *17*(3), 541–558. doi:10.1109/TNN.2006.873284 PMID:16722161

Wu, J.-M., Wu, C.-C., & Huang, C.-W. (2014, July). Annealed cooperative-competitive learning of Mahalanobis-NRBF neural modules for nonlinear and chaotic differential function approximation. *Neurocomputing*, *136*, 56–70. doi:10.1016/j.neucom.2014.01.031

WWDC. (2018). *What's New in Core ML*. Retrieved from Apple Developer: https://developer.apple.com/videos/play/wwdc2018/709

Chapter 4
Handwriting 99 Multiplication on App Store

ABSTRACT

The Modified NIST (MNIST) database, consisting of 70,000 handwritten digit images, in partition to 60,000 training patterns and 10,000 testing patterns, serves as a typical benchmark of evaluating performance of handwritten digit classification. After the LeNet CNNs model proposed by LeCun, researchers regarded this example as "Hello, World" in the field of deep learning. This chapter compares traditional approaches with the CNN model. The dataset of training and testing CNN models here is expanded to the Extension-MNIST (EMNIST) database. It will be employed to pre-train a CNN model for recognizing the handwritten digit image and installation on the iOS device. The user of the presented App can directly write digits on the touchscreen, and the smartphone instantly recognizes what were written. The pre-trained model subject to EMNIST database with a test accuracy of 99.4% has been integrated to an iOS App, termed as handwriting 99 multiplication, which has been successfully published on Apple's App Store.

METHODS OF ANALYZING MNIST

MNIST is a database of handwritten digits (LeCun, Cortes, & Burges, n.d.), which is induced from Special Database 1 and Special Database 3 of NIST. The MNIST database is more suitable than the NIST database for training machine learning models. The MNIST database has been pre-processed and

DOI: 10.4018/978-1-7998-1554-9.ch004

digitized. The handwritten digit patterns of the MNIST database have been size-normalized and centered in a 28x28 pixel size image. Each pattern of the database is a grayscale image. This database contains 60,000 training samples and 10,000 test samples. It is a basic database for researchers who are practicing machine learning. Researchers can spend less time on data pre-processing. In addition to the method of convolutional neural networks proposed by LeCun, researchers have applied many learning techniques and classification methods to solve the problem of handwritten digits recognition, such as radial basis function networks (LeCun, Bottou, Bengio, & Haffner, 1998), neural networks (Ciresan, Meier, Gambardella, & Schmidhuber, 2010) (Salakhutdinov & Hinton, 2007), convolutional neural networks (LeCun, Bottou, Bengio, & Haffner, 1998) (Cireşan, Meier, Masci, Gambardella, & Schmidhuber, 2011), support vector machine (Decoste & Schölkopf, 2002), and k-nearest neighbor (Keysers, Deselaers, Gollan, & Ney, 2007), etc. Before entering our theme, let's review the research methods of analyzing MNIST in the past.

First, the K-Nearest Neighbor (KNN) method is an intuitive classification method. Researchers believe that sample data of the same class will be clustered together in the raw or feature space. During the training phase, the KNN model will retain the training data and disperses the data in the feature space. Furthermore, during the test phase, we need to calculate the distances between the testing pattern and all training patterns in the raw or feature space. The KNN method will require the labels of the K training patterns that are closest to the testing pattern. The class of the testing pattern will be labeled as the category of the highest proportion of the K training labels. In other words, K training labels will vote to determine the class of the testing pattern. The concept of the KNN method is simple, but the pre-processing of the data set will affect the accuracy of the model. Lower the relevance of the data classes, better the classification ability of the model. Currently, the KNN classification method can achieve an error rate of 0.52% in the MNIST example (Keysers, Deselaers, Gollan, & Ney, 2007). Although the accuracy of KNN is higher than many machine learning methods, it seems to be unreasonable in the topic of artificial intelligence to simulate brain recognition by reserving all training patterns like the KNN method for classification.

When it comes to using machine learning to deal with classification problems, the first method that comes to mind is the Support Vector Machine (SVM). The technology of SVM has accumulated for decades. In 1963,

Vladimir Naumovich Vapnik and Alexey Yakovlevich Chervonenkis proposed the basic algorithm of SVM. Furthermore, two SVM-related papers (Boser, Guyon, & Vapnik, 1992) (Cortes & Vapnik, 1995) were proposed in 1992 and 1993 and published in 1992 and 1995. The SVM is built on rigorous mathematical theory. This method is to find an optimal separating hyperplane to separate the data points of different groups. For example, given P-dimension data points come from two different groups, the SVM will look for an optimal hyperplane of the (P-1)-dimension to divide the data points into two categories. In the field of machine learning, the hyperplane is also called the decision boundary. It means that the label of the test data point depends on one side of the decision boundary. In the course of the experiment, we will find a lot of hyperplanes that can divide the data points into two categories, but there is only one optimal separating hyperplane. The optimal separating hyperplane is also called the maximum interval hyperplane. This concept is like the problems of mathematical optimization. The optimal decision boundary of the SVM will maximize the distance of the nearest data point on each side. For the MNIST example, the SVM method can achieve an error rate of 0.56% (Decoste & Schölkopf, 2002).

Before talking about the Radial Basis Function (RBF) Network, we need to understand the Multilayer Perceptron (MLP) model in advance. The MLP model is a typical feedforward neural network architecture. Feedforward neural network means that the connections between nodes in the architecture do not form a cycle. The MLP model will map an input vector to an output vector. The architecture of MLP consists of multiple nodes, as shown in Figure 1. The MLP is a special case of the deep neural networks. The neurons of the upper layer and lower layer in the network architecture must be fully connected. For the MLP model in the Figure 1 we can use the function (4.1) to represent. The continuous function in the hidden layer can be linear or non-linear, and the parameters in the MLP model can be trained by the backpropagation method.

$$f\left(x;\theta\right) = r_0 + \sum_{i=1}^{M} r_i \tanh\left(a_i^{\mathrm{T}} x + b_i\right), \ \theta = \left\{r_i \in \mathrm{R}\right\} \cup \left\{a_i \in \mathrm{R}^d\right\} \cup \left\{b_i\right\} \tag{4.1}$$

However, the Radial Basis Function (RBF) Network of deep learning is similar to the MLP model, as shown in Figure 2. Each node in the RBF architecture is a Gaussian function. The RBF networks will be initialized with the data points μ, in accompany with posterior connections and variances, which will be further refined during the training process and are considered as most representatives of training data for classification. During testing

Figure 1. The basic architecture of the Multilayer Perceptron (MLP) model

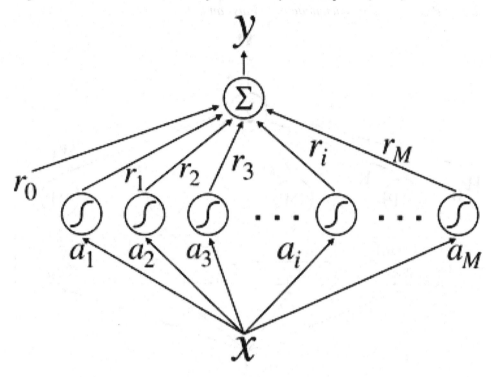

phase, the model calculates the distance and the Gaussian function between the input data and the representative data points. Finally, the output of the nodes will be weighted by w to obtain the predicted result of the model. In the RBF model, smaller the distance between the input data and the representative data point of a certain group, more influential the representative point. Therefore, the choice of representative data points in the group will affect the accuracy of the model. The method of finding representative data points is an issue of research. Currently, the RBF model mostly uses k-means or annealed k-means method for initialization and a hybrid of mean field annealing and gradient descent methods to optimize the representative points and built-in parameters. LeCun's 1998 paper (LeCun, Bottou, Bengio, & Haffner, 1998) used the RBF model to recognize the MNIST dataset with an error rate of 3.6%.

For the problem of the MNIST handwritten digits dataset, the deep neural network (NN) and the convolutional neural network (CNN) model are indispensable. We have explained the architecture and learning methods of deep neural networks and convolutional neural networks in the previous chapters.

Figure 2. The architecture of the radial basis function (RBF) Network is similar to the MLP model and its each node is a Gaussian function

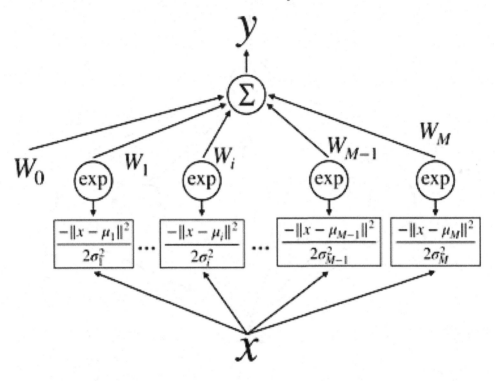

After the publication of the paper by LeCun in 1998, many researchers also made in-depth research and improvement for the two models of deep learning. In 2010, Ciresan et al. published the paper (Ciresan, Meier, Gambardella, & Schmidhuber, 2010), which constructs the deep neural network with six hidden layers for solving the MNIST problem. Each hidden layer in the model architecture contains 25000, 2000, 1500, 1000, 500, 10 neurons respectively. The activation function for each hidden layer is a scaled hyperbolic tangent. The error rate of this model is 0.35%. However, the most accurate model for solving the problem of the MNIST handwritten digits dataset is the convolutional neural network. Cireasan et al published the paper "High-Performance Neural Networks for Visual Object Classification" in 2011 (Cireşan, Meier, Masci, Gambardella, & Schmidhuber, 2011). In the paper, they used six convolutional layers and a fully connected in the CNN model to achieve an error rate of 0.27% for the MNIST problem. In the paper, they used six convolutional layers and a fully connected layer to achieve an error rate of 0.27%. Through the literature, we have found that convolutional neural network model of deep learning can effectively solve problems of pattern recognition.

Both the machine learning model and the deep learning model are designed to develop artificial intelligence systems. In the phase of data preparation, we will divide the given database into a training data set and a test data set. They are like textbooks and exam papers, respectively. Model simulates the brain to recognize objects accurately after training and testing. Although these methods have accuracy in pattern classification, some are not suitable for simulating recognition systems of the brain. Artificial intelligence systems should be like the brain to recognize the features of images and classify them afterward. The model should recognize the class of image after the learning process rather than retaining a large number of training data to calculate the class of test data. For example, K-Nearest Neighbor, although the model can achieve an error rate of 0.52% for the MNIST example, it retains a large number of training data that causes the model unportable. Conversely, the deep neural network or the convolutional neural network is a portable model. The model retains only the network architecture and built-in parameters after training. This book presents a total solution for the deep learning model. The goal is to import the portable model into the iOS App. We will demonstrate the total solution with the example of recognizing handwritten digits.

The total solution we propose will train the deep learning model in Matlab and import the pre-trained model into the iOS devices finally. Nowadays, data-driven deep learning will learn the information that comes with the data set. The richness of the images in the dataset affects the recognition ability of the model in the real-world application. We want to develop an iOS App that recognizes everyone's handwritten digits and applies it to a single digit multiplication. Therefore, we alternatively employ the Digits dataset of the Extension-MNIST (EMNIST) database (Cohen, Afshar, Tapson, & Schaik, 2017) from the MARCS Institute for Brain, Behaviour and Development of Western Sydney University to train our model. The Digits dataset expands the handwritten digit dataset of MNIST. We hope to increase the ability of the model to recognize complexly handwritten digits by expanding the data set.

DATASET

The Extension-MNIST database (EMNIST) (Cohen, Afshar, Tapson, & Schaik, 2017) is a database extended by MNIST. It not only contains the basic MNIST, but also provides multiple set of datasets, including *Balanced*,

By_Merge, *By_Class*, *Letters*, *Digits*, and *MNIST*. Each pattern of the EMNIST database is a 28x28 pixel grayscale image like the MNIST dataset. Here we use the Digits dataset of EMNIST as the data used by our training model. The Digits dataset contains 280,000 handwritten digits from 0 to 9, with 240,000 (86%) training samples and 40,000 (14%) test images respectively. The training and test images are evenly spread over ten categories. It is a balanced dataset, such as Figure 3. The model constructed based on Digits

Figure 3. Digits of extension-MNIST database

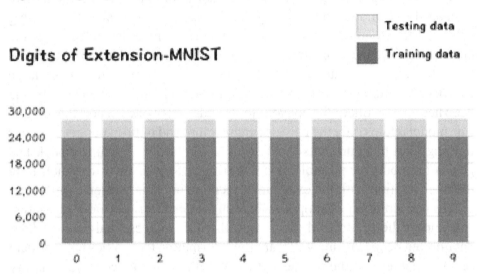

dataset will be able to cope with more complicated handwritten digits than the model trained by MNIST.

CNN Architecture

After determining the data set, we constructed a suitable CNN framework based on the data set. We hope that this model can accurately classify 0 to 9 categories. We use the architecture of MNIST example provided by MatConvNet as the architecture of this problem, as shown in Figure 5, and choose to use *SimpleNN* as the wrapper for CNNs. We think the architecture is sufficient for recognizing handwritten digits and no need to modify it. MatConvNet provides two wrappers for deep learning models, which are Simple Neural Network (SimpleNN) and Directed Acyclic Graph Neural

Network (DagNN). These two wrappers help us store the network architecture and model parameters in the defined format. Although DagNN is more flexible than SimpleNN, it is more slightly slower for small CNNs. In the CNN architecture here, the hidden layer uses four Convolutional layers, two Max Pooling layers, and one ReLU activation function. For the first convolutional layer, we used 20 kernels (channels), where each kernel size (filter size) was 5x5x1 and with stride 1 as shown in Figure 6. We can get that the output of the first convolutional layer is 24x24x20 (Figure 7), and downsampling through Max Pooling layer to the output of 12x12x20 afterward, as indicated by Figure 4. In the last layer of the hidden layer, we used the convolutional layer to emulate the fully connected layer, which includes 10 kernels (channels), and each kernel was 1x1x500. The fully connected layer is a case of the convolutional layer. Because both the convolutional layer and the fully connected layer compute dot products, they can be converted to each other when the kernel size of the convolutional layer is equal to the size of the input map (Johnson & Yeung, 2018). Finally, the Softmax is used to convert

Figure 4. CNN architecture for digit recognition of extension-MNIST

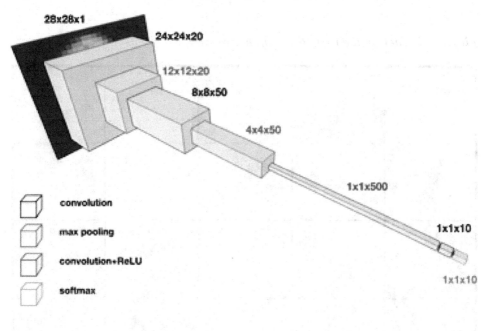

the ten outputs of the last hidden layer into the ten probability values as the

Figure 5. CNN organization for digit recognition of extension-MNIST

Layers	1	2	3	4	5	6
Type	CONV	maxPool	CONV	maxPool	CONV+ReLU	CONV
Channels	20	-	50	-	500	10
Filter Size	5x5x1	-	5x5x20	-	4x4x50	1x1x500
Convolution Stride	1x1	-	1x1	-	1x1	1x1
Pooling Size	-	2x2	-	2x2	-	-
Pooling Stride	-	2x2	-	2x2	-	-

Figure 6. Kernels of the first convolution layer

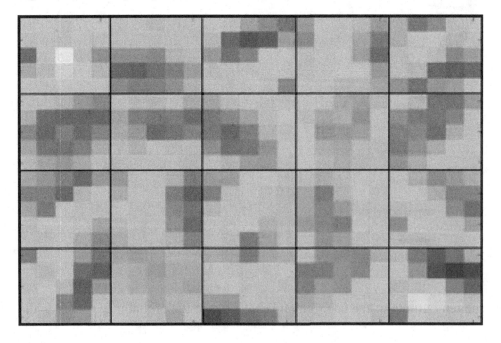

Figure 7. Result of first convolution for an input digit 9

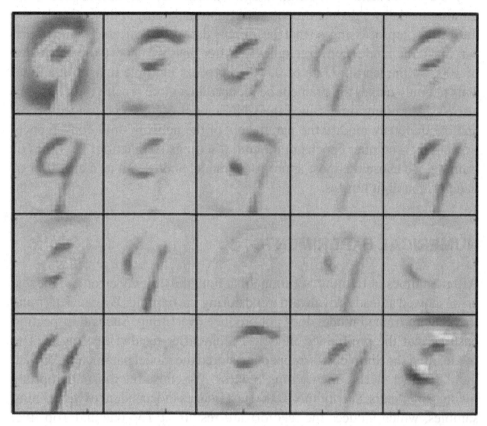

output of the CNNs. The largest of the ten probability values represents the recognition result of the network.

Training Strategies

Since the Digits of EMNIST database is a problem of pattern recognition, we use the CNN model to solve it. With deep learning, we can eliminate the need of defining the axiom or function for discriminating digits from 0 to 9, and we also don't need to use traditional methods of extracting image features to solve the problem of pattern recognition. Because the CNN architecture allows deep learning to automatically extract image features through the self-learning method of BP. We believe that using CNNs to deal with the problem of handwritten digits is the best choice.

For 280,000 handwritten digit images, in order to increase the speed of the training model, we deduct the mean of training data from the entire dataset during the preprocessing, so that the training data is zero-mean. This approach can make the model converge quickly. After that, we choose the batch size of 100 and the learning rate of 0.001 to process multiple images at a time. This not only makes the gradient be reduced in a more precise direction, but also saves training time. Since the CNN model needs to be trained by BP and continuously modify the parameters of the network until convergence, we set up 10 number epochs in the initial settings so that after ten times of training, we chose the most appropriate model and used it as a classifier of handwritten digit images.

NUMERICAL EXPERIMENTS

After ten times of training, we found that both the training error and the test error showed a steady downward trend during the training. We can determine that the pre-trained model does not produce overfitting. Such an inspection ensures that the pre-trained model is a classifier handwritten digits. The model used the SimpleNN wrapper and stored the model parameters for each number epoch during the training process. We chose the most appropriate model parameters, and for the 40,000 test images independent of the training samples, which induces the feedforward results of Top one and Top five, 0.0052 and $5.0*10^{-5}$, respectively. We believe that this pre-trained model can accurately recognize handwritten digits. Next, we will install this model into the iOS device through the Caffe third-party framework, and see how it works.

Execution on iOS Devices and Publishing to App Store

After the experiment, we have obtained the pre-trained CNN model using MatConvNet on Matlab. We hope that this model with the function of recognizing handwritten digits can be used to deal with more practical problems and can have a positive impact on humans. If we can write the model to the wafer and make it into a machine with capabilities for identifying, it must be the primary choice. However, we consider that following the current trend the software made into App and published on App Store is most accessible by users. Almost every person has one or more mobile devices now, and can conveniently download the App from the internet, and use the software on the mobile device without having to re-purchase a machine because of the new software. Therefore, we finally chose to make the model into an iOS App.

We refer to the *NeuralNet-Handwriting-iOS* software (Hundley, 2017), which publish on GitHub by Collin Hundley of Swift AI. Their software is consistent with our philosophy, but we consider that in addition to basic identification of handwritten digits, handwriting digits recognition is also can be used to help children learn. Let children learn the basic one-digit multiplication of mathematics through interaction with software, so we added the single digit multiplication in the app software. Through pattern recognition, the app can not only teach children how to write numbers from 0 to 9 but also learn single digit multiplication. Additionally, the sound effects of mobile phone can increase the fun of children learning.

We don't want to reconstruct a complex CNN architecture in the Xcode environment, so here we will use the pre-trained CNN model of Matlab as a classifier for handwritten digit recognition of iOS App. We used the Caffe deep learning framework, installed the MatCaffe interface, and re-created the pre-trained model into a Caffe model on Matlab. On Caffe framework, we created the *.prototxt* and *.caffemodel* files to record the CNN architecture

Figure 8. We can integrate the .prototxt and .caffemodel files on the Caffe framework into the Core ML model via Core ML Tools

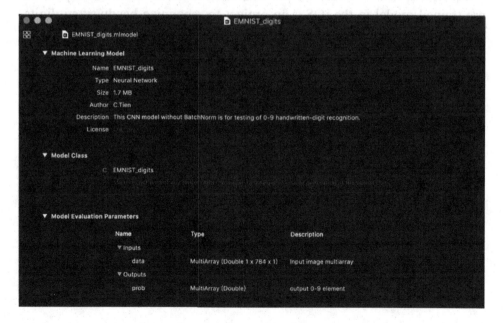

Figure 9. The pre-trained model of Matlab was converted into the Core ML model through the total solution and imported into the Xcode App project

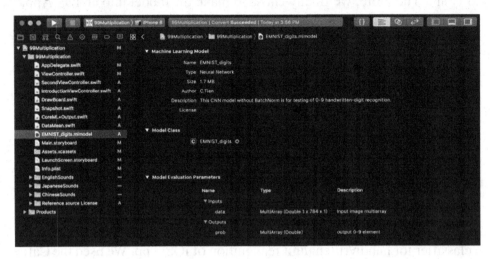

and weight of pre-trained model on MatConvNet. After that, we convert the above two files into the *.mlmodel* file through Core ML Tools and import it into the Xcode project to complete the core of our app, as shown in Figure 8 and Figure 9.

After deep learning cross-platform conversion, the Core ML model is equivalent to the model we pre-trained on Matlab. We will import the pre-trained model in the iOS App project to recognize handwritten digits. After that, we built the user interface in the *Main.Storyboard* of Xcode project, added the handwriting area, the result area and the sound effect of announcing digits. As shown in Figure 10, we can add any UI element from the Xcode library to construct the user interface in Main.Storyboard. After the user interface of the App is completed, we can write the code in the ViewController.swift and activate the UIView, UIButton, and UILabel, etc. in the Main.Storyboard. If you're using Xcode to create an iOS App for the first time, there are many experts on the internet that provide the examples for making iOS Apps. After making the user interface of the iOS App, we can use the code of Table 1 to activate the Core ML model. In Table 1, we let the "inputDataMatrix" variable store the digit pattern of the user-entered and the "results" variable store the ten output probability values of the Core ML model. The digit pattern has been digitized and stored in a matrix of 784x1. We transpose the matrix of input and feed it into the Core ML model

Figure 10. We can add any UI element from the Xcode library to construct the user interface in Main.Storyboard

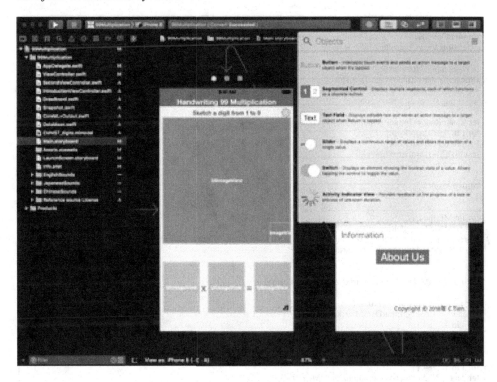

for recognition. Finally, we compare the probability values of the output to determine the prediction results of the model.

In the course of the experiment, we made a huge mistake. We did not add the mean of training data to the App project, so the results of testing the Core ML model on iOS devices broke our expectations. It is against our training strategy that the digital image hasn't be deducted the mean of the training data before feed into the Core ML model. Therefore, we need to add the file which includes the mean of training data to the Xcode project. When the user writes the digit, it will deduct the training data mean before entering the ML model recognition, just like the *inputDataDMean* variable in the table. Finally, the *Handwriting 99 Multiplication* (Tien, 2018) App was completed and published on the App Store, realizing the concept of artificial intelligence deep learning software to assist human learning, in Figure 11. We believe that it is the most appropriate choice to demonstrate the total solution through the Hello World of deep learning but use the extended dataset. It helps us understand how to construct a deep learning model, train network

Table 1. The code was added in the handwriting 99 multiplication app for executing the core ML model

```
import UIKit
import CoreML
extension ViewController{

///Trans input data matrix
func transMatrix(matrix:[Int])-> [Int] {
var result = [Int] (
repeating: 0, count: matrix.count
)
let squareRoot = Int(sqrt(Double(matrix.count)))
for i in 0..<squareRoot{
for j in 0..<squareRoot{
result[i*28+j] = matrix[28*j+i]
}
}
return result
}

///CoreML model
func EMNIST_model(inputDataMatrix:[Int]) -> Int {
guard let input_data = try? MLMultiArray(shape:[1,784,1], dataType:MLMultiArrayDataType.float32) else {
fatalError("MLMultiArray init. barfed")
}

let inputDataMatrix = transMatrix(matrix: inputDataMatrix)

var inputDataDMean = [Float] (
repeating: 0, count: inputDataMatrix.count)
for j in 1...784 {
inputDataDMean[j - 1] =. Float(inputDataMatrix[j - 1]) - Float(data_mean[j - 1])
}

for i in 1...784 {
let data = NSNumber(value: inputDataDMean[i - 1])
input_data[i - 1] = NSNumber(value: (data.floatValue))
}

let i = EMNIST_digitsInput(data: input_data)

guard let digit_prediction = try? model.prediction(input: i) else {
fatalError("Error")
}

let results = digit_prediction.prob

var maxIndex = -1

var maxPredection: NSNumber = -1

// select output label
for i in 0...9 {
let prediction = results[i]

if prediction.floatValue >. maxPredection.floatValue {
maxPredection = prediction
maxIndex = i
}
}
return maxIndex
}
}
```

Figure 11. Testing digit recognition of the CNN model on iOS devices

parameters, transfer the pre-trained model to the third-party deep learning framework, integrate the model into the Xcode App project, and publish pattern recognition App to the App Store. The total solution fully embodies the application of AI deep learning. In the following chapters, we will increase the difficulty of the problem and try to solve problem in the same approach.

REFERENCES

Boser, B. E., Guyon, I. M., & Vapnik, V. N. (1992). A training algorithm for optimal margin classifiers. In *COLT '92 Proceedings of the fifth annual workshop on Computational learning theory* (pp. 144-152). Pittsburgh, PA: ACM.

Ciresan, D. C., Meier, U., Gambardella, L. M., & Schmidhuber, J. (2010, December). Deep Big Simple Neural Nets Excel on Handwritten Digit Recognition. *Neural Computation*, 22(12), 3207–3220. doi:10.1162/NECO_a_00052 PMID:20858131

Cireşan, D. C., Meier, U., Masci, J., Gambardella, L. M., & Schmidhuber, J. (2011). Flexible, High Performance Convolutional Neural Networks for Image Classification. In *IJCAI'11 Proceedings of the Twenty-Second international joint conference on Artificial Intelligence* (vol. 2, pp. 1237-1242). Barcelona, Spain: AAAI Press.

Cohen, G., Afshar, S., Tapson, J., & Schaik, A. V. (2017). *EMNIST: an extension of MNIST to handwritten letters.* arXiv:1702.05373

Cortes, C., & Vapnik, V. (1995, February 20). Support-Vector Networks. *Machine Learning*, 20(3), 273–297. doi:10.1007/BF00994018

Decoste, D., & Schölkopf, B. (2002, January). Training Invariant Support Vector Machines. *Machine Learning*, 46(1-3), 161–190. doi:10.1023/A:1012454411458

Hundley, C. (2017). *NeuralNet-Handwriting-iOS*. Retrieved Jul 2017, from Swift AI on GitHub: https://github.com/Swift-AI/NeuralNet-Handwriting-iOS

Johnson, J., & Yeung, S. (2018). *CS231n Convolutional Neural Networks for Visual Recognition*. Retrieved from Converting Fully-Connected Layers to Convolutional Layers: http://cs231n.github.io/convolutional-networks/#convert

Keysers, D., Deselaers, T., Gollan, C., & Ney, H. (2007, August). Deformation Models for Image Recognition. *IEEE Transactions on Pattern Analysis and Machine Intelligence*, *29*(8), 1422–1435. doi:10.1109/TPAMI.2007.1153 PMID:17568145

LeCun, Y., Bottou, L., Bengio, Y., & Haffner, P. (1998, November). Gradient-Based Learning Applied to Document Recognition. *Proceedings of the IEEE*, *86*(11), 2278–2324. doi:10.1109/5.726791

LeCun, Y., Cortes, C., & Burges, C. J. (n.d.). *The MNIST Database of handwritten digits*. Retrieved from THE MNIST DATABASE of handwritten digits: http://yann.lecun.com/exdb/mnist/

Salakhutdinov, R., & Hinton, G. (2007). Learning a Nonlinear Embedding by Preserving Class Neighbourhood Structure. In *Proceedings of the Eleventh International Conference on Artificial Intelligence and Statistics* (pp. 412-419). Proceedings of Machine Learning Research.

Tien, C.-Y. (2018). *Handwriting 99 Multiplication*. Retrieved Dec 2018, from iOS App Store: https://itunes.apple.com/us/app/handwriting-99-multiplication/id1419757476?mt=8

Chapter 5
Pattern Recognition of Handwritten English Characters

ABSTRACT

After success of a total solution to handwriting 99 multiplication by deep learning, this chapter further addresses on the problem with increased complexity. In addition to handwritten digital dataset, the EMNIST database provides multiple balanced or unbalanced datasets. These datasets contain different combinations of handwritten digit and letter images. It is believed that well trained deep CNNs can handle unbalanced datasets, so this chapter chose By_Class of EMNIST database as a dataset to increase the difficulty of problem solving and extend the application of iOS Apps. This chapter discusses classification of handwritten English character, including uppercase and lowercase, data audition due to requirement of further improvement, and online tests on iOS devices. After a long time of training, the developer got the pre-trained CNN model. For 58,405 testing images, the recognition accuracy rate was as high as 97.0%.

DOI: 10.4018/978-1-7998-1554-9.ch005

AUDITED DATASET OF HANDWRITTEN ENGLISH LETTERS

After the appearance of the CNN model, the pattern recognition of handwritten characters seems basic and simple. But it is more difficult than imagined actually. Different from printed characters, handwritten characters may be irregular, sloped, and distorted. As a human being, to distinguish others' handwritten characters is also not simple. After solving the recognition problem of handwritten digits, we believe that the recognition of handwritten letters will be another valuable topic for research. In present, there are many consumer electronics with touch-screen surrounding, such as smartphone, iPad, computer, GPS, camera and so on. The touch-screen not only retains the function of display but also replaces physical type-in buttons. We can watch videos, draw pictures, type, command transmission and so on via touch-screen. We used to store information on paper, but now we tend to store electronically in the hard disk or cell phone. The developed recognition model of handwritten letters can efficiently convert handwritten characters on photos or touch-screens into electronic characters and store them. We can import the recognition model of handwritten letters to iOS devices and realize practical applications, such as handwriting crossword puzzles, handwriting notepads, handwriting translator and so on. If the recognition model of handwritten letters combines with handwritten digits in Chapter 4, we can also import to traffic enforcement cameras to detect the license plate of the speeding vehicle. Obviously, the recognition model of handwritten letters could be widely applied in real life.

In Chapter 4, handwriting 99 multiplication employs off-line handwritten digit recognition. Relative to on-line character recognition, off-line handprinted character recognition possesses more extensible applications to iOS pattern recognition App design. The App design in this chapter adopts off-line handwritten English character recognition (Grother P. J., 1995) (Grother & Hanaoka, 2016) (Netzer, et al., 2011) (Grother & Hanaoka, 2016) which is feasible for handprinted document recognition (LeCun, Bottou, Bengio, & Haffner, 1998) (Netzer, et al., 2011) (Radtke, Sabourin, & Wong, 2008).

NIPS special database 19 was released in 1995 (Grother P. J., 1995) for automatic handprinted document and character recognition. The original version of NIPS special database 19 contains 3669 handprinted documents and 814,255 segmented handprinted digit and alphabetic characters, each occupying 128x128 pixel.

Its second edition (Grother & Hanaoka, 2016) released in 2016 contains four directories in addition to the images of full page HSF (Handwriting Sample Form) form. The file, termed as by_write, partitions all segmented handprinted digits and characters by author. The file, termed as by_field, discards writer information and stores all segmented sub-images, according their appearance in fields of HSF, in directories of digit, upper, lower, and const. The file, termed as by_class, discards both writer and field information, directly partitions all segmented sub-images into directories, respectively storing sixty-two types of characters for class recognition. The file, termed as by_merge, follows the storage structure of by_class, but merging the uppercase and lowercase letters. For example, handprinted sub-images of "W" and "w" are merged to one class. Merging the uppercase and lowercase of some letters is reasonable due to their similarity for recognition. In this version, letters including "C", "I", "J", "K", "L", "M", "O", "P", "S", "U", "V", "W", "X", "Y" and "Z" are regarded invariant to their lowercase letters respectively. The by_merge file has forty-seven classes. Each segmented character is attached with a predetermined label that indicates its exclusive membership to 47 classes. Excluding 10 classes of digits induces 37 classes of merged English letters.

In 2011, the previous work (Ciresan, Meier, Gambardella, & Schmidhuber, 2011) applied a committee of CNNs to deal with handprinted English letter recognition using NIPS special database 19, where a subset of by_merge file was employed in (Ciresan, Meier, Gambardella, & Schmidhuber, 2011). It is composed of 162559 segmented handprinted characters of 37 merged classes, 85.27% for training and 14.73% for testing. The work (Ciresan, Meier, Gambardella, & Schmidhuber, 2011) reported an average testing error rate, 8.21 ± 0.11 in percentage, and stated no comparative results due to lacking published works that summarize results of similar experimental setups for handprinted English letter recognition.

Chapter 4 has used the digits data set of the EMNIST database (Cohen, Afshar, Tapson, & Schaik, 2017) to replace the MNIST data set (LeCun, Cortes, & Burges, n.d.). The EMNIST database provided by the Western Sydney University also contains many different types of handwritten data set, such as Balanced, By_Merge, By_Class, Letters, Digits, and MNIST. These data sets are composed of handwritten digits and handwritten English letters. To begin with, the Balanced data set is a balanced data set with 131,600 sample images, and images are equally spread over 47 classes. The

47 classes are numbers ranging from 0 to 9 and 37 English letter classes. In Balanced Dataset, letter classes combine 15 lowercase letters into their own uppercase letters. By_Merge dataset, containing 47 classes and 814, 255 sample images, is similar with Balanced dataset approximately. It is different from the Balanced Dataset in size and is with unbalanced numbers of patterns in classes. In the dataset, all sample images are unevenly spread over 10 digit classes and 37 English letter classes. EMNIST database also provides an English letter classes dataset called Letters. Letters dataset contains a total of 145,600 sample images, which are evenly spread over 26 English letter classes. Each of 26 classes contains uppercase and lowercase. Finally, Digits and MNIST Database are familiar handwritten digits dataset. They are both balanced datasets, which contains 280,000 and 70,000 sample images separately. These datasets only have the handwritten digits, but not letter classes.

We want to select the suitable dataset from EMNIST Database in order to expand the application domain of iOS Apps and increase the difficulty of problem solving. This chapter uses the CNN model to recognize handwritten English letters. In addition to the problem of recognizing handwritten digits, the problem of recognizing handwritten letters is also the basic issues of pattern recognition. The English alphabet contains a total of 52 classes of uppercase and lowercase letters. However, some uppercase and its lowercase in 52 classes are over similar. This problem of pattern recognition is basic, but we think it is harder than recognizing handwritten digits.

Similar to Letters dataset in NIPS special database 19, EMNIST Letters dataset contains 88,800 training segmented characters and 14,800 testing characters in 37 classes, where the training and testing segmented characters are formed by random drawing. By using EMNIST Letters dataset, the OPIUM (Online Pseudo-Inverse Update Method) classifiers (Schaik & Tapson, 2015) (Grother & Hanaoka, 2016) in the original paper (Cohen, Afshar, Tapson, & Schaik, 2017) attained a maximal accuracy of 85.15% ± 0.12% and a committee of CNNs (Ciresan, Meier, Gambardella, & Schmidhuber, 2011) resulted in an accuracy of 92.42%. As stated in the previous work (Baldominos, Sáez, & Isasi, 2019), By_Class dataset and By_Merge dataset in the EMNIST database was too new to serve as a benchmark for published works.

This chapter selects the By_Class dataset from the EMNIST database, which contains handwritten English letters and handwritten digits, in a total of 814,255 images. But we only deal with handwritten English characters here, so we removed the handwritten digits from the dataset and created a new dataset, containing 411,302 images, with 352,897 (86%) training samples and 58,405 (14%) test images. For this data set, each image is a 28x28 pixel grayscale image. The dataset is unbalanced. The new dataset is bigger than the Letters dataset in size. We hope the proposed approach feasible for developing handprinted letter recognition App on iOS devices. Unfortunately, directly applying MatConvNet deep learning to the new dataset attained an unacceptable testing accuracy. As argued previously, the EMNIST By_Class dataset is so new that there is no published comparative results. Facing the difficulty of unacceptable testing accuracy, the authors choose data audition for further developing the iOS App of handprinted English letter recognition based on the EMNIST dataset.

After the preliminary experiment, we decided to examine the cleanliness of the new dataset intensively and extensively. The process of developing the iOS App will not go straightforward like the previous chapter. Being in the era of Big Data, accessing information is easier than in the past. On the other hand, the accuracy and reliability of information may be questioned and guaranteed for further usage. A large amount of information is the motivation of promoting data-driven deep learning. We train deep learning model subject to a large-scale dataset. If the training dataset contains a large number of incorrect messages, it will seriously affect the recognition ability of the model. In other words, the model derived from incorrect training data, its accuracy and reliability cannot be accepted for online testing on iOS devices. Therefore, data audition is an important issue in the era of Big Data.

A convenient sub-image displaying tool is developed under Matlab environment for screening and examining more than four hundred thousand segmented letters and relabeling their categories manually. The auditing process is critical for deriving an effective and reliable classifier for pattern recognition of handprinted English letters on iOS devices.

By reviewing the data of By_Class dataset, we found that the dataset contains two types of confusing labels, which are either the confused mark for the uppercase letter and lowercase letter or the incorrect mark. For example, the small *a* is marked as big *A* category, big *Q* is marked as small *q* category, big *G* is marked as small *g* category, etc. All are with a confused mark for identifying the uppercase letter and lowercase letter. According to the definition given by NIPS special database 19, some uppercase letters, such as "A", "Q" and "G", should be distinguishable to lowercases. The original labelling is apparently incorrect and should be corrected during the auditing process. The other incorrect marks, such as small *p* is marked as small *q* category, small *j* is marked as small *i* category, etc., and even we have found that small *y* is marked as small *e*. We believe that all of these incorrect or confusing marks

Figure 1. Category distribution of the By_Class dataset after data audition

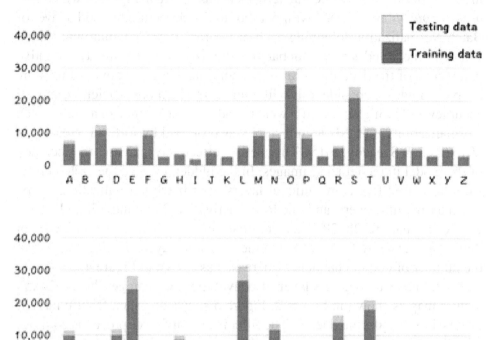

will substantially increase the burden of deep neural network training, so we spent a few weeks reorganizing the dataset and re-marking these images for audition. After the check, the category distribution of the By_Class dataset is shown in Figure 1.

CNN Architecture

Convolutional neural networks (LeCun, Bottou, Bengio, & Haffner, 1998) (Ciregan, Meier, & Schmidhuber, 2012) (Ciresan, Meier, Gambardella, & Schmidhuber, 2011) have been regarded as most competitive neural architecture for document and character recognition. We use MatConvNet (Vedaldi & Lenc, 2015) to construct a CNN architecture subject to constraints proposed by the handwritten English characters dataset, where the network input is a segmented gray-level sub-image and the network output is a binary unitary vector for indicating the exclusive membership to categories of English letters. Similar to the process of learning handwritten digits, details of hidden layers in the deep convolutional neural network are as shown in Figure 3, which also uses *SimpleNN* as the CNN wrapper. For this architecture, we add a layer of Batch Normalization following each of the first four Convolutional layers, where the mean and variance for batch normalization are regarded as adaptive parameters of the deep convolutional neural network and are optimized by deep learning. We consider this will train the model more efficiently, and the accuracy will be higher than if it were not added. The method of adding Batch Normalization into CNN architecture was proposed by Ioffe an Szegedy in 2015 (Ioffe & Szegedy, 2015). This method effectively increases the accuracy of the model in recognizing images. In the hidden layer of the architecture, we totally used five convolutional layers, four batch normalization layers, two max-pooling layers, and one ReLU activation. For handwritten English characters that are 28x28 pixel grayscale images as same as handwritten digits, the same size filter is used in the first three layers of convolution, but the number of output channels is increased as shown in Figure 4.

Therefore, after the first layer of convolution, we can get the 24x24x50 feature map as shown in Figure 2. Figure 5 shows one such feature map of processing a handprinted letter. The filter in size of 5x5x1 proceeds 24 times of valid convolutions over the input that is in size of 28x28x1. There are 50 filters in the first convolution layer, so the feature map is in size of 24x24x50.

Figure 2. Deep CNN architecture for English characters recognition of By_Class dataset

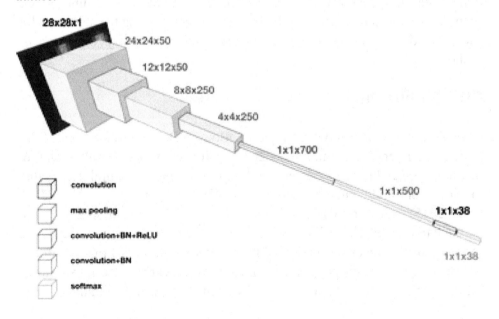

The deep CNN executes batch normalization after each convolution layer, as shown in the Figure 2.

It is easy to verify sizes of features maps of different convolution layers. In this CNN architecture, let **nxnxm** denote the size of the feature map to one convolution layer. Assume there are L filters in this convolution layer. Since the convolution here performs planar movement, the size of the filter can be expressed as **kxkxm**, where the third number in size of the filter is identical to that of the feature map and k is an odd number. There k-1 pixels at each row or the first dimension of the feature map that can not be a center for valid convolution. Therefore the size of the resulted feature of the convolution is **(n-k+1)x(n-k+1)xL**. For the second convolution layer, n equals 8, k equals 5 and L equals 250. It can be verified that the second feature map in figure 2 is in size of 4x4x250.

Finally, we add a new layer of convolution in the last hidden layer, whose action is same as the fully-connected inner product layer. There are 38 channels in this layer, each of which has a size of 1x1x500, allowing the last hidden layer generate 38 output elements. Lastly, the generated output elements are further passed through Softmax to induce the output vector of the deep convolutional neural network. After the output of the last convolutional layer is converted by the Softmax function, each output value of the deep

Figure 3. CNN organization for English character recognition of By_Class dataset

Layers	1	2	3	4	5	6	7
Type	CONV+BN	maxPool	CONV+BN	maxPool	CONV+BN+ReLU	CONV+BN	CONV
Channels	50	-	250	-	700	500	38
Filter Size	5x5x1	-	5x5x50	-	4x4x250	1x1x700	1x1x500
Convolution Stride	1x1	-	1x1	-	1x1	1x1	1x1
Pooling Size	-	2x2	-	2x2	-	-	-
Pooling Stride	-	2x2	-	2x2	-	-	-

Figure 4. Kernels of the By_Class model's first convolution layer

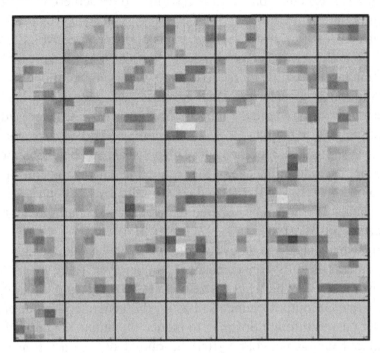

Figure 5. Result of first convolution in response to input S

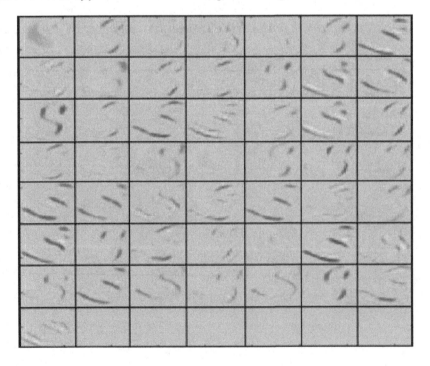

convolution neural network will be within the range [0 1], and the sum of all elements in the output vector is 1.

Training Strategies

The empirical experiences of developing handprinted digit classification App in chapter 4 depict that CNNs are simpler and more straightforward than traditional methods of designing classifiers, and that BP enables CNNs to automatically learn important features. With regard to the grayscale images of handwritten English characters 28x28 pixel, we believe that CNN can easily classify them accurately. Therefore, we choose to use the same initial value to train the model, and the images we used have been deducted from the mean of the training data before training. For pattern recognition of 52 handwritten English letter classes, we adjust the CNN architecture. Different from pattern recognition of handwritten digits, the value of number epoch is set to 20 here. When 52 classes were directly fed into the training model through experiments, the results were not as good as expectation. Although what we did is reasonable, the pre-trained model does not accurately recognize 52 classes of online handwritten letters. We consider that among 52 categories, some categories of the characters are too similar, for example, big *C* and small *c*, big *O* and small *o*, big *S* and small *s*, etc. to be distinguished. Therefore, the model tends to recognize the uppercase as the lowercase or recognize the lowercase as the uppercase. Both are concluded as the errors of the model output, resulting in the error rate of the model unable to fall steadily. But these behaviors are permissible from an application perspective. Therefore, based on the experience of data cleaning, it is suggested that some lowercase letters, including "c", "f", "j", "k", "m", "o", "p", "s", "u", "v", "w", "x", "y", "z", due to similarity to uppercase, are merged to the class of uppercase separately. The result is shown in Figure 6, where we only train and test the remaining 38 categories afterward.

NUMERICAL EXPERIMENTS

Based on data collation and training strategies for merging categories, the model has been significantly improved in reducing the errors caused by the labels, so that we can be more convinced accuracy of this model after training. After training with 20 number epochs using MatConvNet in Matlab, we

Figure 6. Based on the experience of data cleaning, we know that there are 14 lowercase letters in By_Class dataset similar to uppercase, therefore, we filter out 14 lowercase letters and merge them in uppercase separately.

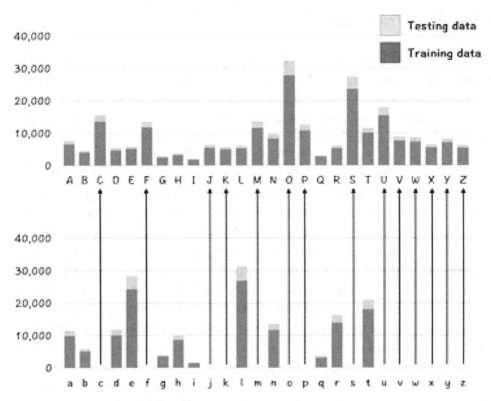

sequentially tested the model to ensure that no over-fitting was produced. We selected the model with the highest accuracy rate for 58,405 testing images, where in the feed-forward mode the obtained test errors of the top one and top five are 0.0307 and 0.0015, respectively. This result is much better than the traditional classification method (Cohen, Afshar, Tapson, & Schaik, 2017). Non-cursive regular handwritten English characters can be identified accurately. Therefore, we consider that this model is very suitable for being used in iOS devices. We will install this model into the iOS device through the Caffe third-party framework and execute it to see how it work.

Execution on iOS Devices and Publishing to App Store

The classifier model of handwritten English characters was trained by MatConvNet. The model will be tested on iOS devices for other users, whose handwritten English characters are not part of the By_Class dataset. Next, this model is made into an app for artificial intelligence image recognition, which is expected to deal with more practical problem or assist human learning. Through the mobile device interface, interaction with the AI app can enhance the life quality of user.

Here we import the Core ML model to the Xcode app project in the same way as Chapter 4. For the purpose, the pre-trained CNN model is made into the *.prototxt* and *.caffemodel* files through the MatCaffe, where the CNN architecture and built-in parameters are recorded respectively. Ensuring that the feedforward of the Caffe model is consistent with the testing results on Matlab, one can further translate the Caffe model into a *.mlmodel* file and import into the Xcode project. It is important to check whether the feedforward of the Caffe model and the pre-trained model are consistent with each other. If we don't check that the feedforward results of the two models are consistent, the iOS App will not be able to recognize patterns accurately, just as subsequence of forgetting to deduct the mean of all training patterns in the fourth chapter. As shown in Figure 7, we have integrated the handwritten letter recognition model in MatConvNet into the Core ML model. We created an App that recognizes handwriting English letters and installed Core ML model on an iOS device to test online usage of the model.

The predictors in training and testing data are segmented handprinted characters in form of 28x28 grayscale images. The classifier makes use of no online information involving moving tracking. Therefore, the obtained classifier on iOS devices is applicable for both offline and online handwritten English letter recognition. This App allows the user to write an English letter (both upper and lower case) through the touch-screen. The online handwritten letter image will be captured and stored as a 28x28 pixel grayscale image, like the thumbnail in the lower left corner of the App. After the image is digitized, the iOS App feeds it into the Core ML model. The pre-trained model will execute feedforward and output the recognition result of the model. The recognition result will belong to one of the 38 categories, but we set the user to see only one of the uppercase A to Z for easy output, such as those in Figure 8, Figure 9 and Figure 10.

According to the test results, we found that most of the handwritten letters in the database are regularly written in non-cursive way. For the people nowadays, the fonts of A to Z are usually mixing the standard, cursive and even more different fonts. The App can only accurately identify the A to Z of the standard writing. Even though the recognition rate of the model for 58,405 testing images is as high as 97.0%, it seems that the application is not

Figure 7. We integrated the deep learning model of MatConvNet into the Core ML model through Caffe third-party deep learning framework. After that, we can use this Core ML model to develop an App that recognizes handwritten letters.

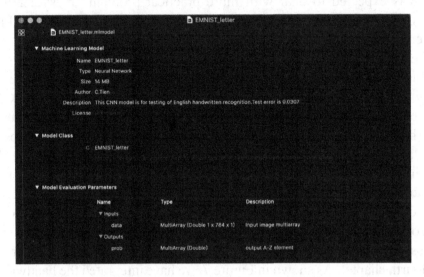

Figure 8. Testing English character recognition of the CNN model for By_Class dataset on iOS devices

Figure 9. Testing English character recognition of the CNN model for By_Class dataset on iOS devices

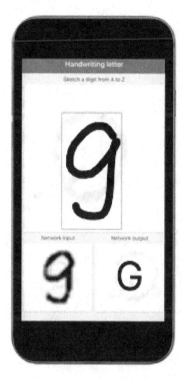

enough to be competent on the broad level. But making a standard teaching app to narrow the application may be a good choice. Through the application of the image recognition of the App, learning the writing of the English letter or the use of word recitation, children will be more interested in learning. After the handwritten pattern is recognized, the result of the recognition or the English word pronunciation is played through the speaker of the iOS device, so that the App becomes plentiful. Finally, publishing it to the iOS App Store and practicing the idea of the AI assist English learning.

Although it seems to only increase the number of classes for recognition in this chapter, the involved problem solving is obviously harder than problem of recognizing handwritten digits. Since large-scale database affects data-driven deep learning models, it will seriously affect the recognizing ability of the model if we do not ensure the correctness of the database and the labeling process. Besides, the convolution layers in CNN take place of hand-crafted textural descriptors. The model automatically extracts the local information from input data and sends it to the next layer for dealing with

Figure 10. Testing English character recognition of the CNN model for By_Class dataset on iOS devices

complex features. The filters of convolutional layers can also self-learning through the backpropagation method. With this mechanism, we no longer need to define axioms and rules for handwritten characters. However, the pre-process of data is still important, especially in the stage of data correcting and data auditing. Data-driven deep learning will self-learn based on paired data, so the accuracy of recognition models will be affected when the paired data contains incorrect information. The pre-process of data takes time of experts, but it significantly increases reliability of recognition model for current task. An artificial intelligence assistant system is what we pursue, which is a model with high accuracy of recognition and high reliability. In the fourth chapter and this chapter, the total solution realizes the application of deep learning models in numerical-analysis software. Additionally, we found through the total solution that the test accuracy of the experiment can only provide a reference in real-life applications. Although the handwritten letter recognition model can achieve a test accuracy of 97.0% in the experiment, it cannot accurately recognize the cursive handwritten letters in the application.

In the future, we can expand the richness of the characters in the dataset to solve this problem. Next chapter, we will introduce how to use the CNN model to aid in the diagnosis of breast cancer images.

REFERENCES

Baldominos, A., Sáez, Y., & Isasi, P. (2019, March). Hybridizing Evolutionary Computation and Deep Neural Networks: An Approach to Handwriting Recognition Using Committees and Transfer Learning. *Complexity, 2019,* 2952304. doi:10.1155/2019/2952304

Ciregan, D., Meier, U., & Schmidhuber, J. (2012, Jul 26). Multi-column deep neural networks for image classification. In *2012 IEEE Conference on Computer Vision and Pattern Recognition*, (pp. 3642–3649). Providence, RI: IEEE. 10.1109/CVPR.2012.6248110

Ciresan, D. C., Meier, U., Gambardella, L. M., & Schmidhuber, J. (2011, Nov 3). Convolutional Neural Network Committees for Handwritten Character Classification. In *2011 International Conference on Document Analysis and Recognition*, (vol. 10, pp. 1135-1139). Beijing, China: IEEE. 10.1109/ICDAR.2011.229

Cohen, G., Afshar, S., Tapson, J., & Schaik, A. V. (2017). *EMNIST: an extension of MNIST to handwritten letters.* arXiv:1702.05373

Grother, P. J. (1995, March). *NIST Special Database 19 – Handprinted Forms and Characters Databas 1st Edition User's Guide.* National Institute of Standards and Technology.

Grother, P. J., & Hanaoka, K. K. (2016). *NIST special database 19 handprinted forms and characters 2nd Edition.* Retrieved 2019, from National Institute of Standards and Technology: https://www.nist.gov/srd/upload/nistsd19.pdf

Grother, P. J., & Hanaoka, K. K. (2016). *NIST special database 19 handprinted forms and characters database. National Institute of Standards and Technology.*

Ioffe, S., & Szegedy, C. (2015). *Batch Normalization: Accelerating Deep Network Training by Reducing Internal Covariate Shift.* arXiv:1502.03167

LeCun, Y., Bottou, L., Bengio, Y., & Haffner, P. (1998, November). Gradient-Based Learning Applied to Document Recognition. *Proceedings of the IEEE, 86*(11), 2278–2324. doi:10.1109/5.726791

LeCun, Y., Cortes, C., & Burges, C. J. (n.d.). *The MNIST database of handwritten digits*. Retrieved from THE MNIST DATABASE of handwritten digits: http://yann.lecun.com/exdb/mnist/

Netzer, Y., Wang, T., Coates, A., Bissacco, A., Wu, B., & Ng, A. Y. (2011). Reading Digits in Natural Images with Unsupervised Feature Learning. In *NIPS Workshop on Deep Learning and Unsupervised Feature Learning 2011*, (pp. 1-9). Granada, Spain: Academic Press.

Radtke, P. V., Sabourin, R., & Wong, T. (2008, Mar 16). Using the RRT algorithm to optimize classification systems for handwritten digits and letters. In *SAC '08 Proceedings of the 2008 ACM symposium on Applied computing*. Fortaleza, Brazil: ACM.

Schaik, A. v., & Tapson, J. (2015, Feb. 3). Online and adaptive pseudoinverse solutions for ELM weights. *Neurocomputing, 149*(Part A), 223-238.

Vedaldi, A., & Lenc, K. (2015). MatConvNet: Convolutional Neural Networks for MATLAB. In *MM '15 Proceedings of the 23rd ACM international conference on Multimedia* (pp. 689-692). New York, NY: ACM.

Chapter 6
Mobile–Aided Breast Cancer Diagnosis by Deep Convolutional Neural Networks

ABSTRACT

After verifying the capability of deep learning for basic image recognition, this chapter further extends image recognition to App-aided breast cancer diagnosis. Human cancer has been considered as the most important health problem. For medical image recognition of breast cancer, the presented approach is no longer the same as the traditional. It needs no axioms for distinguishing malignant and benign tumors, and no hand-crafted textural descriptors for feature extraction. The goal is to develop a mobile-aided diagnosis system of directly processing raw medical images. It automatically extracts features and learn filters of a deep CNN subject to labelled medical images in advance. This chapter presents a CNN architecture for diagnosing breast cancer images, illustrating effectiveness of problem solving by designing classifiers, respectively diagnosing lobular carcinoma breast cancer against phyllodes tumor and papillary carcinoma against adenosis. The performances of two classifiers for breast cancers diagnosis are separately summarized by the testing accuracy rates of 94.9% and 87.3%.

DOI: 10.4018/978-1-7998-1554-9.ch006

BREAST CANCER DIAGNOSIS BY DIRECT
MEDICAL IMAGE RECOGNITION

Beyond pattern recognition of handwritten digits and characters, developing intelligent-assisted diagnostic systems is also an interesting problem. In the current society, the laborers are slowly decreasing, whereas the elders are gradually increasing. This problem has spawned expensive labor and high demand for healthcare resources in the future. The pressure on medical staff is also increasing. Therefore, developing the intelligent diagnostic system helps relieve the pressure of the medical staff (Boyle & Levin, 2008) (Lakhani, Ellis., Schnitt, Tan, & van de Vijver, 2012). Today, cancer is the second cause of leading death in the world. The number of people worldwide who died of cancer was about 9.6 million in 2018 (Wold Health Organization, 2018) and will increase to 27 million until 2030 according to prediction in (Boyle & Levin, 2008). Among the 9.6 million cancer deaths, breast cancer is the second common cancer. After verifying the capability of deep learning for basic pattern recognition, we hope to develop the diagnostic system of breast cancer by deep learning of the CNN models.

In fact, research on the development of intelligent diagnosis of breast cancer has been around for a long time, where those based on histopathological analysis are especially important for BC diagnosis (Lakhani, Ellis., Schnitt, Tan, & van de Vijver, 2012). BC diagnosis based on automatic image processes has been also developed over 40 years (Stenkvist, et al., 1978). The previous work in (Kowal, Filipczuk, Obuchowicz, Korbicz, & Monczak, 2013) applies image processes for segmenting nuclei of breast cancer. We can trace back to the Breast Cancer Wisconsin (Original) dataset (Wolberg, Breast Cancer Wisconsin (Original) Data Set, 1992) created by Dr. William H. Wolberg in the 1990s. This data set contains 699 instances, with 458 benign and 241 malignant samples. Each sample is described by nine cytological characteristics, each with an integer ranging from 1 to 10. The cell of the breast mass was obtained via the medical method of fine-needle aspirates (FNAs) for analysis and recorded as benign or malignant by analysis of cytological characteristics. Scientists selected nine characteristics from eleven cytological characteristics of breast FNAs by statistical analysis to differed significantly between benign and malignant masses. The nine characteristics are including cell size, uniformity of cell size, uniformity of cell shape, bare nuclei, normal nucleoli, clump thickness, clump cohesiveness, mitosis and nuclear chromatin (Wolberg & Mangasarian, 1990). In the past, researchers have solved the problem by defining mathematical functions or axioms for nine cytological characteristics. Many methods of machine learning or statistical model have been used to solve the recognition problem of Wisconsin breast cancer dataset, such as artificial neural networks (Abbass, 2002) (Wu, 2006), decision trees (Grąbczewski & Duch, 2002), K-Means (Bradley, Bennett, & Demiriz, 2000), logical analysis of data (Boros, et al., 2000) and support vector machines (Lee, 2001), etc. Although traditional classification methods can effectively classify benign and malignant masses, these build on the leadership of expert. These methods are called expert systems because they require the expert to define the characteristics of the medical image, and the researchers construct the classifier through the defined features afterward. The researches in (Filipczuk, Fevens, Krzyżak, & Monczak, 2013) (George, Zayed, Roushdy, & Elbagoury, 2014) (Zhang, Zhang, Coenen, & Lu, Breast cancer diagnosis from biopsy images with highly reliable random subspace classifier ensembles, 2013) report BC diagnosis of FNA cytological images and techniques of one-class classification (Zhang, Zhang, Coenen, Xiau, & Lu, 2014), spectral clustering (Doyle, Agner, Madabhushi, Feldman, & Tomaszewski, 2008) and telepathology (Evans, Krupinski, Weinstein, & Pantanowitz, 2015) have been applied for BC diagnosis.

Today, deep learning methods different from expert systems. It needs no axioms for distinguishing malignant and benign masses, and no hand-crafted textural descriptors for feature extraction. Deep learning model will be trained via the medical image with the correct label. The convolutional layer of the deep learning model replaces the hand-crafted textural descriptors and expertly defined cytological characteristics. The backpropagation method of deep learning is based on the gradient descent to modify the parameters of each layer to achieve self-learning. In this chapter, we use deep learning to solve the medical image recognition problem of breast cancer. We constructed a deep learning model for the Breast Cancer Histopathological Dataset. The 40X breast cancer microscopic images can be directly fed into the model for recognition. Finally, we hope that the portable deep learning model can develop an App-aided breast cancer diagnosis through the total solution.

Dataset

The Breast Cancer Histopathological Database (BreakHis) (Spanhol F. A., Oliveira, Petitjean, & Heutte, 2016) provided by the Laboratory of Vision, Robotics and Imaging (VRI), contains a total of 9,109 microscopic images of breast cancer tumor. These images were created by VRI in collaboration with P&D Laboratory - Pathological Anatomy and Cytopathology, Parana, Brazil. The BreakHis Database has attracted many attentions in the field of deep learning (Aresta, et al., 2019) (Brancati, De Pietro, Frucci, & Riccio, 2019) and pattern recognition (Bayramoglu, Kannala, & Heikkilä, 2016) (Nawaz, Ahmed, Tahir, & Khan, 2018). This chapter aims to demonstrate applicability of proposed total solution for developing iOS pattern recognition of breast histopathology images for BC diagnosis. Images in the BreakHis Database were taken from 82 patients and contained four different magnification factors images (40X, 100X, 200X, 400X). For all images, there were 2,480 benign and 5,429 malignant samples, each with 460x700 pixels, 3-channel RGB, 8-bit depth in each channel, in PNG format (Spanhol F., Oliveira, Petitjean, & Heutte, 2017).

The most difference between benign and malignant tumors is their diffusion properties. There is a capsular around the tumor that separates normal tissue from tumor tissue. Benign tumors usually remain localized and slow-growing. It will oppress the surrounding tissue but will not destroy or invade surrounding tissue. After the benign tumor is removed, the symptoms of nerves or blood vessels compression caused by it will be eliminated and the original function will be restored. In histopathology, the structure of benign tumors looks similar to the original cell. However, the cells of the malignant tumor are different from the original cells and abnormally differentiated. Malignant tumors easily invade other organs via lymph or blood. Even if a malignant tumor is removed, it will still recur or metastasize to other organs. The damage caused by malignant tumors is usually unrecoverable. The benign and malignant in the BreakHis dataset contain four different categories respectively. The types of benign tumors are adenosis, fibroadenoma, phyllodes tumor, and tubular adenoma; the types of malignant tumors are ductal carcinoma, lobular carcinoma, mucinous carcinoma, and papillary carcinoma.

Microscopic images in the BreakHis database were collected by the surgical open biopsy method. Different from the FNAs method in the Breast Cancer Wisconsin dataset, the surgical biopsy method will remove the tissue samples of the tumors and requires general anesthesia during surgery. Although the FNAs method can avoid unnecessary surgery and high diagnostic accuracy, this method can only identify whether there are malignant cells and cannot assess the type and intrusion situation of the tissue. The surgical biopsy method is also named excisional biopsy. The surgeon will attempt to remove the entire area of the lesion during the surgical operation. Additionally, the surgeon will collect non-tumorous tissue around the lesion to check for spread.

In the experiment, only the microscope images of the 40X magnification factor are processed. The images of the 40X magnification factor cover a wide range and include more information than other magnification factors, and no area has been amplified by pathologists. We hope that the constructed classifier can recognize the whole image. Even in the future, the machine can automatically capture the area with malignant cancer cells through the features learned in the past, whether to enlarge or not, and no longer depending on the pathologist.

We simplify the problem into two small examples for demonstration of BC diagnosis, and use the state-of-the-art deep learning of CNNs to deal with it. The first example is to recognize lobular carcinoma breast cancer against phyllodes tumor (LC vs. P) as shown in Figure 1, which respectively contain 156 malignant images and 109 benign images. The second example is to discriminate papillary carcinoma against adenosis (PC vs. A) as shown in Figure 2, which respectively include 124 malignant images and 114 benign images.

Figure 1. Lobular carcinoma breast cancer against phyllodes tumor

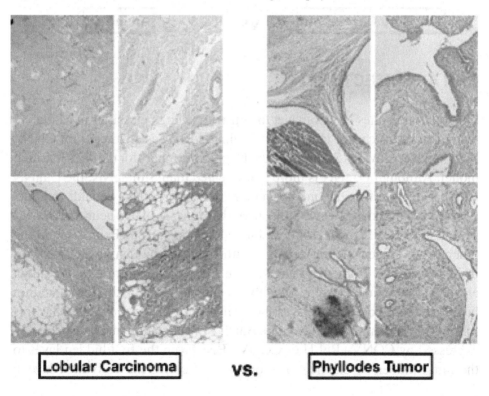

Lobular Carcinoma　　　VS.　　　**Phyllodes Tumor**

Figure 2. Papillary carcinoma against adenosis

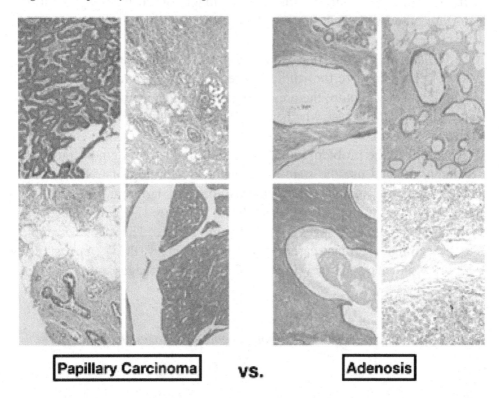

CNN ARCHITECTURE

This section applies MatConvNet to construct a large classifier in Matlab to recognize breast cancer images, employing *DagNN* as a wrapper for CNNs. MatConvNet provides SimpleNN and DagNN wrappers for the deep learning model. Although DagNN is more complicated than SimpleNN, the DagNN wrapper is more flexible and convenient for large CNNs (Vedaldi & Lenc, 2015). The large classifier we built on Matlab consists of two neural networks. The first is a CNN model with 25 hidden layers, such as Figure 3, and the other is a nonlinear neural network with only one hidden layer, as shown in Figure 5. The 25 hidden layers of the CNN architecture totally contain eleven Convolutional layers, five ReLU layers, five Batch Normalization layers, and four Pooling layers, as shown in Figure 4. The convolution layer is followed by either a ReLU layer or a Batch Normalization layer, respectively expressed by CONV+ReLU or CONV+BN. From the first hidden layer to the ninth hidden layer, there are four sets of concatenated hidden layers, consisting of CONV+ReLU, CONV+BN and one Pool. The tenth hidden layer, CONV+ReLU, is especially followed by two CONV+BN hidden layers. The input layer receives a 200x200x3 patch image, which is a sample from the original 460x700 image and the output layer is softmax, which generates the probability value for the benign or malignant of the patch image.

Since the first classifier focuses on classification of the patches, we constructed a second classifier that contains only a non-linear hidden layer. The responses of the CNN model to all patches regularly sampled from the whole image are fed into the second classifier for recognition, and the output of the second classifier represents the recognition result of the whole full image.

Figure 3. CNN architecture for patch recognition of breast cancer

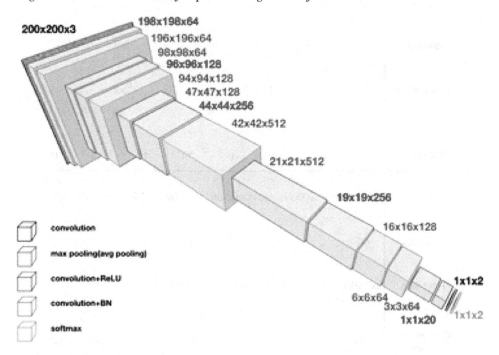

Training Strategies

Before model training, the data set for each of the two examples has been randomly divided into 70% training set and 30% test set as shown in Figure 6, They are independent of each other and there is no duplicate image. For the original cancer image (460x700 pixels, 3-channels RGB) in the dataset,

Figure 4. CNN organization for patch recognition of breast cancer

Layers	1	2	3	4	5	6	7
Type	CONV+ReLU	CONV+BN	maxPool	CONV+ReLU	CONV+BN	avgPool	CONV+ReLU
Channels	64	64	-	128	128	-	256
Filter Size	3x3x3	3x3x64	-	3x3x64	3x3x128	-	4x4x128
Convolution Stride	1x1	1x1	-	1x1	1x1	-	1x1
Pooling Size	-	-	2x2	-	-	2x2	-
Pooling Stride	-	-	2x2	-	-	2x2	-

Layers	8	9	10	11	12	13	14	15
Type	CONV+BN	avgPool	CONV+ReLU	CONV+BN	CONV+BN	maxPool	CONV+ReLU	CONV
Channels	512	-	256	128	64	-	20	2
Filter Size	3x3x256	-	3x3x512	4x4x256	5x5x128	-	3x3x64	1x1x20
Convolution Stride	1x1	-	1x1	1x1	2x2	-	1x1	1x1
Pooling Size	-	2x2	-	-	-	2x2	-	-
Pooling Stride	-	2x2	-	-	-	2x2	-	-

Figure 5. The nonlinear classifier with one hidden layer for breast cancer recognition

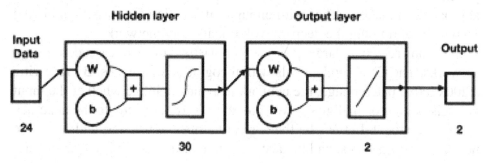

Figure 6. Breast cancer dataset for two models

Model	Training Data (70%)	Testing Data (30%)
lobular carcinoma (M) vs. phyllodes tumor (B)	186	79
papillary carcinoma (M) vs. adenosis (B)	167	71

we can't handle it intuitively. Because the image is too large, it will cause a huge load on the deep neural network and need to construct a deeper model and more parameters for recognition.

We refer to the approach of the paper (Spanhol F. A., Oliveira, Petitjean, & Heutte, 2016). The author uses the AlexNet architecture to deal with breast cancer images, and trains and tests the model with the patch images of 32x32 pixels or 64x64 pixels. However, we consider the problem of extracting a whole image into the patches of 32x32 pixels or 64x64 pixels. For malignant images, some patches will contain areas without the information of malignancy, but they will be marked as the malignant image. We hope that the patches have enough information and reduce the burden of training the deep convolutional neural network, so each original image in the dataset of LC vs. P or PC vs. A generates 24 patches by moving a window of 200x200 regularly, with marks same as the original image. Each patch is composed of 200x200 pixels with 3-channels RGB. Finally, there are 4,467 training patches and 1,896 test patches in the LC vs. P dataset, and 4,008 training patches and 1704 test patches in the PC vs. A dataset. We believe that this approach can make patches with enough information for classification and no burden of training the deep convolutional neural network.

We constructed a large classifier consisting of two cascaded neural networks. The CNN model deals with recognition of patches. By receiving a 200x200x3 patch image, the network responds to judge whether the input patch is benign or malignant. We provide a way to calculate the accuracy rate of the model. Let N_{res} be the correct number of patches, and N_{all} is the number of test patches, and the accuracy rate of the model is calculated as

$$Accuracy\ rate\ of\ patches = \frac{N_{res}}{N_{all}} \qquad (6.1)$$

We can get the benign and malignant probability values of each patch image through the first convolutional neural network. We hope that the diagnostic system can diagnose the whole image rather than a patch image. Therefore, in the training strategies of the second neural network, we used the result of classifying 24 patches from the same original image in the training data as input to the network. These input values are the malignant probability values that the patch images are recognized by the CNN model. After that, through a hidden layer to get the output of the second network, the output result represents the probability of benign and malignant of the original image. As shown in Figure 7, 24 patches regularly extracted from a test image are processed by the deep convolutional neural networks and 24 probabilities form a vector that is further processed by a multilayer network for classification.

Numerical Experiments

After 10 hours training subject to sampled patches from the dataset of LC vs. P (without GPU), we obtained the CNN model (the first classifier) with the test error of 0.0723. The same experiment for training the CNN model subject to patches sampled from the PC vs. A dataset attained the test error of 0.1414.

The empirical results show benign patches distinguishable from malignant patches for both problems. So a neural network (the second classifier) with only one hidden layer is trained subject to the correspondent training dataset. Finally, a large classifier consisting of two cascaded classifiers is used to

Figure 7. The large diagnosis system of breast cancer consists of a CNN model and a nonlinear model with one hidden layer

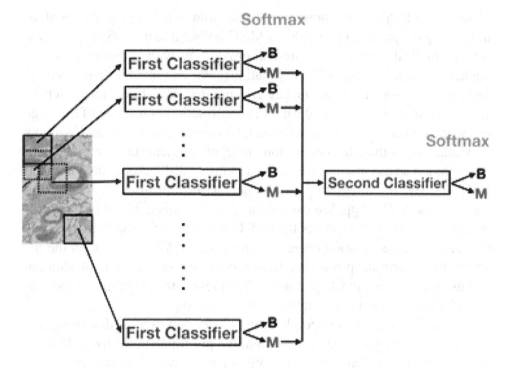

recognize individual test data (raw images). The test accuracy rate obtained was 94.9% and 87.3%, respectively for the problems of LC vs. P and PC vs. A. Although there is still much room for improvement in the accuracy rate of recognition, there is an apparent breakthrough in the results compared to the traditional approach (Spanhol F. A., Oliveira, Petitjean, & Heutte, 2016). Especially in the process of training, there is no artificial interference from input to output, and the deviation caused by interference classification is also avoided. Therefore, we believe that this approach is a good beginning and the results are encouraging. In the future, an automatic mobile-aided diagnosis system can be developed. Through the pre-trained CNN model, the histopathologist can directly input an image of a fixed size, and the mobile-aided diagnosis system will make a recognition on the whole image. The doctor or scholar can identify this as a preliminary judgment to alleviate the pressure on diagnosis.

Execution on iOS Devices and Future App Publication

Chapter 3 of this book presents a total solution, keeping the goal of integrating the pre-training model of MatConvNet into the iOS App. Matlab is mathematical analysis software that provides us with an environment for mathematical modeling and computations. We can use the mathematical toolboxes to input medical images and preprocess dataset. In particular, when execution errors occur during the construction or training of the large classifier, we can easily debug it through Workspace and Command Window on Matlab. After that, the recognition model of deep learning combined with the mobile App has gradually become a trend. In 2017, Apple Inc. provided the Core ML for integrating the model of the third-part deep learning frameworks to iOS App. We can import the pre-trained model of the third-part deep learning frameworks through Cor ML to make the iOS App have the function of recognition objects. Unfortunately, Matlab is not on the list of the third-party deep learning frameworks. We provide a total solution and use the example in Chapter 4 and 5 to present the pre-trained model of Matlab that can also be integrated into the iOS App.

In this chapter, we use deep learning to develop models that recognize breast cancer images. Finally, we obtain the pre-trained models on Matlab. With the model for diagnosis of the breast cancer, we can import the model into an iOS App through the Caffe third-party framework and finally publish on App Store for sale. Today, iOS mobile devices possess amazing computing power and fruitful hardware equipment for data acquisitions. Apple iPhone 4 with computing power in CPU speed of 800 MHz and 1.9 GFLOPS has been recognized compatible with Cray-2 supercomputer. Therefore, we believe that it is a good choice to make the pre-trained breast cancer recognition model into an iOS App for execution on iOS devices. The doctors or scholars can easily find and download it from the App Store via iPhone. During the operating stage, the device is connected to the microscope, and the image is directly transmitted into the App software, and the device will immediately output the diagnosis result. In particular, this stand-alone diagnostic system is portable. For remote areas or resource-poor areas, doctors can use the stand-alone diagnostic system for medical diagnosis at any time. Nowadays, mobile devices are gradually replacing computers and many medical devices are able to connect to mobile devices, such as Bluetooth Stethoscope and Personal Ultrasound. This diagnosis system can not only reduce the doctor's fatigue on diagnosis, but also reduce the misjudgment caused by the doctor's fatigue or lack of experience, and even reduce the waiting time of the patient. We believe that this idea can not only reduce the burden of manpower, but also enhance social benefits, and the overall value of existence is high.

Deep Learning for Classification of Bluetooth Stethoscopic Heart Sounds

The author in the work (Chen, 2017) proposes the methodology of learning convolution neural networks (CNN) for classifying MFCC (Mel-Frequency Cepstral Coefficients) (Huang, Acero, Hon, & Reddy, 2001) (Wojcicki, 2020) (Fu, Yang, & Wang, 2010) features of heart sounds recorded by bluetooth stethoscopes. The goal is to train a CNN classifier that is able to distribute immediate heart sounds from Bluetooth stethoscope into its suitable condition. The database of the heart sound recordings used in (Chen, 2017) is the PASCAL Classifying Heart Sounds Challenge (Bentley, Nordehn, Coimbra, Mannor, & Getz, 2011). The proposed methodology mainly translates time-domain heart sounds to distributed two-dimensional feature patterns and applies deep learning for training the CNN classifier of heart sounds.

Let τ denote the size of a moving window and S denote a heart sound recording. Starting from time instance $S[t]$, consecutive instances framed by such a window, denoted by $S[t: t+\tau - 1]$, are processed by the mfcc Matlab function in (Huang, Acero, Hon, & Reddy, 2001) to form a feature vector v. The first element in v denotes the log energy and the remaining, denoted by $v[2: L+1] \equiv u$, are MFCC coefficients, corresponding human ear perception in different frequency, where $L=12$ denotes the number of coefficients in (Chen, 2017). The technique of extracting the MFCC feature was developed by Davis and Mernelstein in 1980's. The MFCC feature extraction is powerful for audio analysis.

Sliding the window forward K steps results in consecutive overlapping or non-overlapping windows, inducing K sets of MFCC coefficients which constitute a feature pattern well represented by a $K \times L$ matrix, where $K=16$ in (Chen, 2017). A feature pattern is labeled as zero when its source is normal and is labeled as one when its source is murmur. The experiment in (Chen, 2017) processes 200 normal and 66 murmur heart sound recordings in dataset B, always generating N feature patterns from each heart sound source by randomly setting the starting instances, where N = 1500. By stratified sampling, the experiment in (Chen, 2017) selects $N_0=31$ normal heart sounds and $N_1=10$ murmur heart sounds, totally forming $(N_0+N_1) \times N \equiv M$ feature patterns, each being a *K×L* matrix. Sampled from each source heart sound, N labeled feature patterns are randomly partitioned to two exclusive subsets, in ratio of 4:1, respectively for training and testing. The training and testing sets respectively contain $\frac{4M}{5}$ and $\frac{M}{5}$ labeled feature patterns.

The experiment in (Chen, 2017) organizes a deep convolutional neural network for classification of MFCC feature patterns. The network input is a *K×L* matrix and the output is a single sigmoid unit for two-alternative classification. The architecture contains two convolutional blocks and a fully connected layer. The first block contains a convolution layer, which possesses ten 5×5 convolutional filters, followed by a 2×2 average pooling layer. The second block contains a convolution layer, which possesses twenty 3×3×10 convolutional filters, followed by a 2×2 average pooling layer. The experiment in (Chen, 2017) applies the deep learning framework in Matlab to train the CNN classifier subject to labeled training feature patterns. Deep leaning of the CNN classifier subject to labeled training feature patterns in (Chen, 2017) attains the accuracy 90.8% for training and 89.3% for testing.

The CNN classifier of feature patterns is further employed for classifying the whole heart sound recording. Given a heart sound recording, the stepwise procedure (Chen, 2017) is sketched as follows for classification.

1. Generate N feature patterns, denoted by $\{u_i\}_i^N = 1$, from a given heart sound recording by randomly selecting N starting instances.
2. Apply the trained CNN classifier to infer the type of each feature pattern, denoted by $F(u_i)$, where F denotes the network function of the trained CNN classifier.
3. Calculate $z = \frac{1}{n}\sum_{i=1}^{N} F(u_i)$.
4. If z > 0.5 , Z = 1, otherwise Z = 0. Output Z.

The given heart sound recording is murmur if Z = 1 and is normal if Z = 0. The above heart sound classification is applied to classify N_0 normal heart sounds and N_1 murmur heart sounds, which have been employed for generating labeled training and testing feature patterns of the CNN classifier. The numerical experiment in (Chen, 2017) shows an accuracy of 97.6% for classification.

Figure 8. A bluetooth stethoscope

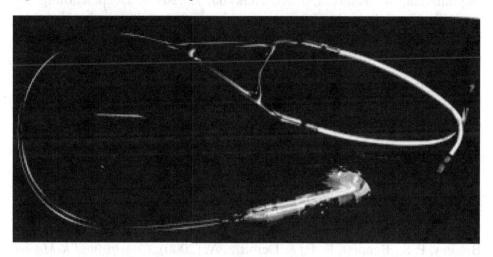

Applying the above heart sound classification to process 200 normal and 66 murmur heart sound recordings in dataset B. The numerical experiment in (Chen, 2017) attains an encouraging accuracy of 84.6%.

Another fourteen heart sounds for testing were obtained by recording heart sounds of the author of the work (Chen, 2017) using the bluetooth stethoscope in Figure 8. The experiment in (Chen, 2017) also gives the results of using the above classification procedure to classify newly recorded fourteen cases, which are all classified as normal heart sounds. There still are 120 cases of noisy normal heart sounds and 29 cases of noisy murmur heart sounds in Dataset B. The experiment further applies the above classification procedure to classify these 149 cases noisy heart sounds. The numerical experiment in (Chen, 2017) shows an accuracy of 76.5%.

REFERENCES

Abbass, H. A. (2002). An Evolutionary Artificial Neural Networks Approach for Breast Cancer Diagnosis. *Artificial Intelligence in Medicine*, *25*(3), 265–281. doi:10.1016/S0933-3657(02)00028-3 PMID:12069763

Aresta, G., Araújo, T., Kwok, S., Chennamsetty, S. S., Safwan, M., Alex, V., ... Ludwig, F. (2019, August). BACH: Grand challenge on breast cancer histology images. *Medical Image Analysis*, *56*, 122–139. doi:10.1016/j. media.2019.05.010 PMID:31226662

Bayramoglu, N., Kannala, J., & Heikkilä, J. (2016). Deep learning for magnification independent breast cancer histopathology image classification. In *2016 23rd International Conference on Pattern Recognition (ICPR)*. Cancun, Mexico: IEEE.

Bentley, P., Nordehn, G., Coimbra, M., Mannor, S., & Getz, R. (2011). *Classifying Heart Sounds Challenge*. Retrieved from Classifying Heart Sounds Challenge: http://www.peterjbentley.com/heartchallenge/

Boros, E., Hammer, P. L., Ibaraki, T., Kogan, A., Mayoraz, E., & Muchnik, I. (2000). An implementation of logical analysis of data. IEEE, 292-306.

Boyle, P., & Levin, B. (2008). *World Cancer Report 2008*. Lyon, France: IARC Press, International Agency for Research on Cancer.

Bradley, P. S., Bennett, K. P., & Demiriz, A. (2000). *Constrained K-Means Clustering*. Microsoft Research Dept. of Mathematical Scences One Microsoft Way Dept. of Decision Sciences and Eng. Sys.

Brancati, N., De Pietro, G., Frucci, M., & Riccio, D. (2019). A Deep Learning Approach for Breast Invasive Ductal Carcinoma Detection and Lymphoma Multi-Classification in Histological Images. *Deep Learning for Computer-aided Medical Diagnosis.*, *7*, 44709–44720. doi:10.1109/ACCESS.2019.2908724

Chen, S.-S. (2017). *Classification of Bluetooth stethoscopic heart sounds using convolution neural network* (Master Thesis). National Dong Hwa University.

Doyle, S., Agner, S., Madabhushi, A., Feldman, M., & Tomaszewski, J. (2008). Automated grading of breast cancer histopathology using spectral clustering with textural and architectural image features. *2008 5th IEEE International Symposium on Biomedical Imaging (ISBI): From Nano to Macro, 61*.

Evans, A. J., Krupinski, E. A., Weinstein, R. S., & Pantanowitz, L. (2015, March 24). 2014 american telemedicine association clinical guidelines for telepathology: Another important step in support of increased adoption of telepathology for patient care. *Journal of Pathology Informatics*, *6*(1), 6. doi:10.4103/2153-3539.153906 PMID:25838965

Filipczuk, P., Fevens, T., Krzyzak, A., & Monczak, R. (2013, December). Computer-aided breast cancer diagnosis based on the analysis of cytological images of fine needle biopsies. *IEEE Transactions on Medical Imaging*, *32*(12), 2169–2178. doi:10.1109/TMI.2013.2275151 PMID:23912498

Fu, W., Yang, X., & Wang, Y. (2010). Heart Sound Diagnosis Based on DTW and MFCC. In *2010 3rd International Congress on Image and Signal Processing*. Yantai, China: IEEE.

George, Y. M., Zayed, H. L., Roushdy, M. I., & Elbagoury, B. M. (2014, September). Remote computer-aided breast cancer detection and diagnosis system based on cytological images. *IEEE Systems Journal, 8*(3), 949–964. doi:10.1109/JSYST.2013.2279415

Grąbczewski, K., & Duch, W. (2002). Heterogeneous Forests of Decision Trees. In *International Conference on Artificial Neural Networks* (pp. 504-509). Madrid, Spain: Springer.

Huang, X., Acero, A., Hon, H.-W., & Reddy, R. (2001). *Spoken Language Processing: A guide to theory, algorithm, and system development.* Prentice Hall PTR.

Kowal, M., Filipczuk, P., Obuchowicz, A., Korbicz, J., & Monczak, R. (2013, October). Computer-aided diagnosis of breast cancer based on fine needle biopsy microscopic images. *Computers in Biology and Medicine, 43*(10), 1563–1572. doi:10.1016/j.compbiomed.2013.08.003 PMID:24034748

Lakhani, S., Ellis, I., Schnitt, S., Tan, P., & van de Vijver, M. (2012). *WHO Classification of Tumours of the Breast* (4th ed.). Lyon, France: WHO Press.

Lee, Y.-J., & Mangasarian, O. L. (2001, October). SSVM: A Smooth Support Vector Machine for Classification. *Computational Optimization and Applications, 20*(1), 5–22. doi:10.1023/A:1011215321374

Nawaz, W., Ahmed, S., Tahir, A., & Khan, H. A. (2018). Classification Of Breast Cancer Histology Images Using ALEXNET. In *International Conference Image Analysis and Recognition (ICIAR) 2018: Image Analysis and Recognition* (pp. 869-876). Springer. 10.1007/978-3-319-93000-8_99

Spanhol, F., Oliveira, L. S., Petitjean, C., & Heutte, L. (2017). *Breast Cancer Histopathological Database (BreakHis).* Retrieved from The Laboratory of Vision, Robotics and Imaging (VRI): https://web.inf.ufpr.br/vri/databases/breast-cancer-histopathological-database-breakhis/

Spanhol, F. A., Oliveira, L. S., Petitjean, C., & Heutte, L. (2016, July). A Dataset for Breast Cancer Histopathological Image Classification. *IEEE Transactions on Biomedical Engineering, 63*(7), 1455–1462. doi:10.1109/TBME.2015.2496264 PMID:26540668

Spanhol, F. A., Oliveira, L. S., Petitjean, C., & Heutte, L. (2016, Nov 3). Breast Cancer Histopathological Image Classification Using Convolutional Neural Networks. In *2016 International Joint Conference on Neural Networks (IJCNN)*. Vancouver, Canada: IEEE. 10.1109/IJCNN.2016.7727519

Stenkvist, B., Westman-Naeser, S., Holmquist, J., Nordin, B., Bengtsson, E., Vegelius, J., ... Fox, C. (1978, December). Computerized nuclear morphometry as an objective method for characterizing human cancer cell populations. *Cancer Research, 38*(12), 4688–4698. PMID:82482

Vedaldi, A., & Lenc, K. (2015). MatConvNet: Convolutional Neural Networks for MATLAB. In *MM '15 Proceedings of the 23rd ACM international conference on Multimedia* (pp. 689-692). New York, NY: ACM.

Wojcicki, K. (2020, January 30). *HTK MFCC MATLAB*. Retrieved from MATLAB Central File Exchange: https://www.mathworks.com/matlabcentral/fileexchange/32849-htk-mfcc-matlab

Wolberg, W. H. (1992, Jul 15). *Breast Cancer Wisconsin (Original) Data Set*. Retrieved from UCI Machine Learning Repository: https://archive.ics.uci.edu/ml/datasets/breast+cancer+wisconsin+(original)

Wolberg, W. H., & Mangasarian, O. L. (1990, Dec). Multisurface Method of Pattern Separation for Medical Diagnosis Applied to Breast Cytology. *Proceedings of the National Academy of Sciences*, 9193-9196. 10.1073/pnas.87.23.9193

Wold Health Organization. (2018, Sep 12). *Cancer*. Retrieved from Wold Health Organization: https://www.who.int/news-room/fact-sheets/detail/cancer

Wu, J.-M. (2006, March 12). Natural Discriminant Analysis Using Interactive Potts Models. *Neural Computation*, 689–713. PMID:11860688

Zhang, Y., Zhang, B., Coenen, F., & Lu, W. (2013). Breast cancer diagnosis from biopsy images with highly reliable random subspace classifier ensembles. *Machine Vision and Applications, 24*(7), 1405–1430. doi:10.100700138-012-0459-8

Zhang, Y., Zhang, B., Coenen, F., Xiau, J., & Lu, W. (2014, December). One-class kernel subspace ensemble for medical image classification. *EURASIP Journal on Advances in Signal Processing, 2014*(17), 1–13. doi:10.1186/1687-6180-2014-17

Conclusion

The field of deep learning has made major breakthroughs in recent years, and there are already many deep learning frameworks in both business and academia. Those frameworks provide feasible approaches for easy use of deep learning to solve problems of interest to us. By stepping on the shoulders of giants, we can solve more problems. Using deep learning to deal with problems such as image recognition, speech, natural language, etc., can all achieve a good result. Here we constructed the deep learning model based on mathematical knowledge. With mathematical calculus and linear algebra, the deep learning model can execute feedforward for recognizing objects and execute backpropagation by gradient descent to achieve self-learning. As we discussed in the second chapter, there is a strong connection between mathematics and AI. Mathematics is an engine that contributes to the successful development of deep learning. In the future, the mathematical subjects that developers have studied in the past have great opportunities to enhance the recognition accuracy of the deep learning model or create novel training models for future AI. In this book, we also integrated large scale data set, applying the deep learning framework to build CNN architecture, training and detection model, transforming the pre-trained model into the Xcode environment through the third-party framework and eventually executing the model on the iOS device. We complete an App of pattern recognition and present the total solution from the dataset to App. Through handwritten digit recognition, we have a preliminary understanding of the use of deep learning and model transformation cross platforms. The handwritten digit dataset of LeCun, consisting of sixty thousand training patterns and ten thousand testing patters, has been considered as a benchmark of performance evaluation of variant approaches for handwritten digits recognition. We use the method of the extended dataset in numerical experiments to make the model achieve high recognition accuracy in real-life applications. We also use this basic example to present the feasibility of the total solution, even though MatConvNet is not in the list of third-party deep learning frameworks for Core ML Tools. After solving the Hello World of deep learning filed, we used handwritten English character recognition to enhance the difficulty of the pattern recognition problem. Finally, we used breast cancer image recognition to understand how to use deep learning to solve the problem of medical image recognition.

In the course of experiments, we found that today's "data-driven" artificial intelligence and the overall training process of the model are thoroughly based on the information that comes with the data. Although the effect is apparently better than the traditional approach, it also makes the training set seriously affect the recognition result of the model in future applications. Just like the model trained by By_Class dataset is not able to accurately identify cursive English characters, even if it has 97.0% accuracy rate of the test set. Therefore, it is particularly important for the prior selection, processing, and analysis of the database. Especially when the complexity of the data set is not enough to face the real problem, then the accuracy rate of the test set of the model can only be used for reference only. However, nowadays it is an era of big data. The quantity and complexity of the data also increase the difficulty of the data in the pre-processing stage. So here is a total solution to the problem. Let the model be written into the iOS device, make the App and receive the data directly in the iOS device. Through the data of output, we can quickly and apparently understand how the effect of the model in the real problem and how the status of each output category is. For the current era of big data and database severely impacting models, we believe this is the most direct and quick solution. Also, we learned the importance of data audition in the research in Chapter 5. Whenever the assumption that training and testing patterns have been well labeled does not stand according to evidence shown by numerical experiments, we require data audition. We can easily explore data audition in Matlab and re-mark or delete the confused paired data. Audited training set and testing set feedback to deep learning model for classification. Data audition is an important and essential part of the development of the deep learning model.

In the diagnosis of breast cancer images, this work uses the MatConvNet to construct the CNN architecture, and train the model to assist in the diagnosis of cancer images afterward, avoiding the manual feature extraction. This method is more direct than the traditional hand-crafted textural descriptors, and there are obvious breakthroughs in the effect. Finally, integration of the pre-trained model into the Xcode environment well develops an App. This total solution allows the mobile-assisted diagnosis of breast cancer that can be used more directly and conveniently. Today's mobile devices are like the supercomputers of the past. In addition to being updated every year on hardware, iOS devices are constantly pursuing progress in software. With such a pipeline, developers and users can get closer, regardless of installation or updates have become more convenient, and no longer need to be obsessed with making the software into a machine. With the total solution provided in this book, you will have a quick and detailed understanding in three dividing fields of deep learning, the architecture, the work and the application in real life. We consider this is a good beginning for the total solution of deep learning. There is still much room for improvement in the future, whether the pre-processing of the data, the architecture of CNN, the gradient descent of the backpropagation, or even the integration of software onto iOS devices, etc., we will continue to track and research.

Related Readings

To continue IGI Global's long-standing tradition of advancing innovation through emerging research, please find below a compiled list of recommended IGI Global book chapters and journal articles in the areas of software development, software engineering, and machine learning. These related readings will provide additional information and guidance to further enrich your knowledge and assist you with your own research.

Abramek, E. (2019). Maturity Profiles of Organizations for Social Media. In R. Lenart-Gansiniec (Ed.), *Crowdsourcing and Knowledge Management in Contemporary Business Environments* (pp. 134–145). Hershey, PA: IGI Global. doi:10.4018/978-1-5225-4200-1.ch007

Abu Talib, M. (2018). Towards Sustainable Development Through Open Source Software in the Arab World. In M. Khosrow-Pour, D.B.A. (Ed.), Optimizing Contemporary Application and Processes in Open Source Software (pp. 222-242). Hershey, PA: IGI Global. doi:10.4018/978-1-5225-5314-4.ch009

Adesola, A. P., & Olla, G. O. (2018). Unlocking the Unlimited Potentials of Koha OSS/ILS for Library House-Keeping Functions: A Global View. In M. Khosrow-Pour, D.B.A. (Ed.), Optimizing Contemporary Application and Processes in Open Source Software (pp. 124-163). Hershey, PA: IGI Global. doi:10.4018/978-1-5225-5314-4.ch006

Akber, A., Rizvi, S. S., Khan, M. W., Uddin, V., Hashmani, M. A., & Ahmad, J. (2019). Dimensions of Robust Security Testing in Global Software Engineering: A Systematic Review. In M. Rehman, A. Amin, A. Gilal, & M. Hashmani (Eds.), *Human Factors in Global Software Engineering* (pp. 252–272). Hershey, PA: IGI Global. doi:10.4018/978-1-5225-9448-2.ch010

Amrollahi, A., & Ahmadi, M. H. (2019). What Motivates the Crowd?: A Literature Review on Motivations for Crowdsourcing. In R. Lenart-Gansiniec (Ed.), *Crowdsourcing and Knowledge Management in Contemporary Business Environments* (pp. 103–133). Hershey, PA: IGI Global. doi:10.4018/978-1-5225-4200-1.ch006

Anchitaalagammai, J. V., Samayadurai, K., Murali, S., Padmadevi, S., & Shantha Lakshmi Revathy, J. (2019). Best Practices: Adopting Security Into the Software Development Process for IoT Applications. In D. Mala (Ed.), *Integrating the Internet of Things Into Software Engineering Practices* (pp. 146–159). Hershey, PA: IGI Global. doi:10.4018/978-1-5225-7790-4.ch007

Bhavsar, S. A., Pandit, B. Y., & Modi, K. J. (2019). Social Internet of Things. In D. Mala (Ed.), *Integrating the Internet of Things Into Software Engineering Practices* (pp. 199–218). Hershey, PA: IGI Global. doi:10.4018/978-1-5225-7790-4.ch010

Biswas, A., & De, A. K. (2019). *Multi-Objective Stochastic Programming in Fuzzy Environments* (pp. 1–420). Hershey, PA: IGI Global. doi:10.4018/978-1-5225-8301-1

Callaghan, C. W. (2017). The Probabilistic Innovation Field of Scientific Enquiry. *International Journal of Sociotechnology and Knowledge Development*, 9(2), 56–72. doi:10.4018/IJSKD.2017040104

Chhabra, D., & Sharma, I. (2018). Role of Attacker Capabilities in Risk Estimation and Mitigation. In R. Kumar, A. Tayal, & S. Kapil (Eds.), *Analyzing the Role of Risk Mitigation and Monitoring in Software Development* (pp. 244–255). Hershey, PA: IGI Global. doi:10.4018/978-1-5225-6029-6.ch015

Chitra, P., & Abirami, S. (2019). Smart Pollution Alert System Using Machine Learning. In D. Mala (Ed.), *Integrating the Internet of Things Into Software Engineering Practices* (pp. 219–235). Hershey, PA: IGI Global. doi:10.4018/978-1-5225-7790-4.ch011

Dorsey, M. D., & Raisinghani, M. S. (2019). IT Governance or IT Outsourcing: Is There a Clear Winner? In A. Mukherjee & A. Krishna (Eds.), *Interdisciplinary Approaches to Information Systems and Software Engineering* (pp. 19–32). Hershey, PA: IGI Global. doi:10.4018/978-1-5225-7784-3.ch002

Dua, R., Sharma, S., & Kumar, R. (2018). Risk Management Metrics. In R. Kumar, A. Tayal, & S. Kapil (Eds.), *Analyzing the Role of Risk Mitigation and Monitoring in Software Development* (pp. 21–33). Hershey, PA: IGI Global. doi:10.4018/978-1-5225-6029-6.ch002

Dua, R., Sharma, S., & Sharma, A. (2018). Software Vulnerability Management: How Intelligence Helps in Mitigating Software Vulnerabilities. In R. Kumar, A. Tayal, & S. Kapil (Eds.), *Analyzing the Role of Risk Mitigation and Monitoring in Software Development* (pp. 34–45). Hershey, PA: IGI Global. doi:10.4018/978-1-5225-6029-6.ch003

Fatema, K., Syeed, M. M., & Hammouda, I. (2018). Demography of Open Source Software Prediction Models and Techniques. In M. Khosrow-Pour, D.B.A. (Ed.), Optimizing Contemporary Application and Processes in Open Source Software (pp. 24-56). Hershey, PA: IGI Global. doi:10.4018/978-1-5225-5314-4.ch002

Ghafele, R., & Gibert, B. (2018). Open Growth: The Economic Impact of Open Source Software in the USA. In M. Khosrow-Pour, D.B.A. (Ed.), Optimizing Contemporary Application and Processes in Open Source Software (pp. 164-197). Hershey, PA: IGI Global. doi:10.4018/978-1-5225-5314-4.ch007

Gilal, A. R., Tunio, M. Z., Waqas, A., Almomani, M. A., Khan, S., & Gilal, R. (2019). Task Assignment and Personality: Crowdsourcing Software Development. In M. Rehman, A. Amin, A. Gilal, & M. Hashmani (Eds.), *Human Factors in Global Software Engineering* (pp. 1–19). Hershey, PA: IGI Global. doi:10.4018/978-1-5225-9448-2.ch001

Gopikrishnan, S., & Priakanth, P. (2019). Web-Based IoT Application Development. In D. Mala (Ed.), *Integrating the Internet of Things Into Software Engineering Practices* (pp. 62–86). Hershey, PA: IGI Global. doi:10.4018/978-1-5225-7790-4.ch004

Guendouz, M., Amine, A., & Hamou, R. M. (2018). Open Source Projects Recommendation on GitHub. In M. Khosrow-Pour, D.B.A. (Ed.), Optimizing Contemporary Application and Processes in Open Source Software (pp. 86-101). Hershey, PA: IGI Global. doi:10.4018/978-1-5225-5314-4.ch004

Hashmani, M. A., Zaffar, M., & Ejaz, R. (2019). Scenario Based Test Case Generation Using Activity Diagram and Action Semantics. In M. Rehman, A. Amin, A. Gilal, & M. Hashmani (Eds.), *Human Factors in Global Software Engineering* (pp. 297–321). Hershey, PA: IGI Global. doi:10.4018/978-1-5225-9448-2.ch012

Jagannathan, J., & Anitha Elavarasi, S. (2019). Current Trends: Machine Learning and AI in IoT. In D. Mala (Ed.), *Integrating the Internet of Things Into Software Engineering Practices* (pp. 181–198). Hershey, PA: IGI Global. doi:10.4018/978-1-5225-7790-4.ch009

Jasmine, K. S. (2019). A New Process Model for IoT-Based Software Engineering. In D. Mala (Ed.), *Integrating the Internet of Things Into Software Engineering Practices* (pp. 1–13). Hershey, PA: IGI Global. doi:10.4018/978-1-5225-7790-4.ch001

Juma, M. F., Fue, K. G., Barakabitze, A. A., Nicodemus, N., Magesa, M. M., Kilima, F. T., & Sanga, C. A. (2017). Understanding Crowdsourcing of Agricultural Market Information in a Pilot Study: Promises, Problems and Possibilities (3Ps). *International Journal of Technology Diffusion, 8*(4), 1–16. doi:10.4018/IJTD.2017100101

Karthick, G. S., & Pankajavalli, P. B. (2019). Internet of Things Testing Framework, Automation, Challenges, Solutions and Practices: A Connected Approach for IoT Applications. In D. Mala (Ed.), *Integrating the Internet of Things Into Software Engineering Practices* (pp. 87–124). Hershey, PA: IGI Global. doi:10.4018/978-1-5225-7790-4.ch005

Kashyap, R. (2019). Big Data and Global Software Engineering. In M. Rehman, A. Amin, A. Gilal, & M. Hashmani (Eds.), *Human Factors in Global Software Engineering* (pp. 131–163). Hershey, PA: IGI Global. doi:10.4018/978-1-5225-9448-2.ch006

Kashyap, R. (2019). Systematic Model for Decision Support System. In A. Mukherjee & A. Krishna (Eds.), *Interdisciplinary Approaches to Information Systems and Software Engineering* (pp. 62–98). Hershey, PA: IGI Global. doi:10.4018/978-1-5225-7784-3.ch004

Kaur, J., & Kaur, R. (2018). Estimating Risks Related to Extended Enterprise Systems (EES). In R. Kumar, A. Tayal, & S. Kapil (Eds.), *Analyzing the Role of Risk Mitigation and Monitoring in Software Development* (pp. 118–135). Hershey, PA: IGI Global. doi:10.4018/978-1-5225-6029-6.ch008

Kaur, Y., & Singh, S. (2018). Risk Mitigation Planning, Implementation, and Progress Monitoring: Risk Mitigation. In R. Kumar, A. Tayal, & S. Kapil (Eds.), *Analyzing the Role of Risk Mitigation and Monitoring in Software Development* (pp. 1–20). Hershey, PA: IGI Global. doi:10.4018/978-1-5225-6029-6.ch001

Kavitha, S., Anchitaalagammai, J. V., Nirmala, S., & Murali, S. (2019). Current Trends in Integrating the Internet of Things Into Software Engineering Practices. In D. Mala (Ed.), *Integrating the Internet of Things Into Software Engineering Practices* (pp. 14–35). Hershey, PA: IGI Global. doi:10.4018/978-1-5225-7790-4.ch002

Köse, U. (2018). Optimization Scenarios for Open Source Software Used in E-Learning Activities. In M. Khosrow-Pour, D.B.A. (Ed.), Optimizing Contemporary Application and Processes in Open Source Software (pp. 102-123). Hershey, PA: IGI Global. doi:10.4018/978-1-5225-5314-4.ch005

Kumar, A., Singh, A. K., Awasthi, N., & Singh, V. (2019). Natural Hazard: Tropical Cyclone – Evaluation of HE and IMSRA Over CS KYANT. In A. Mukherjee & A. Krishna (Eds.), *Interdisciplinary Approaches to Information Systems and Software Engineering* (pp. 124–141). Hershey, PA: IGI Global. doi:10.4018/978-1-5225-7784-3.ch006

Kumar, N., Singh, S. K., Reddy, G. P., & Naitam, R. K. (2019). Developing Logistic Regression Models to Identify Salt-Affected Soils Using Optical Remote Sensing. In A. Mukherjee & A. Krishna (Eds.), *Interdisciplinary Approaches to Information Systems and Software Engineering* (pp. 233–256). Hershey, PA: IGI Global. doi:10.4018/978-1-5225-7784-3.ch010

Kumar, U., Kumar, N., Mishra, V. N., & Jena, R. K. (2019). Soil Quality Assessment Using Analytic Hierarchy Process (AHP): A Case Study. In A. Mukherjee & A. Krishna (Eds.), *Interdisciplinary Approaches to Information Systems and Software Engineering* (pp. 1–18). Hershey, PA: IGI Global. doi:10.4018/978-1-5225-7784-3.ch001

Lal, S., Sardana, N., & Sureka, A. (2018). Logging Analysis and Prediction in Open Source Java Project. In M. Khosrow-Pour, D.B.A. (Ed.), Optimizing Contemporary Application and Processes in Open Source Software (pp. 57-85). Hershey, PA: IGI Global. doi:10.4018/978-1-5225-5314-4.ch003

Latif, A. M., Khan, K. M., & Duc, A. N. (2019). Software Cost Estimation and Capability Maturity Model in Context of Global Software Engineering. In M. Rehman, A. Amin, A. Gilal, & M. Hashmani (Eds.), *Human Factors in Global Software Engineering* (pp. 273–296). Hershey, PA: IGI Global. doi:10.4018/978-1-5225-9448-2.ch011

Lenart-Gansiniec, R. A. (2019). Crowdsourcing as an Example of Public Management Fashion. In R. Lenart-Gansiniec (Ed.), *Crowdsourcing and Knowledge Management in Contemporary Business Environments* (pp. 1–19). Hershey, PA: IGI Global. doi:10.4018/978-1-5225-4200-1.ch001

Lukyanenko, R., & Parsons, J. (2018). Beyond Micro-Tasks: Research Opportunities in Observational Crowdsourcing. *Journal of Database Management*, 29(1), 1–22. doi:10.4018/JDM.2018010101

Mala, D. (2019). IoT Functional Testing Using UML Use Case Diagrams: IoT in Testing. In D. Mala (Ed.), *Integrating the Internet of Things Into Software Engineering Practices* (pp. 125–145). Hershey, PA: IGI Global. doi:10.4018/978-1-5225-7790-4.ch006

Mansoor, M., Khan, M. W., Rizvi, S. S., Hashmani, M. A., & Zubair, M. (2019). Adaptation of Modern Agile Practices in Global Software Engineering. In M. Rehman, A. Amin, A. Gilal, & M. Hashmani (Eds.), *Human Factors in Global Software Engineering* (pp. 164–187). Hershey, PA: IGI Global. doi:10.4018/978-1-5225-9448-2.ch007

Memon, M. S. (2019). Techniques and Trends Towards Various Dimensions of Robust Security Testing in Global Software Engineering. In M. Rehman, A. Amin, A. Gilal, & M. Hashmani (Eds.), *Human Factors in Global Software Engineering* (pp. 219–251). Hershey, PA: IGI Global. doi:10.4018/978-1-5225-9448-2.ch009

Mookherjee, A., Mulay, P., Joshi, R., Prajapati, P. S., Johari, S., & Prajapati, S. S. (2019). Sentilyser: Embedding Voice Markers in Homeopathy Treatments. In A. Mukherjee & A. Krishna (Eds.), *Interdisciplinary Approaches to Information Systems and Software Engineering* (pp. 181–206). Hershey, PA: IGI Global. doi:10.4018/978-1-5225-7784-3.ch008

Mukherjee, S., Bhattacharjee, A. K., & Deyasi, A. (2019). Project Teamwork Assessment and Success Rate Prediction Through Meta-Heuristic Algorithms. In A. Mukherjee & A. Krishna (Eds.), *Interdisciplinary Approaches to Information Systems and Software Engineering* (pp. 33–61). Hershey, PA: IGI Global. doi:10.4018/978-1-5225-7784-3.ch003

Nandy, A. (2019). Identification of Tectonic Activity and Fault Mechanism From Morphological Signatures. In A. Mukherjee & A. Krishna (Eds.), *Interdisciplinary Approaches to Information Systems and Software Engineering* (pp. 99–123). Hershey, PA: IGI Global. doi:10.4018/978-1-5225-7784-3.ch005

Omar, M., Rejab, M. M., & Ahmad, M. (2019). The Effect of Team Work Quality on Team Performance in Global Software Engineering. In M. Rehman, A. Amin, A. Gilal, & M. Hashmani (Eds.), *Human Factors in Global Software Engineering* (pp. 322–331). Hershey, PA: IGI Global. doi:10.4018/978-1-5225-9448-2.ch013

Onuchowska, A., & de Vreede, G. (2017). Disruption and Deception in Crowdsourcing. *International Journal of e-Collaboration*, *13*(4), 23–41. doi:10.4018/IJeC.2017100102

Papadopoulou, C., & Giaoutzi, M. (2017). Crowdsourcing and Living Labs in Support of Smart Cities' Development. *International Journal of E-Planning Research*, *6*(2), 22–38. doi:10.4018/IJEPR.2017040102

Patnaik, K. S., & Snigdh, I. (2019). Modelling and Designing of IoT Systems Using UML Diagrams: An Introduction. In D. Mala (Ed.), *Integrating the Internet of Things Into Software Engineering Practices* (pp. 36–61). Hershey, PA: IGI Global. doi:10.4018/978-1-5225-7790-4.ch003

Pawar, L., Kumar, R., & Sharma, A. (2018). Risks Analysis and Mitigation Technique in EDA Sector: VLSI Supply Chain. In R. Kumar, A. Tayal, & S. Kapil (Eds.), *Analyzing the Role of Risk Mitigation and Monitoring in Software Development* (pp. 256–265). Hershey, PA: IGI Global. doi:10.4018/978-1-5225-6029-6.ch016

Persaud, A., & O'Brien, S. (2017). Quality and Acceptance of Crowdsourced Translation of Web Content. *International Journal of Technology and Human Interaction*, *13*(1), 100–115. doi:10.4018/IJTHI.2017010106

Phung, V. D., & Hawryszkiewycz, I. (2019). Knowledge Sharing and Innovative Work Behavior: An Extension of Social Cognitive Theory. In R. Lenart-Gansiniec (Ed.), *Crowdsourcing and Knowledge Management in Contemporary Business Environments* (pp. 71–102). Hershey, PA: IGI Global. doi:10.4018/978-1-5225-4200-1.ch005

Pohulak-Żołędowska, E. (2019). Crowdsourcing in Innovation Activity of Enterprises on an Example of Pharmaceutical Industry. In R. Lenart-Gansiniec (Ed.), *Crowdsourcing and Knowledge Management in Contemporary Business Environments* (pp. 58–70). Hershey, PA: IGI Global. doi:10.4018/978-1-5225-4200-1.ch004

Pramanik, P. K., Pal, S., Pareek, G., Dutta, S., & Choudhury, P. (2019). Crowd Computing: The Computing Revolution. In R. Lenart-Gansiniec (Ed.), *Crowdsourcing and Knowledge Management in Contemporary Business Environments* (pp. 166–198). Hershey, PA: IGI Global. doi:10.4018/978-1-5225-4200-1.ch009

Priakanth, P., & Gopikrishnan, S. (2019). Machine Learning Techniques for Internet of Things. In D. Mala (Ed.), *Integrating the Internet of Things Into Software Engineering Practices* (pp. 160–180). Hershey, PA: IGI Global. doi:10.4018/978-1-5225-7790-4.ch008

Priyadarshi, A. (2019). Segmentation of Different Tissues of Brain From MR Image. In A. Mukherjee & A. Krishna (Eds.), *Interdisciplinary Approaches to Information Systems and Software Engineering* (pp. 142–180). Hershey, PA: IGI Global. doi:10.4018/978-1-5225-7784-3.ch007

Rath, M. (2019). Intelligent Information System for Academic Institutions: Using Big Data Analytic Approach. In A. Mukherjee & A. Krishna (Eds.), *Interdisciplinary Approaches to Information Systems and Software Engineering* (pp. 207–232). Hershey, PA: IGI Global. doi:10.4018/978-1-5225-7784-3.ch009

Realyvásquez, A., Maldonado-Macías, A. A., & Hernández-Escobedo, G. (2019). Software Development for Ergonomic Compatibility Assessment of Advanced Manufacturing Technology. In M. Rehman, A. Amin, A. Gilal, & M. Hashmani (Eds.), *Human Factors in Global Software Engineering* (pp. 50–83). Hershey, PA: IGI Global. doi:10.4018/978-1-5225-9448-2.ch003

Saini, M., & Chahal, K. K. (2018). A Systematic Review of Attributes and Techniques for Open Source Software Evolution Analysis. In M. Khosrow-Pour, D.B.A. (Ed.), Optimizing Contemporary Application and Processes in Open Source Software (pp. 1-23). Hershey, PA: IGI Global. doi:10.4018/978-1-5225-5314-4.ch001

Sanga, C. A., Lyimo, N. N., Fue, K. G., Telemala, J. P., Kilima, F., & Kipanyula, M. J. (2019). Piloting Crowdsourcing Platform for Monitoring and Evaluation of Projects: Harnessing Massive Open Online Deliberation (MOOD). In R. Lenart-Gansiniec (Ed.), *Crowdsourcing and Knowledge Management in Contemporary Business Environments* (pp. 199–217). Hershey, PA: IGI Global. doi:10.4018/978-1-5225-4200-1.ch010

Sedkaoui, S. (2019). Data Analytics Supporting Knowledge Acquisition. In R. Lenart-Gansiniec (Ed.), *Crowdsourcing and Knowledge Management in Contemporary Business Environments* (pp. 146–165). Hershey, PA: IGI Global. doi:10.4018/978-1-5225-4200-1.ch008

Sen, K., & Ghosh, K. (2018). Designing Effective Crowdsourcing Systems for the Healthcare Industry. *International Journal of Public Health Management and Ethics*, *3*(2), 57–62. doi:10.4018/IJPHME.2018070104

Sen, K., & Ghosh, K. (2018). Incorporating Global Medical Knowledge to Solve Healthcare Problems: A Framework for a Crowdsourcing System. *International Journal of Healthcare Information Systems and Informatics*, *13*(1), 1–14. doi:10.4018/IJHISI.2018010101

Sharma, A., Pal, V., Ojha, N., & Bajaj, R. (2018). Risks Assessment in Designing Phase: Its Impacts and Issues. In R. Kumar, A. Tayal, & S. Kapil (Eds.), *Analyzing the Role of Risk Mitigation and Monitoring in Software Development* (pp. 46–60). Hershey, PA: IGI Global. doi:10.4018/978-1-5225-6029-6.ch004

Sharma, A., Pawar, L., & Kaur, M. (2018). Development and Enhancing of Software and Programming Products by Client Information Administration in Market. In R. Kumar, A. Tayal, & S. Kapil (Eds.), *Analyzing the Role of Risk Mitigation and Monitoring in Software Development* (pp. 150–187). Hershey, PA: IGI Global. doi:10.4018/978-1-5225-6029-6.ch010

Sharma, A. P., & Sharma, S. (2018). Risk Management in Web Development. In R. Kumar, A. Tayal, & S. Kapil (Eds.), *Analyzing the Role of Risk Mitigation and Monitoring in Software Development* (pp. 188–203). Hershey, PA: IGI Global. doi:10.4018/978-1-5225-6029-6.ch011

Sharma, I., & Chhabra, D. (2018). Meta-Heuristic Approach for Software Project Risk Schedule Analysis. In R. Kumar, A. Tayal, & S. Kapil (Eds.), *Analyzing the Role of Risk Mitigation and Monitoring in Software Development* (pp. 136–149). Hershey, PA: IGI Global. doi:10.4018/978-1-5225-6029-6.ch009

Sharma, S., & Dua, R. (2018). Gamification: An Effectual Learning Application for SE. In R. Kumar, A. Tayal, & S. Kapil (Eds.), *Analyzing the Role of Risk Mitigation and Monitoring in Software Development* (pp. 219–233). Hershey, PA: IGI Global. doi:10.4018/978-1-5225-6029-6.ch013

Shilohu Rao, N. J. P., Chaudhary, R. S., & Goswami, D. (2019). Knowledge Management System for Governance: Transformational Approach Creating Knowledge as Product for Governance. In R. Lenart-Gansiniec (Ed.), *Crowdsourcing and Knowledge Management in Contemporary Business Environments* (pp. 20–38). Hershey, PA: IGI Global. doi:10.4018/978-1-5225-4200-1.ch002

Sidhu, A. K., & Sehra, S. K. (2018). Use of Software Metrics to Improve the Quality of Software Projects Using Regression Testing. In R. Kumar, A. Tayal, & S. Kapil (Eds.), *Analyzing the Role of Risk Mitigation and Monitoring in Software Development* (pp. 204–218). Hershey, PA: IGI Global. doi:10.4018/978-1-5225-6029-6.ch012

Srao, B. K., Rai, H. S., & Mann, K. S. (2018). Why India Should Make It Compulsory to Go for BIM. In R. Kumar, A. Tayal, & S. Kapil (Eds.), *Analyzing the Role of Risk Mitigation and Monitoring in Software Development* (pp. 266–277). Hershey, PA: IGI Global. doi:10.4018/978-1-5225-6029-6.ch017

Srinivasa, K., Deka, G. C., & P.M., K. (2018). Free and Open Source Software in Modern Data Science and Business Intelligence: Emerging Research and Opportunities (pp. 1-189). Hershey, PA: IGI Global. doi:10.4018/978-1-5225-3707-6

Srivastava, R. (2018). An Analysis on Risk Management and Risk in the Software Projects. In R. Kumar, A. Tayal, & S. Kapil (Eds.), *Analyzing the Role of Risk Mitigation and Monitoring in Software Development* (pp. 83–99). Hershey, PA: IGI Global. doi:10.4018/978-1-5225-6029-6.ch006

Srivastava, R., Verma, S. K., & Thukral, V. (2018). A New Approach for Reinforcement of Project DEMATEL-FMCDM-TODIM Fuzzy Approach. In R. Kumar, A. Tayal, & S. Kapil (Eds.), *Analyzing the Role of Risk Mitigation and Monitoring in Software Development* (pp. 234–243). Hershey, PA: IGI Global. doi:10.4018/978-1-5225-6029-6.ch014

Tolu, H. (2018). Strategy of Good Software Governance: FLOSS in the State of Turkey. In M. Khosrow-Pour, D.B.A. (Ed.), Optimizing Contemporary Application and Processes in Open Source Software (pp. 198-221). Hershey, PA: IGI Global. doi:10.4018/978-1-5225-5314-4.ch008

Trad, A. (2019). The Business Transformation Framework and Enterprise Architecture Framework for Managers in Business Innovation: Knowledge Management in Global Software Engineering (KMGSE). In M. Rehman, A. Amin, A. Gilal, & M. Hashmani (Eds.), *Human Factors in Global Software Engineering* (pp. 20–49). Hershey, PA: IGI Global. doi:10.4018/978-1-5225-9448-2.ch002

Vasanthapriyan, S. (2019). Knowledge Management Initiatives in Agile Software Development: A Literature Review. In M. Rehman, A. Amin, A. Gilal, & M. Hashmani (Eds.), *Human Factors in Global Software Engineering* (pp. 109–130). Hershey, PA: IGI Global. doi:10.4018/978-1-5225-9448-2.ch005

Vasanthapriyan, S. (2019). Knowledge Sharing Initiatives in Software Companies: A Mapping Study. In M. Rehman, A. Amin, A. Gilal, & M. Hashmani (Eds.), *Human Factors in Global Software Engineering* (pp. 84–108). Hershey, PA: IGI Global. doi:10.4018/978-1-5225-9448-2.ch004

Vasanthapriyan, S. (2019). Study of Employee Innovative Behavior in Sri Lankan Software Companies. In M. Rehman, A. Amin, A. Gilal, & M. Hashmani (Eds.), *Human Factors in Global Software Engineering* (pp. 188–218). Hershey, PA: IGI Global. doi:10.4018/978-1-5225-9448-2.ch008

Zaei, M. E. (2019). Knowledge Management in the Non-Governmental Organizations Context. In R. Lenart-Gansiniec (Ed.), *Crowdsourcing and Knowledge Management in Contemporary Business Environments* (pp. 39–57). Hershey, PA: IGI Global. doi:10.4018/978-1-5225-4200-1.ch003

Related Readings

Ziouvelou, X., & McGroarty, F. (2018). A Business Model Framework for Crowd-Driven IoT Ecosystems. *International Journal of Social Ecology and Sustainable Development*, *9*(3), 14–33. doi:10.4018/IJSESD.2018070102

Zykov, S. V., Gromoff, A., & Kazantsev, N. S. (2019). *Software Engineering for Enterprise System Agility: Emerging Research and Opportunities.* Hershey, PA: IGI Global. doi:10.4018/978-1-5225-5589-6

About the Authors

Jiann-Ming Wu is a mathematics educator in Taiwan. He currently serves National Dong Hwa University as a professor and head in the department of Applied Mathematics. In addition to holding a career in education, Dr. Jiann-Ming is known for the design of multilayer Potts perceptrons, generalized adalines, natural elastic nets, Mahalanobis-NRBF neural networks, state-regulated inverse neural networks, Potts ICA neural networks, Sudoku associative memory, and deep learning, inluding annealed Kullback-Leibler divergence minimization learning, annealed cooperative-competitive learning, hybrid mean-field-annealing and gradient descent deep learning, among others. Prior to entering a career in mathematics education, Dr. Jiann-Ming received a Bachelor of Science in Engineering and Computer Science from National Chiao Tung University in 1988. He went on to attend National Taiwan University, where he completed a Master of Science in Computer Science and Information Engineering in 1990 and a PhD in 1994. Dr. Jiann-Ming is certified in engineering through the International Neural Network Society.

Chao-Yuan Tien was born in Taiwan in 1995. He published Handwriting 99 Multiplication App on Apple's App Store in 2018. He received the M.S. degree in applied mathematics from National Dong Hwa University, Hualien, Taiwan, in spring 2019, and the B.S. degree in applied mathematics from National Dong Hwa University, Hualien, Taiwan, in 2017. His research interesting includes Deep learning, MatConvNet deep learning, Caffe deep learning, iOS mobile App design.

Index

Ensure Quality Research is Introduced to the Academic Community

Become an IGI Global Reviewer for Authored Book Projects

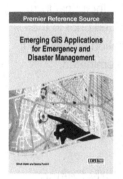

Premier Reference Source

Emerging GIS Applications for Emergency and Disaster Management

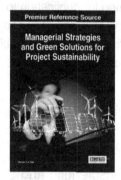

Premier Reference Source

Managerial Strategies and Green Solutions for Project Sustainability

Premier Reference Source

Comparative Approaches to Using R and Python for Statistical Data Analysis

Premier Reference Source

Solutions for High-Touch Communications in a High-Tech World

The overall success of an authored book project is dependent on quality and timely reviews.

In this competitive age of scholarly publishing, constructive and timely feedback significantly expedites the turnaround time of manuscripts from submission to acceptance, allowing the publication and discovery of forward-thinking research at a much more expeditious rate. Several IGI Global authored book projects are currently seeking highly-qualified experts in the field to fill vacancies on their respective editorial review boards:

Applications and Inquiries may be sent to:
development@igi-global.com

Applicants must have a doctorate (or an equivalent degree) as well as publishing and reviewing experience. Reviewers are asked to complete the open-ended evaluation questions with as much detail as possible in a timely, collegial, and constructive manner. All reviewers' tenures run for one-year terms on the editorial review boards and are expected to complete at least three reviews per term. Upon successful completion of this term, reviewers can be considered for an additional term.

If you have a colleague that may be interested in this opportunity, we encourage you to share this information with them.

IGI Global Proudly Partners With
eContent Pro International
Receive a 25% Discount on all Editorial Services

Editorial Services

IGI Global expects all final manuscripts submitted for publication to be in their final form. This means they must be reviewed, revised, and professionally copy edited prior to their final submission. Not only does this support with accelerating the publication process, but it also ensures that the highest quality scholarly work can be disseminated.

English Language Copy Editing

Let eContent Pro International's expert copy editors perform edits on your manuscript to resolve spelling, punctuaion, grammar, syntax, flow, formatting issues and more.

Scientific and Scholarly Editing

Allow colleagues in your research area to examine the content of your manuscript and provide you with valuable feedback and suggestions before submission.

Figure, Table, Chart & Equation Conversions

Do you have poor quality figures? Do you need visual elements in your manuscript created or converted? A design expert can help!

Translation

Need your documjent translated into English? eContent Pro International's expert translators are fluent in English and more than 40 different languages.

Email: customerservice@econtentpro.com   **www.igi-global.com/editorial-service-partners**